Fernweh

CROSSING BORDERS AND
CONNECTING PEOPLE
IN ARCHAEOLOGICAL
HERITAGE MANAGEMENT

Sidestone Press

Fernweh

CROSSING BORDERS AND
CONNECTING PEOPLE
IN ARCHAEOLOGICAL
HERITAGE MANAGEMENT

edited by
Monique H. van den Dries, Sjoerd J. van der Linde
& Amy Strecker

© 2015 individual authors

Published by Sidestone Press, Leiden
www.sidestone.com

ISBN 978-90-8890-350-2

Lay-out & cover design: Sidestone Press
Photographs cover: Johan van der Heijden Fotografie
www.johanvanderheijdenfotografie.nl
(permission for use also granted by Gemeente Goes)

Also available as:
e-book (PDF): ISBN 978-90-8890-351-9

Universiteit Leiden

Contents

Willem J.H. Willems (1950-2014)	9
Fernweh: Introduction	13
Monique van den Dries, Sjoerd van der Linde and Amy Strecker	
Taking the next steps	21
Douglas C. Comer	
TIME TRAVELS	27
FACING CHALLENGES IN HERITAGE MANAGEMENT	
Challenging values	29
Adrian Olivier	
The aftermath of Malta	34
Arkadiusz Marciniak	
Preservation *in situ*	38
Not an ethical principle, but rather an option amongst many	38
Tim Williams	
Making futures from the remains of the distant past	42
Timothy Darvill	
From the preservation of cultural heritage to critical heritage studies	47
Kristian Kristiansen	
Creative archaeology	51
Sjoerd J. van der Linde and Monique H. van den Dries	
Sustainable archaeology in post-crisis scenarios	56
Felipe Criado-Boado, David Barreiro and Rocío Varela-Pousa	
Yours, mine, and ours	61
Pei-Lin Yu, Chen Shen and George S. Smith	
Mapping stakeholders in archaeological heritage management	64
Alicia Castillo	
Solving the puzzle	68
Annemarie Willems and Cynthia Dunning	
"Willem, give me an excuse to attend WAC!"	72
Nelly M. Robles Garcia	
Heritage from the heart	77
Pieter ter Keurs	

CROSSING BORDERS AND BOUNDARIES
GLOBAL INTERACTIONS IN HERITAGE MANAGEMENT
 … 81

'This is not Australia!' … 83
Ian Lilley

A personal memoir of the early years of ICAHM … 87
Henry Cleere

A view from the 'far side' … 91
Margaret Gowen

On translating the untranslatable, African heritage … in African … 96
Nathan Schlanger

The Oyu Tolgoi cultural heritage program, Mongolia … 101
Jeffrey H. Altschul and Gerry Wait

The Caribbean challenge … 105
Corinne L. Hofman

The organic nature of monuments' use … 110
Jay B. Haviser

Why history (still) matters … 114
Mariana de Campos Françozo

The problem of landscape protection … 118
Amy Strecker

Scientific illiteracy … 122
Sander van der Leeuw

HOME SWEET HOME
MANAGING ARCHAEOLOGICAL RESOURCES IN THE NETHERLANDS
 … 127

Veni, vidi, vici … 129
Leonard de Wit

Paving the way … 132
Monique Krauwer

Visualizing the unknown … 136
Jos Deeben and Bjørn Smit

A plea for ethics … 141
Tom Bloemers

Preservation *in situ* at Almere, the downside of our success … 145
Dick de Jager

The invisible treasures of our past … 149
Martijn Manders

Fluctuating boundaries … 153
Ruurd B. Halbertsma

People rather than things, the *Haka* and the *Waka* *Steven Engelsman*	157
'Make it happen' *Dieke Wesselingh*	160
Crossing borders along the Dutch *limes* *Tom Hazenberg*	164
Bibliography W.J.H. Willems	169
Contributors	183

Wat ik heb heeft een naam, 'Fernweh'.

Willem J.H. Willems

(What I have has a name, 'Wanderlust')

Willem J.H. Willems (1950-2014)

Professor dr. Willem J.H. Willems was one of the most prominent Dutch archaeologists. He steered three main national organizations, played a major role in the restructuring of the archaeological heritage management system in the Netherlands, produced an impressive list of academic publications and was also very active in the international arena of heritage management. Willem was unparalleled in the extent of his participation in committees and boards, in presidencies, in academic professorships, in the vast size of his network and in air miles. During his long and impressive career, his professional passion was threefold: Roman archaeology, archaeological heritage management and international collaboration.

After his academic training in Roman archaeology and anthropology at the University of Amsterdam, and in anthropology at the University of Michigan (USA), he started his professional career in 1979 as the provincial archaeologist of Limburg, the province in the southern part of the Netherlands where he was born. He continued in Roman archaeology with a PhD dissertation (1986, *cum laude*) entitled 'Romans and Batavians' and published numerous articles and monographs. Both in the Netherlands and internationally, he was considered as one of the leading Roman specialists. In 1985 he was appointed as project manager for the Roman period at the State Service for Archaeology (ROB, now *Rijksdienst Cultureel Erfgoed* or Cultural Heritage Agency) in Amersfoort and two years later he became professor of Roman archaeology at Leiden University.

Inspired by the CRM developments he witnessed in the US, he not only developed his taste for excavating Roman sites but also tackled the challenges of preserving them, as well as other types of sites. Heritage management even became his main concern when in 1989 he became the director of the ROB. As such he began to develop an interest in the social role of archaeology, especially the relationship between science and society. He would also bring these interests into practice on an international scale, when in the early nineties he was part of a committee of experts from the Council of Europe that drafted the European Convention for the Protection of the Archaeological Heritage (also known as the Malta Convention). His approach and views on heritage management and academic quality were put to the test when he was asked (in 1999) to become the director of quality management for archaeology at the Ministry of Education, Culture and Science. His main task was to direct the adaptation of the Dutch archaeological heritage management system to the principles of the Malta Convention, a complex and delicate process. However he successfully ensured that the future commercially-based heritage management system would be accompanied by quality assurance measures. Later he dynamically chaired the committee that successfully developed the Dutch Quality Standard. After its completion he was appointed as Inspector General for Archaeology (2001) and began to mold the State Inspectorate for Archaeology (now Heritage Inspectorate). His remit was to monitor in practice the quality of the archaeological work that was undertaken under the new regime and in a commercial setting. In 2006 Willem exchanged this position for one in Leiden, where he became the Dean of the Faculty of Archaeology. At the same time he obtained his second professorship in Leiden, on International Archaeological Resource Management. He established a research group with PhD-candidates from all over the world and in 2009 began the first Masters degree specialization in heritage management with a global orientation. He has also published extensively on this subject, as his bibliography in this volume demonstrates.

His wide horizons and endless affiliation with archaeological matters is reflected in the huge number of Dutch committees, executive boards and editorial boards in which he participated (such as the Dutch Archaeology Foundation, the RAAP-foundation, RING Foundation, Central Committee of Experts for Archaeology – CCvD, the Van Es Award Committee; ICOMOS Netherlands, the Centre for International Heritage Activities (CIE), etc.). He even ran an advisory company, with his good friend Roel Brandt († 2009). At the international level, the list of boards and committees is even longer; ever since his studies in the United States he remained intensely involved in the international arena, for instance through his membership of the Society for American Archaeology, the Register of Professional Archaeologists, the Conservation and Heritage Management Committee of the American Institute of Archaeology (AIA), and the World Archaeological Congress (WAC). In Europe, he was vice-president for Europe of the ICOMOS International Committee for Archaeological Heritage Management (ICAHM), the president of the founding committee of the Europae Archaeologiae Consilium (1996-1999) and in 1998 he became president of the European Association of Archaeologists (EAA) and served two full terms. After that he chaired the Archaeological Heritage Prize

Committee of the latter (2004-2010). In 2009 he was elected co-president (with Douglas C. Comer) of ICAHM. In 2010, Willem was elected as one of the twelve members of the European Union's academic committee, the Joint Programming Initiative on Cultural Heritage and Global Change.

On top of all this, he travelled all over the world to evaluate nominations for World Heritage Sites. His own heritage management projects on the ground were geographically scattered across the globe too, from Europe and the Near-East, to Africa and Mongolia. His final major research activities were taking place under the Caribbean sun – where, as of 2013, he directed the heritage component of the ERC Synergy project NEXUS 1492 – when he was confronted with his awful illness.

Willem was honored for his achievements with many prizes and honorary memberships. To mention just some of the most prestigious ones; in 2004 he was the recipient of the Rheinlandtaler, which is awarded by the Landschaftsverband Nordrhein-Westfalen in Bonn, and in 2010 he received the Special Achievement Award of the Register of Professional Archaeologist's for his efforts in the Malta Convention and in heritage management in Europe and internationally. The last prize he received in person from colleagues was in 2012 when he was the laureate of 'his' EAA Heritage Prize. It showed an appreciation for his significant contribution to widening perspectives in archaeological heritage management, to position European archaeology and heritage in a broader global context. In hindsight, this beautifully closed the circle of his work for EAA. His highest reward was yet to come however. In September 2013, when he stepped down as dean of the Faculty of Archaeology, he was knighted into the Order of the Dutch Lion, a distinction reserved only for those with exceptional achievements. In April 2015 the Society for American Archaeology honoured Willem posthumously with the Presidential Recognition Award in recognition of his extraordinary work and to thank him for being 'a guiding light in the development of cultural heritage management throughout the world'.

***

More on Willem Willem's work can be found in the bibliographic entry on him in the Encyclopedia of Global Archaeology (Van den Dries 2014) and in the many obituaries and homages that were published about him on the internet and in print (*e.g.* De Waard 2015; Kristiansen 2015; Maas 2014; Marciniak 2015; Olivier and De Wit 2015; Schatorjé 2015; Van den Dries 2015).

De Waard, P. 2015. 'Willem Willems 1950-2014', *De Volkskrant – 6th January 2015*.

Kristiansen, K. 2015. 'Willem in memoriam (1950-2014)', *The European Archaeologist* 43: 12-14.

Maas, R. 2014. 'Willems, zelf een monument in de archeologie', *Limburgs Dagblad – 15th December 2014*.

Marciniak, A. 2015. 'On the memory of Willem Willems', *The European Archaeologist* 43: 19-20.

Olivier, A. and L.C. de Wit. 2015. 'In memoriam Willem Willems', in P.A.C. Schut, D. Scharff and L.C. de Wit (eds), *"Setting the Agenda": Giving new meaning to the European archaeological heritage*. Brussels: Europae Archaeologiae Consilium (EAC Occasional Paper no. 10), 7.

Schatorjé, J. 2015. 'In memoriam Willem Willems', *De Maasgouw* 134: 3-4.

Van den Dries, M.H. 2014. 'Willems, Willem J.H.', in C. Smith (ed.), *Encyclopedia of Global Archaeology*. New York: Springer, 7822-7824.

Van den Dries, M.H. 2015. 'In memoriam Willem J.H. Willems (1950-2014)', *The European Archaeologist* 43: 15-18.

Fernweh: Introduction

Normally and ideally, a book honouring a person is presented to this person during life. That is precisely what the editors and contributors to this volume had in mind. But sadly, while this book was on its way, things developed differently and ended up being far from normal and ideal.

The idea to create a *Festschrift* for professor dr. Willem J.H. Willems was born in the early summer of 2014. In academia it is *un bon usage* to honour a respected person with a celebration publication and the editors wanted to surprise Willem on the occasion of his official retirement as head of the Chair Group of Archaeological Heritage Management at the Faculty of Archaeology (Leiden University, The Netherlands), which was due for the autumn of 2015. We worked with him for many years, joined in several of his trips, projects and endeavours and had become much more than just colleagues. By means of a *liber amicorum* we wanted to thank him and express our gratitude for this successful collaboration.

The work was in full progress when in November 2014 disaster struck; Willem turned out to be very seriously ill and his prognosis was terribly bad. We, the editors, decided to inform him about the work that was under construction and to somewhat adapt the plans by including an interview with him in which he could react to issues put forward in 'his' book. Willem was very surprised and deeply moved to hear about the book and immediately agreed to have this interview. We set a date for the interview to be taken swiftly, but unfortunately this plan could not be carried out either; Willem's condition deteriorated unexpectedly fast and already on 13th December 2014, only a few days after we had shared our plans with him, he passed away.

When Willem heard about the book, he expressed his deep regret that he would not see the *result*. By explicitly expressing this, he clearly expected us to finish this enterprise and to actually produce the book. And so we did. But what started off as a *festschrift* suddenly became a *gedenkschrift*, a memorial volume. At times it was hard, for most – if not all – contributors. It was painful to continuously think of him while writing about and for him. Yet in a way it was also comforting and healing. Reading all those warm words about Willem, the thoughts he provoked and the ideas for future developments in heritage management he helped to shape, helped us to come to terms with his inevitable departure. It is in his honour that this volume was produced. We are confident that the discussions would have pleased him; one of our contributors said 'Willem would smile and make bad jokes about how many people were cajoled into writing scurrilous things about him'. He is probably right.

Aim of the book

When we initiated the book Willem was still working in various areas of the archaeological discipline, on all kinds of subjects. While he started off as an archaeologist specialized in the Dutch Roman period, during the last few decades he increasingly and passionately promoted and studied heritage management issues. He still shared a love for the past, but was arguably more interested in the present. He used to say that whilst archaeology was about investigating the past, heritage management was about dealing with that past in the present. So, this has become our main driver in composing 'his' book. We aimed to combine policies and science, theory and practice and to address important issues such as the effects of heritage legislation, conventions and policies; selection; *in situ* and *ex situ* preservation; commercial archaeology and quality management; implications of World Heritage and global heritage; heritage tourism and public engagement.

Willem loved discussions and – foremost – to stir things up a little bit by being provocative. He also did not shy away from trying to break down barriers where he experienced or saw them. For him, building bridges between disciplines and various worlds, between people with different expertise and experience, was instrumental to finding suitable answers to the challenges the profession was facing. So the *festschrift* we intended to create, aimed to celebrate the debate. We decided to compose a book of short, critical essays rather than academically justified elaborations on archaeological topics. We aimed for contributions that would evoke discussions and perhaps transcend the barriers of the academic world and the wider heritage discipline in order to also connect the heritage debate with wider societal debates.

Willem also had a gift for meeting and connecting people across cultures, countries, continents and disciplines. It has already been recounted how he was almost continuously travelling to undertake projects and setting up initiatives and networks all over the world. His contributions to the EAC, EAA, ICAHM and SAA are important examples, as well as his latest projects in Mongolia, in the Caribbean, and the evaluation missions for World Heritage nominations for ICOMOS, UNESCO's advisory body. His latest ventures included setting up the first EAA-SAA conference in the Caribbean, connecting several continents within one project. And due to his long, intense and varied career, his global explorations and his amicable, humorous personality, this gift resulted in an immense national and international network. Across all continents he knew a vast number of colleagues in archaeology and heritage management. If there were ever archaeologists on Mars, he would have made connections with them too. We therefore wanted to include as many people as possible with whom he (had) closely worked with – colleagues and friends working in a museum context, in state agencies, local or national authorities, universities, companies, etc. – that would also cover the various geographical regions and research areas Willem was involved in. We soon realised however that we could never be complete or exhaustive. We were not able to include all of the people whom he worked with and were inevitably forced to make a selection of contributors for him. We made an effort to have at least most of his main endeavours represented in this book, and apologize to those who could not be included although they may have wished to contribute, in particular after they learned about his passing away.

Fernweh

Willem travelled an awful lot. For his professional interests and activities he was almost continuously flying around the world, but also his family holidays brought him to remote places. It was already at a very young age that he discovered his desire to roam, to explore new worlds. His younger brother, Gerrit Willems, shared stories about Willem's wanderlust with the audience at the warm and impressive memorial service (22nd December 2014) in the large theatre in Amersfoort, which characterized Willem so neatly and beautifully. When Willem was a young boy he told his brother that his 'condition', this longing to explore what is out there, to get to know the worlds beyond his own, to absorb the flavours of different cultures, actually had a name. He said that his everlasting and continuous desire to new encounters was called *fernweh*. It is the opposite of longing for home, having *heimweh* (being home sick). To us, Willem used to say 'The past is a foreign country', after David Lowenthal (1985), whose work he hugely admired. Perhaps studying the past was also a means for him to wander off from the here and now. A visit to the past would presumably have been his ultimate journey.

Due to his *fernweh* there were actually not many countries left that Willem had not visited; he loved it when he could tick the box of yet another World Heritage site he had seen. But there was one particular place he had not been, even though it had been at the top of his bucket list for many years. He really would have loved to go to Rapa Nui, the isolated island in the Pacific Ocean, located west of Chile, also known as Easter Island. He wanted to see and feel the overwhelming presence of the hundreds of massive *moai*, the large men-like stone statues which the island's first inhabitants erected. But perhaps it was more than just the fascination for its heritage that attracted him to this – for us – remote destination. Part of his fascination may also have lain in the idea that this part of the world was rather difficult for him to reach, even with modern transportation means, while people living back (around 400 A.D.) had managed to colonize it and to start a thriving culture on this isolated 'big rock' in the middle of the South Pacific Ocean.

It was this unfulfilled dream that dictated our choice for the photo on the cover. This picture of some reconstructed *moai* from Rapa Nui, erected in the typical Dutch scenery of a green and flat arable field in Zeeland, right next to a highway and an industrial area, tells all the stories we wanted to convey. It first of all tells the story of the place Willem was longing for. It also symbolizes the destination (Zeeland) of the excursion we had planned with the heritage management chair group and to which he was very much looking forward, but which we had to do without him. He facilitated the trip and made us promise to go there anyway, no matter what. And we did.

The cover photo also symbolizes for us how Willem firmly stood up if he experienced that the interests of the past and the profession were at stake. The picture is taken not far from the plot where a field inspection was carried out under his supervision when he was chief inspector at the Dutch inspectorate and which triggered him to strongly voice his discontent about some aspects of the development-led archaeological practice he witnessed in those days. It was the start of a discussion and controversy that would chase him for many years.

But most of all the picture symbolizes the thread running through this book, how society connects with the past and vice versa and how objects, architectural remains and other features from the past can obtain a life of their own in the present, how they can become a new symbol, be re-interpreted, re-used, etc. (see foremost Haviser this volume). It illustrates how many if not all heritage objects have been reinterpreted recurrently throughout their existence. In this case the city council of Goes erected the reconstructed Easter Island statues in 2013 to celebrate the Goes-Latin America year and to commemorate that it was a Sea Captain from Zeeland, Jacob Roggeveen, who set foot on the Island on Easter Sunday (5th of April) 1722.

Outline of the book

All of the above mentioned worlds, projects and topics are present in this volume. The essays collected reflect upon or contribute to debates in contemporary archaeological heritage management and concern the various dimensions and/or consequences of our current (international) policies, practices and standards. Many essays touch upon more than one of these issues, but in a way, they all address variations of the same theme, which basically comes down to the meaning and use of the world's legacies from the past in and for society, at present and in the future. Interestingly, the overarching theme turned out to be the question of whose heritage are we protecting and how to better valorise research results and connect with society; all contributions more or less stress the importance and potential of archaeology and heritage to find relevance for the world of today. It is not surprising that this was also one of the main themes Willem was working on in the context of ICAHM, as Douglas Comer – Willem's co-president for ICAHM since 2009 – points out in an elaborate account of the work they did and of what needs to be done next.

We have organised the book into three parts. The first part, 'Time Travels' covers the big themes and (global) challenges the archaeological heritage discipline is facing and which Willem was working on, both in the Netherlands and at the international level. As a member of the committee of experts that drafted the Council of Europe's Malta Convention (1992), Willem has exerted a strong influence on the present day practice of archaeology and archaeological heritage management. Nearly 25 years later he had also become increasingly critical of the way things were developing. Most articles in this part refer to his concerns. The title refers to the visions, directions, strategies, approaches and plans the contributions in this part discuss and propose for the future. It starts with two contributions, one by Adrian Olivier and one by Arkadiusz Marciniak, which reflect upon the accomplishments that the Malta Convention has brought about, as well as the unfinished business and the challenges that remain. Interestingly they share many conclusions, although they are not equally optimistic about where we are heading. Tim Williams dives into the discussion of choosing between preserving archaeological resources for the future and developing knowledge by destroying these sources in the present, whereby the second option could increasingly count on Willem's support. Tim urges the discipline to start thinking more strategically than it has done thus far. This is followed by several contributions that in a way follow up on this appeal. Kristian Kristiansen questions the power of the past and the secret behind the success of cultural heritage. He underlines the need for critical, cross-disciplinary heritage research as a response and a possible way to find the answers heritage experts are looking for. Tim Darvil continues by arguing that archaeology should expand its knowledge-building beyond that of primarily constructing narrative knowledge. He proposes a diversified way of using archaeological data, to create connective knowledge that may satisfy a variety of human values, such as well-being and social solidarity, which may help to strengthen the support for our discipline's endeavours. The next two contributions look for answers in a similar but slightly different direction. Sjoerd van der Linde and Monique van den Dries propose to tackle the lack of progress in implementing Malta's aim to connect with society by being creative and innovative in creating societal values and to take these values as the core of the heritage business rather than just the production of knowledge. Felipe Criado-Boado, David Barreiro and Rocía Varela-Pousa also envision archaeology to play a role in social innovation. They propose a 20-point action list to turn the public into 'prosumers' rather than mere passive consumers. This is followed by two contributions, one by Pei-Lin Yu, Chen Shen and George Smith and one by Alicia Castillo, that call upon the sector to first of all be more inclusive. They consider the (continuous) discussion with all stakeholders, in the case of Alicia in particular also with those who oppose heritage activities, as the way forward to find the common ground that is so urgently needed to respectfully manage heritage in modern society. The final three essays explore some of the dilemmas the discipline faces in connecting with society. Annemarie Willems and Cynthia Dunning examine the riddle of 'archaeotourism', how it differs from other cultural tourism and needs a dedicated approach. Nelly Robles and Pieter ter Keurs discuss and analyse (modern and ancient) examples of the abuse of archaeology and heritage by society – for political or other reasons – and the lessons to be learned from this.

The second part of the book, 'Crossing borders and boundaries', consists of essays that consider the international organizations and projects Willem became (directly and indirectly) involved in and his trans-domain and trans-disciplinary interests and endeavours. It is organised in a more or less chronological order. First Ian Lilley introduces the work Willem and he accomplished in the context of ICOMOS and World Heritage, with which Willem was involved since 1988. He covers some of the main issues they were occupied with, through ICAHM, the archaeological advisory committee of ICOMOS, such as connecting with important key players in heritage management, such as large transnational organisations and international development banks, and the implications and problems of imposing 'western' heritage methods and values to the rest of the world. In the last couple of years one of Willem's main 'jobs' concerned the work for ICAHM, of which he become co-president (with Doug Comer) in 2009 and Henry Cleere provides an oral history account of how he witnessed and helped this organisation to come into being in the 1980s. Margaret Gowen writes about some of the work Willem did in Ireland as President of the EAA (in the 1990s) and afterwards, and how things have developed there since. This illustrates his devotion to the development-led heritage regime and the Malta Convention and how he communicated the pros and cons of commercial archaeology. Nathan Schlanger highlights a project that resulted from the 2010 ICAHM 'Africa initiative', an initiative which was intended among other things to counter the western view and hegemony in heritage issues. The project Nathan and his (African) colleagues undertook aimed to translate western concepts, such as museum and heritage into the African languages. Jeff Altschul and Gerry Wait talk about one of Willem's next adventures, that of designing the Oyu Tolgoi cultural heritage programme in Mongolia in which he participated in 2010. The discussion the three of them had with the Mongolian heritage officials led to a reconfiguring of the legislative and regulatory framework. The following three contributions relate to Willem's interest and work in the Caribbean. Jay Haviser shares the conversations Willem and he had – while enjoying the Caribbean sun, food and drink – on how the remnants from the past are given new meaning by present day people. The following two contributions are written in the context of the NEXUS1492 project of the Faculty of Archaeology that is being carried out in the Caribbean since 2013 and within which Willem was the principle investigator for the heritage management component. Corinne Hofman provides an overview of the heritage challenges that this region faces and how the NEXUS1492 project addresses these. Mariana Françozo illustrates the role and importance of studying the history and whereabouts of non-European and Caribbean collections in European museums to better understand heritage as an ever-reinvented present. In the final two essays borders are crossed as well, albeit figurative ones; they take a wider angle to analyse the human dimension of heritage and science. Amy Strecker observes the protection of historic landscapes from a legislative and planning point of view and stresses the need for a more democratic, human rights-based approach in legal designation processes. The final contribution, by Sander van der Leeuw, one of Willem's oldest friends, closes the section by taking a birds eye view on the wider context of the academic world's connection and perceived lack of connection with society.

In the third and final part, 'Home sweet home', we go back home to the Netherlands, just as Willem would always return home after all his travels to be with his family. A warm family that understood and accepted his urge to dedicate most of his time to being an advocate for the past in the present. It is his family that supported him most in this mission and who in fact made it possible. In doing so, they made the tremendous sacrifice of sharing him with all of us. 'Back home', the contributions first discuss Willem's involvement with and dedication to the Dutch archaeological heritage management system. Leonard de Wit recalls the crucial role Willem played in the signing of the Malta Convention by the Netherlands and its subsequent implementation in policies and heritage legislation, and urges the community of professionals to finish what Willem started and to complete what is left to be done. Monique Krauwer stresses the positive influence Willem has had on how governmental policies and legislation are developing in favour of the protection of the archaeological heritage, despite the fact that Willem himself had become less optimistic about the directions things had taken, such as the focus on preservation *in situ* as the foremost adagio for heritage preservation. Jos Deeben and Bjørn Smit go back to the earlier days of the ROB. They talk about Willem's influence on the development of the national and comprehensive predictive archaeological map, a typical Dutch instrument for heritage management that was first developed by the state agency (the ROB) in Amersfoort when Willem was its director. Tom Bloemers and Dick de Jager both continue the discussion on preservation *in situ*, the concept Willem helped to push as the way forward, but about which he increasingly expressed his doubts in the past couple of years. The concept of preservation *in situ* also heavily influences the management of the underwater and maritime heritage, as Martijn Manders shows. The maritime dimension of heritage was always on Willem's radar too. He was, for instance, trying hard to integrate it within the heritage management work for the NEXUS1492 project in the Caribbean. His dedication to maritime heritage is also illustrated by the book Water & Heritage (2015) that he was working on with Henk van Schaik until almost his very last day and which he unfortunately did not live to see either. In his essay Martijn also brings the archaeologists' relationship with the public back to the centre of the debate and the last four contributions continue on this theme. The first two represent the museum world in Leiden with which Willem collaborated intensively. Ruurd Halbertsma goes back to the very beginning of the formation of the collection of the National Museum of Antiquities (RMO), to the discussions and political processes behind it; discussions and politics that often still rule today's collection building strategies. Steven Engelsman, the former director of the Museum of Ethnology in Leiden, shows how they put people before objects and include intangible heritage in museum exhibitions. Although Willem – still first and foremost an archaeologist – personally preferred the 'real stuff' (finds, sites and monuments) rather than intangible heritage he too increasingly advocated for taking the human dimension much more into account in heritage management practices and decisions, in particular the values and needs of present day people. Dieke Wesselingh discusses how a modern city such as Rotterdam, which prefers to look forward rather than back, literally brings the past to its inhabitants. Bringing heritage back to the people is also the topic of Tom Hazenberg's paper. He shows how valuable it is for disabled people in the small rural village of Zwammerdam to be able to take care of remnants from the Roman Empire and its border, the *limes*. This contribution brings the volume full circle, as Willem was in the last couple of years heavily involved in the preparation of the nomination of the Lower German *limes* as World Heritage, a project he clearly liked a lot because he could finally connect his first professional love, Roman Archaeology, with his experience in World Heritage. Unfortunately again this is something of which he will not see the result.

Before bringing this introduction to a close, we would like to sincerely thank our contributors for their efforts in helping to accomplish this book, in particular since all the essays were written under difficult circumstances, while we were all mourning for the loss of a much appreciated colleague and good friend, whom we dearly miss. We are grateful to the board of the Faculty of Archaeology for providing facilities and some of the necessary finances, and to Karsten Wentink and Corné van Woerdekom of Sidestone Press, who wanted to thank Willem for his support to their enterprise by generously offering to lend a hand in bringing this volume to publication.

We hope this book will help to keep the memory of Willem Willems alive and to carry on with his mission in his spirit.

Monique van den Dries
Sjoerd van der Linde
Amy Strecker

Leiden, September 2015

Taking the next steps

Douglas C. Comer

ICOMOS International Committee on Archaeological Heritage Management /
Cultural Site Research and Management, United States of America

*'…February made me shiver
With every paper I'd deliver
Bad news on the doorstep'*
Don McLean (American Pie)

We lost Willem quickly, and I was glad that he did not linger in discomfort, but it was a huge, unexpected blow for all who knew him: his family, most significantly, but also his friends, his colleagues at his university and around the world, his students. For weeks and then months I was occupied in writing obituaries and pieces for memorial services and websites, communicating bad news to the world.

There was a time when people read the news on paper rather than on electronic devices. Young people rose before dawn to carry stacks of newspapers through neighbourhoods, dropping one on each doorstep, seeing the headline for the top story over and over again. That is, at least apocryphally, what stopped a boy named Don McLean in his tracks on the day he delivered newspapers with a headline about the death of three musicians, including Buddy Holley, the works of whom are now seen as being seminal to the form of music emerging in 1959, which became known as rock and roll. In my head I began to hear American Pie, the song that McLean wrote about that experience, each time I sat down to write something about Willem. Unlike McLean, we must keep moving, toward the goals that inspired Willem.

I had known and worked with Willem for years on ICAHM (the ICOMOS International Committee of Archaeological Heritage Management) business, and then we became Co-Presidents of that organization, a decision we made in part because there was so much to do, but really, as much because working together was fun. Willem and I communicated just about every day for years, usually via email, sometimes by telephone or video communication. Then we would see each other in person at conferences or meetings that we would arrange when one of us was traveling to a place near where the other person happened to be, and of course at World Heritage Sites. It is quite easy for me to imagine even now that just because I haven't received an email from him today, I will receive one tomorrow, or if I emailed him, he would email back. When I have to write something like this, of course, I must acknowledge that this is not possible. Taking the step of putting these thoughts into words is therefore difficult for me. I am guessing that these words are probably the last contribution the editors of this volume received.

We were good friends, so we talked a lot, especially making a lot of jokes together, which made us talk more. But something happened during those years of conversation, and our ideas began to change.

Archaeology for archaeologists?

We began by thinking of ourselves as archaeologists, and we never stopped thinking of ourselves in that way, but as time went on, recognized clearly that archaeological heritage management demands more than expertise in archaeology. At the time of his death, we were deep into an ongoing conversation about levels of membership in ICAHM. It is one of many ICOMOS scientific committees, but one of the largest, and because we deal with evaluations and nominations of sites to the World Heritage List, I am sure one of the busiest.

All scientific committees, as directed by the ICOMOS Secretariat, have established a category of membership called Expert. Willem and I were adamant for years that only archaeologists should be considered for Expert membership. We were both convinced that archaeologists, who deal with context every day as they conduct their fieldwork and analysis, understand its importance in a special way. As archaeologists, we know in our bones that when something is taken out of context, the capacity to learn from the find is enormously diminished. Archaeologists follow this principal rigorously in their own work, as they must, but some in influential positions seem unconcerned with preserving context for all archaeological material. In the United States, where archaeology itself has largely been privatized, private property is sacrosanct. In most states it is legal to take artifacts from the ground in any way on one's own property, or with the permission of the property owner. Recreational metal detecting for artifacts has become commonplace. It is legal, but knowing that the artifacts in context are non-renewable, this activity is surely something that archaeologists with a sense of stewardship for public heritage, should discourage in every possible way. It should be clear that effective heritage management requires that the public be made aware that collecting artifacts without following the painstaking protocols employed by archaeologists destroys context.

Many archaeologists were appalled when a spate of television programs, all produced in the United States, appeared a few years ago celebrating the joys of metal detecting for historic artifacts. ICAHM was concerned that by portraying this activity as a harmless pursuit, the public would take away from these programs that context was unimportant, that it was the artifact itself that held value, not the contribution that an artifact in context could make to public heritage. By emphasizing the value of the artifact itself, either monetarily or as a point of departure for an individual, fantasized version of the past, detectorists would likely be more tempted to metal detect on US public lands and in other countries, where it is illegal. In the western US, more than half of some states are public lands, with little effective protection from metal detection. The Bureau of Land Management, which oversees a great percentage of these lands, has only one ranger to patrol each million acres. Nonetheless, the US-based Register of Professional Archaeologists (RPA) had, in a test case, determined that the appearance of a professional archaeologist on the National Geographic *Diggers* television program would not violate the standards of that organization.

This brought into focus a number of issues that are central to archaeological heritage management. One of these issues is the special role that archaeological material plays in the construction, deconstruction, and reconstruction of public heritage. From a heritage management standpoint, the first responsibility of an archaeologist is to preserve the archaeological record. It follows that in conducting research, an archaeologist who is mindful of this responsibility will excavate no more than absolutely necessary. It also follows that such an archaeologist cannot encourage or condone excavation of archaeological materials by a non-archaeologist, simply because the careful steps needed to document how and what was found, and to provide a fact-based interpretation of why it was found there, will not be taken. Laws pertaining to this might vary; as Willem would point out, Anglo-Saxon countries tend to be more lenient in this regard than most of the rest of the world. In England, for example, finding what is legally defined as "treasure" obligates the finder to report this within fourteen days, but the finder usually receives some level of monetary reward (Thomas and Stone 2009: 1-9). This is controversial, but understandable: there are enormously valuable items to be found in England and in many other countries, including hordes of coins, jewelry, bars of silver and gold. This provides great incentive for people to metal detect. The legal framework devised in England is an attempt at damage control, participating in a program that generates enthusiasm for finding belt buckles or a single historic coin that have little or no worth is an incentive to produce damage.

From the past to heritage...

Heritage most essentially deals with how we present the past. It is a term which, until it came under academic scrutiny, was taken to refer to a harmless celebration of a common past that knit certain groups together. David Lowenthal began to look at these common understandings of what heritage was, perhaps most notably in his book, 'The Past is a Foreign Country' (1985). (A quote from that book appeared on the announcement for Willem's memorial service.) This book generated a much greater awareness that heritage could and should be subjected to critical scrutiny. Today, heritage studies has developed into an important way of understanding ourselves, one that draws heavily from an anthropological approach which attends closely to economic and political factors, especially the politics of identity. Willem's contribution to this development was great; he established a thriving chair group in heritage management at Leiden University.

Nations, for example, construct a heritage in many ways. Among them: nations recognize a variety of holidays, which are affirmations of unity, often framed as unity based upon the resolution of historic grievances. In what were once colonies, independence days provide a rationale for the existence of a nation by celebrating the means by which it obtained freedom from another, oppressive one. Further, each person can imagine that they as individuals have obtained freedom along with the nation in which they are citizens, no matter what their personal circumstances. Historical narratives associated with the struggle for independence are inevitably presented on such occasions. Holidays can also be religious in nature, offering an account of past events that provide a basis for the theological underpinnings of a religion. If religious holidays are national in scale (in many places, these are bank holidays and holidays when government employees don't work), they generally represent the religion that is dominant in that society. Many nations, however, also acknowledge the holidays observed by minority religions. This can be done, for example, by granting leave from work or school so that adherents can celebrate religious holidays in their own ways, which will feature an historical narrative that is different from that which is offered by the dominant religion. Such efforts to accommodate alternate accounts of the past must still fit under the national narrative of the past if they are to be successful over the long term.

This holds true, as well, for ethnic groups. In the United States, for example, Columbus Day is celebrated, which commemorates the discovery of the Americas by a person from Europe. For many decades, this fit comfortably within a United States national narrative of discovery and taming of wilderness. At present, however, this presentation of the past is increasingly challenged by Native American groups, who emphasize events previously overlooked by that narrative. They point out, in particular, that the Americas were occupied by humans for millennia before Columbus's arrival, an historical fact established beyond doubt by archaeological research. Further, Native American groups contend that events which ensued after the arrival of Columbus, such as genocide, the enslavement of some indigenous groups, and the forced movement of others to reservations, are hardly suitable causes for celebration. These events are also fully borne out by the archaeological record.

... and back to the past

Such a critical review and subsequent reformulation of heritage assumes that it is possible to ascertain actual events, as opposed to events as they have been recounted by individuals or the consensus of groups in ways promote that the interests of those doing so. Physical evidence plays an essential role in contesting presentations of the past that serve the special interests of individuals and groups. While pure objectivity might be impossible in the search for truth, it is clearly possible to use material evidence to disprove a misrepresentation of the past. If, for example, we have a great body of physical evidence that established the presence of humans in the New World many thousands of years ago, which we do, then Columbus did not discover the Americas.

But material evidence can do more; it can provide the basis for a narrative of the past different from that which dominates the present. Columbus Day, from a charitable standpoint, celebrated the opportunities that the Americas provided to those fleeing from a ridged, class-dominated society. The New Colossus, a poem by Emma Lazarus engraved in the base of the Statue of Liberty in New York, puts it this way:

> *"Keep ancient lands, your storied pomp!" cries she*
> *With silent lips. "Give me your tired, your poor,*
> *Your huddled masses yearning to breathe free,*
> *The wretched refuse of your teeming shore.*
> *Send these, the homeless, tempest-tost to me,*
> *I lift my lamp beside the golden door!"*

In doing so, it ignored the terrible suffering that accompanied the great tide of European immigrants. A revisionist history of these events is based upon more than archaeological findings, but the materials gained from archaeological research occupy a special position in this alternate narrative, making it much more than a difference of opinion, and instead inviting a dialogue that might merge or even reconcile different versions of the past.

While Herodotus is generally referred to as the first historian, others argue that honor should go to Thucydides. Herodotus often provided fanciful reports, which included the interventions of the gods in the affairs of men. Thucydides took great pains not to do this; his position was that the recounting of events should be as factual as possible. Donald Kagan spent two decades comparing the work of Thucydides on the Peloponnesian War (Kagan 2009: 20-21). His conclusion was that Thucydides might as well be known as the *first* revisionist historian. There were histories before his time, but concern with facts was not paramount.

Unfinished business

In the last year of his life, Willem was engaged in using archaeology as a tool that might produce just this kind of revisionist history. His role was that of organizing heritage management for the NEXUS1492-project, a major research effort funded by the European Union. His work promised to make prominent the ways in which material culture can serve to act as a check on ideological presentations of the past that excuse injustice.

In one of his last publications, Willem decried the politicization of the process by which sites are inscribed on the World Heritage List (Willems 2014). Politics here, as it usually does, is based on economic incentives. For example, is the well-publicized 'destruction' of archaeological artifacts and sites by extremists in the Middle East really about ideology, or is it more about lining the pockets of those who use terror to achieve political ends? Looting sites is a way of mining artifacts that can be sold to well-to-do collectors, and many of the artifacts seen destroyed in popular social media were in fact replicas. The genuine items are worth money; why would those who covet money for power destroy them?

More to the immediate point, there is now a widespread belief, one that seems to be becoming a self-fulfilling prophecy, that sites inscribed on the World Heritage List become an economic engine. The tourism industry now seeks out World Heritage Sites located in what were once out of the way places. They provide enticements to travel for those who have done Europe and the National Parks in the Western US, and the most renowned World Heritage Sites from Petra to Machu Picchu to Pompeii to Angkor. Travel is easy now, within reach of the ever expanding global middle class.

And this introduces real threats. There are threats to the way of life of inhabitants of city destinations such as Barcelona and Venice. And, very alarmingly, also threats to the non-renewable resource of archaeological material. Archaeological sites are now being inscribed without anything like an effective management system to protect the sites from damage and destruction. For this reason, Willem and I began the long process of developing standards for the management of archaeological sites that are on, or which are bound for, as witnessed by their appearance on a Tentative List, the World Heritage List. These next years, hopefully culminating in 2017, will see the fulfillment of that goal.

Once we have standards that must be met by sites inscribed on the World Heritage List, they can be applied to the Tentative Lists that all signatories to the World Heritage Convention are supposed to develop. It takes years to put in place an effective management system where one does not exit, or exists only in embryonic form. This sobering fact, however, introduces the possibility of mapping out a multi-year plan, complete with estimated costs for each year, which can be presented to foreign aid organizations in developed countries, or to philanthropic organizations. In effect, a partnership could be formed with such organizations that would provide the resources not available in many nations wishing to inscribe sites on the World Heritage List.

Much work remains to be done: work that will realize the overall objectives of the World Heritage Convention and which will engage the archaeological communities in all countries in the task of preserving the archaeological record, and not attending solely to the interests of the sites in which a particular archaeologist might be conducting investigations on a for-profit basis or for academic purposes. Work to elucidate how heritage is used for political and economic ends. We must proceed with this task, and then devise the means by which to engage the economists and political scientists who exercise immediate influence on public policy. As varied and as important as Willem's accomplishments were, he knew that there was much left to do, and this work should be his legacy.

References

Kagan, D. 2010. *The Reinvention of History*. New York: Viking.

Lowenthal, D. 1985. *The Past is a Foreign Country*. Cambridge: Cambridge University Press.

Thomas, S. and P.G. Stone (eds). 2009. *Metal Detecting and Archaeology*. Woodbridge, England: The Boydell Press.

Willems, W.J.H. 2014. The Future of World Heritage and the Emergence of Transnational Regimes. *Heritage & Society* 7(2): 105-120.

Time travels
Facing challenges in heritage management

Challenging values

Adrian Olivier

Institute of Archaeology, University College London
(formerly Heritage Protection Director, English Heritage), United Kingdom

Willem Willems was a member of the Council of Europe Committee of Experts that drafted the Valletta Convention. He remained deeply interested in the working of the convention throughout his career and published on this topic repeatedly (*e.g.* 1998; 1999; 2014). Most recently (2014) he summarised both the problems that the convention was intended to address and his view of its consequences.

As Willem recognised, the Valletta Convention was the product of a very different world-view of heritage, and of the very different European socio-political and economic context that prevailed in the 1990s. In common with other broadly contemporary instruments, the Valletta Convention placed considerable emphasis on prohibition – focussing more on what should not be done. The cornerstone of the convention was the concept that the fragile, vulnerable, and finite archaeological resource was increasingly under threat from the growing pace of development and that steps needed to be taken to secure its better preservation. Mitigation (through excavation) was regarded as a secondary response, when all other options (particularly for preservation *in situ*) had been eliminated.

Challenging conventions: barriers to democracy

In Willem's opinion the Valletta Convention was directly responsible both for a significant increase in levels of public awareness and interest in archaeology (2014: 152), and an associated focus on public benefit (2014: 155). He ascribed this to the need (foreseen by the drafters of the Convention) to legitimise the increased costs of archaeological work by demonstrating its public benefit through more effective public communications. As a consequence, in recent decades archaeologists throughout Europe have opened up their work to involve public stakeholders. However, Willem also considered that a great deal of the archaeological work carried out across Europe within the framework of the Valletta Convention had been turned into a relatively mechanistic exercise that suffered from bureaucratisation and over-regulation 'that increase the distance between policy and practice and often stand in the way of good research' (2014: 152).

One of the greatest successes of the Valletta Convention has unquestionably been the integration of archaeology with spatial planning. This led directly to an exponential increase in the volume of archaeological work undertaken year on year throughout Europe – and of course a significant growth in the number of practising archaeologists. As a result, field archaeology in particular has become increasingly 'professionalised' (*cf.* the recent granting in the United Kingdom of 'chartered' status to the former Institute for Archaeologists). Increased professionalism is invariably seen as a good thing by the professionals involved but in other quarters, the rise of professionalism can be regarded as a barrier to democracy. The growth of archaeology and of archaeologists has faltered recently as a result of the (continuing) impacts of worldwide economic recession and austerity policies on archaeology (more severe in some countries than others). Nevertheless there are well in excess of 25,000 archaeologists working in Europe today. The recent Discovering the Archaeologists of Europe (DISCO) project identified 24,740 archaeologists working in 21 European countries (see www.discovering-archaeologists.eu).

One of the by-products of this growth was the foundation in 1994 of the European Association of Archaeologists, EAA (now with a membership base in excess of 2000), and in 1999 of the *Europae Archaeologiae Consilium* (the European Archaeological Council, EAC), the network of state heritage agencies which brought together directors and representatives of organisations with legal responsibilities for the management of the archaeological heritage (Willems 2000). Willem of course was a central figure in the genesis of both organisations and a steadfast supporter of, and active participant in their work.

One of the key objectives of the founders of the EAA was to position archaeological heritage in a wider European framework and to combine the academic and the practical, research and heritage (Kristiansen 2015); themes to which Willem would return throughout his career. The focus of the EAC was on heritage management, specifically in the context of standards and the development of evolving approaches to preservation, conservation, and management; again all subjects of deep concern to Willem throughout his career. The EAC built a strong relationship with the Council of Europe and participated directly in activities associated not just in monitoring the implementation of the Council's heritage conventions but in trying to use this process as a platform to develop and then raise standards – another central concern of the Valletta Convention.

It is easy to make subjective judgements about the success or otherwise of conventions, but repeated attempts by the EAC (and others) have consistently demonstrated that it is infinitely more difficult to understand exactly how conventions are implemented and put into practice on the ground and then to measure actual impacts in any meaningful fashion (*e.g.* Olivier and Van Lindt 2014). Nevertheless, notwithstanding subjective judgements to the contrary, it is clear that the articles of the Valletta Convention relating to dissemination, research, and public awareness (Articles 7-9) have seen the least activity – possibly because these topics have generally been accorded a lower priority (by governments and official agencies) (see Van den Dries 2015). Despite significant advances in these areas over the past twenty years, there is still real concern in some quarters that much more remains to be done if these particular objectives of the Valletta Convention are to be achieved. It seems unlikely, however, that these can be operationalised simply through regulatory provisions. The real question rather is how to embed (and resource) such activities properly into the daily work of practicing archaeologists. The answer is likely to lie not in new regulatory frameworks, but in accepting a fundamental change in prevailing archaeological values and approaches.

Challenging attitudes and approaches: placing archaeology at the heart of communities

The creation and successful promulgation of the Valletta Convention was an outstanding achievement, not the least because at the time the relatively limited number of archaeologists did not occupy a strong position in society. The convention gave archaeology a legitimate place (and voice) at the spatial planning table and in turn led to the creation of a (relatively) strong and professional area of practice. As Willem pointed out (with the advantages of hindsight) it is also possible to identify some negative and unlooked for consequences of the convention (2014) – but these should not in any way eclipse its very significant achievements.

Nevertheless, twenty-three years after the Valletta Convention came into force, the socio-political and economic context for archaeology has changed significantly. As a result of the current economic situation, archaeological practice now occurs in an ever more constrained political and economic environment in which deregulation

> 'It is legitimate to question whether the Valletta Convention remains relevant today or whether archaeologists need to move away from such instruments and develop new responses and approaches.'

coupled with delegation and devolution and increasing decentralisation of responsibility to lower and more local levels of administration are changing the regulatory framework under which archaeology has hitherto prospered. In many countries, the consequences of these changes are imposing severe pressures not just on the archaeological resource itself, but also on the practice of archaeology. In this situation it is legitimate to question whether the Valletta Convention (or any such regulatory framework) remains relevant today or whether archaeologists need to move away from such instruments, and develop new responses and approaches that better match new social circumstances by placing archaeology at the heart of communities so that it becomes a more people-centred discipline.

Such a people-oriented approach exemplified by the Florence Convention (Landscape) and Faro Convention (Value of Cultural Heritage for Society), is very easy to aspire to, but much more difficult to operationalise in practice. In reviewing the positives and negatives of the Valletta Convention Willem rightly challenged the existing orthodoxy of *preservation in situ*, and in particular focused on what he saw as the growing failure of the relationship between practice and research which in his view derived in part at least from different pressures resulting from the bureaucratisation and commercialisation of archaeological practice.

Willem was passionate in his unshakable belief that research values *must* lie at the heart of all archaeological work and today there is wide (but not universal) acceptance that contract/commercial archaeology should always be firmly grounded in academic research. However it is certainly true that commercial and academic archaeologists have different visions of the nature and purpose of archaeological practice. These arise from the different value-systems and different drivers that reflect the different needs of different customers and different audiences. The problems identified by Willem may therefore be less about shortcomings of the Valletta Convention (which in practice is interpreted very differently in different national contexts and therefore is actually very adaptable) and more about the readiness (or otherwise) of archaeologists radically to change their ways of thinking and their approaches to their work.

Different tools have been developed in different countries to address this problem (*e.g.* in the UK the development of national and regional research frameworks), but the challenges remain. We must collectively find new and better mutual benefits to underpin and reinforce the reciprocal (and symbiotic) relationship between practice and research. We must foster better dialogue between the worlds of academia and professional practice and recognise the positive contribution that each can make to the work of the other. We need to understand how involvement in commercial archaeology can deliver better research, teaching, and training and how opportunities in contract archaeology can be exploited to develop innovative practice, expanding the social benefits of fieldwork and pushing forward the frontiers of the discipline.

Challenging other orthodoxies

By challenging the orthodoxy of *preservation in situ* Willem challenged the profession to make a fundamental shift in approach and practice that would re-calibrate field archaeology to focus on the primacy of research values and at the same time position archaeology better to serve public value and public benefit. However, in characteristic fashion, this may only have been an opening gambit in a much more deeply rooted and fundamental reappraisal of archaeological values and practice that Willem might have planned for us all in coming years.

There are many other problems facing archaeology today (including the failing relationship between archaeological practice and people), and there are many other questions that Willem might have wanted to ask – and other orthodoxies that he might have wanted to challenge in his inimitable (and invariably humorous) way:

1. What are the appropriate roles for government, voluntary bodies, communities, and private individuals in making decisions about archaeology?

2. Dissemination is a one-way process – how can public engagement be integrated into the skills that archaeologists learn so that it is seen as a fundamental component of archaeological practice that demonstrates *de facto* public benefit?

3. How can we identify what is important, what is valued, and what is significant when difficult choices have to be made about what to preserve and what to excavate?

4. How much archaeological capital should be tied up in conservation and protection *per se* – do we truly understand the relationship between what we value and how we transform it through the archaeological process?

5. In ever more diverse societies with increasing constraints on funding how much and whose heritage should be protected?

6. Recent advances show us that archaeological knowledge is infinite – to what extent should we even continue to worry about the finite nature of the physical archaeological resource?

7. What is the appropriate balance between the role of archaeologist as 'expert' defining heritage values for other people to consume and as 'facilitator' enabling other people's perceptions of heritage values?

8. To what extent should archaeologists recognise and better understand how society values heritage and incorporate other perceptions into our professional belief system?

Willem would have delighted in furnishing us with his *definitive* answers to all these questions (and to ones that we haven't even thought of yet!). These would not always have been answers that we would have expected (or wanted). It is certain too that we would not always have agreed. It is equally certain that we would have taken great pleasure in the discourse accompanied (always) by good fellowship, good food, and good beer. It is our very great loss and with inestimable sadness, that individually, and collectively through the organisations with which he will always be associated (EAA and EAC), we will now have to look for the answers without the benefit of Willem's deep experience, great wisdom, and gentle good humour. His presence will be sorely missed in all our future counsels.

References

Kristiansen, K. 2015. 'Willem in memoriam (1950 – 2014)', *The European Archaeologist* 43: 12-14.

Olivier, A. and P. van Lindt. 2014. 'Valletta Convention perspectives: an EAC survey', in V.M. van der Haas and P.A.C. Schut (eds), *The Valletta Convention: Twenty Years After – Benefits, Problems, Challenges*. Brussels: Europae Archaeologiae Consilium (EAC Occasional Paper No. 9), 165-176.

Van den Dries, M.H. 2015. 'From Malta to Faro, how far have we come? Some facts and figures on public engagement in the archaeological heritage sector in Europe', in P.A.C. Schut, D. Scharff and L.C. de Wit, *"Setting the Agenda": Giving new meaning to the European archaeological heritage*. Brussels: Europae Archaeologiae Consilium (EAC Occasional Paper No. 10), 45-55.

Willems, W.J.H. 1998. 'Archaeology and Heritage Management in Europe', *European Journal of Archaeology* 1(3): 293-312.

Willems, W.J.H. 1999. *The Future of European Archaeology*. Oxbow Lecture 3, Archaeology in Britain conference 1997. Oxford: Oxbow.

Willems, W.J.H. (ed). 2000. *Challenges for European Archaeology*. Zoetermeer: Europae Archaeologiae Consilium.

Willems, W.J.H. 2014. 'Malta and its consequences: a mixed blessing', in V.M. van der Haas and P.A.C. Schut (eds.) *The Valletta Convention: Twenty Years After – Benefits, Problems, Challenges*. Brussels: Europae Archaeologiae Consilium (EAC Occasional Paper No. 9), 151-156.

The aftermath of Malta

Arkadiusz Marciniak

Adam Mickiewicz University, Poznań, Poland

The past is a foreign country. It needs to be constantly understood, conceptualized and institutionalized in an ever-changing present. The last decade of the 1990s was a period of optimism and hope for a better future. After decades of separation and conflict Europeans were again united and had to seek the means of building cohesion and a common identity. The importance of archaeological heritage was acknowledged as an intrinsic element of European civilization and as a valuable source of collective memory.

The foundational role of archaeological heritage was confirmed and codified in the European Convention on the Protection of the Archaeological Heritage. The Malta Convention, as it came to be known, rightly captured the soul and challenges of the time. It adequately and accurately identified efficient means of dealing with the threats archaeological heritage faced in the period of unprecedented large scale investment. For almost two decades, the Malta Convention laid foundations for its management and protection across Europe.

Malta as a landmark

The Convention defined archaeological heritage as an infinite source of the European collective memory, a carrier of the European past and an instrument for historical and scientific study. Its protection was integrated with planning at the regional and national levels. It also paved the way for its inclusion into sustainable development. More importantly, it secured adequate financing for archaeological works from national, regional and private bodies by linking it with investment and development projects. This in turn laid the foundations for the unprecedented growth of the archaeological profession.

The Convention was met with great enthusiasm. As of 2015, it was ratified by 42 Council of Europe member states. It became an undisputable guide and point of reference for a range of solutions in the field of archaeological heritage. Legal measures and administrative practices of a largely similar character were implemented into national legislation across Europe. They triggered a continuous growth of the profession in terms of economic activity, employment and productivity. A new and previously unknown category of professional contract archaeologists emerged and were confronted with the demands of the corporate world and temptations of consumer society (see Kristiansen 2009; Van den Dries 2011).

These developments of the 1990s were effectively institutionalized in the form of two major bodies: the European Association of Archaeologists (EAA) and the Europae Archaeologiae Consilium (EAC). They were aimed at integrating different national archaeologies and merging the hitherto largely separated segments of the profession, including heritage offices, academia, museums and the commercial sector.

Many and major challenges

The outcomes of the Malta Convention in many instances did not match expectations. Instead of becoming a mission of public service, archaeological heritage protection became too much of a business guided by principles of the market economy. It has been overrun by the self-regulating competitive model quintessentially played out in the financial fields of costs and profits (see different chapters in Schlanger and Aitchison 2010). It is not surprising then that any reductions in time and resources would only compromise the quality of the work undertaken, its contribution to knowledge and its benefit to society (Marciniak 2015). By paving

> 'What is required is more understanding of the dynamic conditions of today, in order to find appropriate and accurate responses to them.'

the way for largely uncontrolled commercialisation of archaeological practice, the implemented solutions revealed the previously unknown and in fact unthinkable market-oriented and managerial face of archaeology. It was pretty unpleasant and not surprisingly unwelcome by many. Furthermore, the public and private spending on archaeology reached an unprecedented level, not accompanied by an increase of the quality of work, including excavations, post-excavation and the publication of final results.

Numerous pitfalls and shortcomings of Malta archaeology were already becoming evident around the middle of the first decade of the 2000s. These were amplified and accelerated by a global crisis of 2008. This challenged a relative consensus in this field and ultimately ended the flourishing era for archaeology and archaeological heritage in Europe. It marked the beginning of yet relatively unspecified *modus operandi* in the field.

The most direct consequence of the global crisis was the slowing down of economic growth. The sustainability of the economic model supporting archaeological activities was speedily challenged (see examples in Schlanger and Aitchison 2010), lost its relevance and justification. In particular, public spending cuts directly affected a number of archaeological contracts. This led to the collapse of the archaeological market and ultimately heralded the end of the archaeological boom. With large-scale investments almost over, the dynamically growing sector of contact archaeologists was abruptly stopped and the relevance of archaeological results undermined. The Malta Convention triggered model of archaeological practice was proven to be short-lived and not sustainable for longer than two decades. Consequently, somehow the nostalgic aura of archaeological heritage and the undisputable consensus as to its role for European cohesion and identity has gone. It was deprived of its foundational significance and its significance has been forgotten (see *e.g.* Aitchison 2009).

The reaction to these deficiencies of Malta inclined solutions by national governments, additionally amplified by the economic crisis, was prompt. Different legislative and administrative measures were introduced in different national settings, irrespective of political underpinnings. These mitigation solutions significantly reduced the effectiveness and efficiency of the hitherto existing model. It was no longer seen as feasible and in accordance with newly emerged strategies of sustainable development in the continent. These new legal frameworks significantly jeopardized the idea of archaeology and archaeological heritage, as defined almost two decades earlier, and had a range of profound consequences. One of the most serious was the lowering of the standards of protection of archaeological heritage.

The past few years marks a largely different situation compared to the beginning of the 1990s. A united Europe is no longer a project overwhelmingly supported by Europeans at large and is not seen as a universal remedy to different challenges of the globalizing and increasingly unsecure world. Archaeologists are not seen as partners by the decision makers and their voice is hardly heard in public debate. The disciplinary practice is getting rapidly and uncontrollably dispersed. This creates an uncomfortable situation, often despair, for those who cannot come to terms with these dramatic changes and are unable not only to keep apace but even to conceptualize them.

Looking for new beacons

One cannot expect the situation to change in the foreseeable future. It clearly requires new solutions. A large body of archaeologists has chosen to fiercely fight for the status quo and insist on doing business as usual. This is not a viable solution and will lead us nowhere. Rather than complaining about policies of national governments, the undermined role of archaeology and archaeological heritage, and twisted developments within the discipline, it is necessary to say farewell to the Malta Convention and the bygone world it created. What is required is more understanding of the dynamic conditions of today, in order to find appropriate and accurate responses to them. More efficient modes of engagement with material culture and what is left from the past are needed. Archaeologists need to make a common cause with people and communities seeking to preserve and gain respect for their cultural and archaeological heritage, as they understand it, whether that understanding has an archaeological twist to it or not. They should develop an awareness of numerous economic and social benefits beyond identity, ownership, descent and scholarship. There is also a need to amplify relationships with other practices inspired by the past and the materiality of the past, including artistic creations and design practices. The voice of international corporations and banks, whatever their motivations, should not be left unnoticed. This is particularly timely considering an increasingly evident withdrawal of national states from the domain of archaeological heritage and a shift to global and transnational heritage regimes (*e.g.* Hodder 2010; Willems 2009, 2014).

Willem Willems was and remains to be at the forefront of the pursuit of an ever changing role of the past, archaeology and archaeological heritage. As one of the very few, he kept setting the agenda and tried to grasp their nature in a rapidly changing world, including the post-2008 period of turbulent European and global history. His intellectual wit, critical mind, genuine intuition and extraordinary administrative skill made him well suited to the role. He completed his duty in an unprecedented way throughout his professional life, in a variety of different forms, including numerous publications and presentations and active participation in several bodies: as member of the committee of experts of the Council of Europe that drafted the Malta Convention; as founder and then President of the EAA and the EAC; as Co-President of the ICOMOS Committee for Archaeological Heritage Management (ICAHM) and board member of the Centre for International Heritage Activities. He remained actively engaged in these diverse organizations until his untimely death. In the years to come, his vision will keep inspiring those who are left to ultimately grasp the nature of the past, archaeology, and the archaeological heritage of today.

References

Aitchison, K. 2009. 'After the "gold rush": global archaeology in 2009', *World Archaeology* 41(4): 659-671.

Hodder, I. 2010. 'Cultural heritage rights: From ownership and descent to justice and well – being', *Anthropological Quarterly* 83(4): 861-882.

Kristiansen, K. 2009. 'Contract archaeology in Europe: an experiment in diversity', *World Archaeology* 41(4): 641-648.

Marciniak, A. 2015. 'Archaeology and ethics. The case of Central-Eastern Europe', in C. Gnecco and D. Lippert (eds), *Ethics and Archaeological Praxis*. New York: Springer, 49-60.

Schlanger, N. and K. Aitchison (eds.) 2010. *Archaeology and the global economic crisis. Multiple impacts, possible solutions*. Brussels: Culture Lab Editions.

Van den Dries, M.H. 2011. 'The good, the bad and the ugly? Evaluating three models of implementing the Valletta Convention', *World Archaeology* 43(4): 594-604.

Willems, W.J.H. 2009. 'European and world archaeologies', *World Archaeology* 41(4): 649-658.

Willems, W.J.H. 2014. 'The future of world heritage and the emergence of transnational heritage regimes', *Heritage & Society* 7(2): 105-120.

Preservation *in situ*

Not an ethical principle, but rather an option amongst many

Tim Williams

Institute of Archaeology, University College London, United Kingdom

As Willem Willems stated, with his normal clarity, 'preservation *in situ* has developed into a central dogma of western archaeological heritage management' (Willems 2012: 1). Or rather more bluntly, 'Preservation *in situ* sucks' (his opening slide in a presentation at the 20th European Association of Archaeologists meeting in Istanbul, quoted in Anderson *et al.* 2014: 40). Willem, with his natural perspicacity, had once again challenged an uncritically accepted truism, in this case that preservation *in situ* is always the right response: 'while surely useful and important in some situations, preservation *in situ* is too problematic in several ways to be acceptable as an ethical principle with broad validity' (Willems 2012: 1).

The revised European Convention on the Protection of the Archaeological Heritage (Council of Europe 1992), commonly known as the Valletta Convention, aimed to preserve and protect archaeological heritage; created as a growing awareness that 'archaeologists have become aware that their source material is rapidly disappearing while only a tiny fraction of the information can be recorded. We now know that its survival needs a different approach that requires communication with the outside world, influencing the political and socio-economic decision making process, and enlisting the support of the general public' (Willems 2008: 284).

Major concerns

There are obvious concerns about *in situ* preservation, despite the clear benefits that engaging with a preservation policy bring:

If archaeological remains are left exposed – to fulfil economic, social, educational or interpretative agendas – then degradation is an issue. Sacrificial materials, shelters, protective coatings, and the rest, have developed their own extensive literature – for example see the Preservation of Archaeological Remains In Situ (PARIS) conferences (Corfield *et al.* 1998; Nixon 2004; Kars and van Heeringen 2008; Gregory and Matthiesen 2012), or international journals such as the Conservation and Management of Archaeological Sites (CMAS: http://www.maneypublishing.com/index.php/journals/cma/). But these interventions are potentially costly and, depending upon the context and materials, inevitably a process of managing change. Nevertheless, one might argue, at least the archaeology is being used – interpreted, displayed, debated, engaged with – and thus this process of change or loss can be balanced against the impact it has on contemporary society; it goes beyond simply 'preserving the past for the future' (*e.g.* Spennemann 2011).

If we implement mitigation strategies, where archaeological remains are reburied, or are left 'undisturbed', this sometimes leads to compromises resulting in attrition: for example, digging pile caps and peripheral walls, often with poor access and under difficult conditions. We are degrading the quality of the remaining resource in the very act of preserving it. Perhaps more significantly, do we understand what is happening to the buried resources? Is it stable or is it degrading? How will changing ground water, pollutants, compression, etc., impact upon the quality of the remains? Again, we have invested research into monitoring impacts (see CMAS & PARIS above), although not as much as we need to. However, the issue is that even if we are confident that the remains are stable, for these archaeological deposits there is no access (intellectual or physical), no contribution to understanding past societies, no benefit for contemporary society. So we need to be confident that they will 'benefit' future generations; and by 'benefitting' we must mean that we are not compromising their ability to make the decision to actually use, rather than simply preserve, the resource. This, of course, raises the question of when does the future become the present? When is it better to explore past societies, communicate values and engage communities through narratives, rather than preserve?

The above result in digging less, but as Willem argues, 'fewer and fewer sites are excavated, which leads to less new knowledge and which in turn leads to fewer stories to be told and in the end the public is going to lose its interest in archaeology' (Willem paraphrased by Anderson *et al.* 2014: 40). Rather, 'archaeological monuments, in the sense of movable as well as immovable parts of the cultural heritage, are no longer seen primarily as objects of study but as cultural resources to be of use and benefit in the present and future' (Willems 2008: 284).

How do we move forward? 'One might look at combining the Valletta and Faro treaties – one calling for preservation, the other for communication and dissemination of heritage to increase value of life' (Anderson *et al.* 2014: 40). Therein lies the rub. Most of the legislative and planning guidance that has come out in Europe, and been copied around the world, whether directly influenced by the Valetta Convention or not, places the emphasis on preservation, not on understanding, communicating, or contributing. As a result, heritage, and particularly buried archaeological resources, are often portrayed as in some way being in opposition to the needs of 21st century communities: obstacles to development, not an asset for society.

Lack of critical engagement

Willem rightly pointed to the growing disparity that has developed through this tension between preservation and research/communication: a tension between archaeological research and resource management, in which bureaucratization and commercialization have become the important drivers behind heritage policy (Willems 2012: 2-4). The declining opportunities for field archaeology to undertake substantive and complex research can be seen as a consequence of the increase in development-led work on evaluation, monitoring mitigation strategies, and only excavating the archaeology no one deems important enough to preserve. This work, while potentially high in volume, is low in critical engagement. Will we develop a new generation of field archaeologists capable of pushing the discipline forward in such an environment? Ironically the failure of most states to have the political will or legislative tools to ensure preservation strategies are implemented in the face of commercial and political pressures, means that large-scale archaeological work does still take place; but more by luck than any coherent strategy.

> 'The future of archaeology must lie in demonstrating it has relevance to twenty-first century communities.'

The dislocation of our discipline between heritage managers and archaeologists, between academics and commercial archaeologists, remains a real cause for concern. Is archaeological work seen as research on behalf of the state or as a service, not unlike many other services that can be bought and sold (Willems 2008: 285)? Perhaps most significantly, 'does the state wish to control the quality of archaeological work or does it not?' (*loc. cit*). The United Kingdom, for example, has never satisfactorily addressed these issues and desperately needs to consider a more sustainable response: currently too much depends on the relationship between developer, contractor and consultant, without effective quality control. The increasingly under-resourced country/city archaeological curatorial structure does not have the capacity, political will or legislative instruments to achieve this. (For general strengths and weaknesses of European approaches see for example Willems and Van den Dries 2007).

Anderson *et al.* argue that 'we need to discuss which sites can be preserved and which should be excavated' (2014: 39). We certainly do. By applying a simple 'one rule fits all' approach we compromise a society's ability to make informed choices. The problem is the 'polluter pays' principle. It does not encourage strategic thinking, but rather a plot-by-plot piecemeal response. This is hardly a new call to arms: the pioneering Scottish urban planner Sir Patrick Geddes (1915) argued that planning must be based on a thorough appreciation of context and a review of available data: and especially that it cannot be left to the casual dynamics of market forces or the improvisations of high-profile architects.

Demonstrating relevance

Spennemann (2011) points out that the cost of archaeological preservation is incurred today and its benefits should also be clear today. So 'in order to be relevant for the world of today, archaeological heritage can contribute in various ways to the economic and social well-being of present-day nations or communities, it can be "a driver of development", a source of income through tourism and it can be used to provide identity and a sense of rootedness' (Willems 2012: 4). Furthermore, 'preservation in situ is either misused by uncritical application in situations where research and other objectives might have been better served by proper investigation, or it is consciously misused to prevent additional costs and investment' (Willems 2012: 6). The future of archaeology must lie in demonstrating it has relevance to twenty-first century communities. In general, archaeology has enormous potential to create narratives that help to develop a sense of place and a sense of purpose. To achieve this we need to ensure the quality of the process: high quality excavation and properly funded research, clear and transparent decision-making on *in situ* preservation, creative strategies for on-site presentation, and valuing and developing interpretation. It is about enabling complex narratives to be developed that explore the historic landscapes, not isolate fragments of it, despite the fact that *in situ* archaeological remains, and archaeological excavations, will by their very nature, be fragmentary windows into these (Williams 2014).

References

Anderson, C., D. de Jager, E. Kars and V. Vandrup Martens. 2014. 'Preservation *in situ* or excavation?', *The European Archaeologist* 42: 39-40.

Corfield, M., P. Hinton, T. Nixon and M. Pollard (eds). 1998. *Preserving archaeological remains in situ: proceedings of the conference of 1st – 3rd April, 1996*. London: Museum of London Archaeology Service.

Geddes, P. 1915. *Cities in evolution: an introduction to the town planning movement and to the study of civics*. London: Williams & Norgate.

Gregory, D. and H. Matthiesen (eds). 2012. Preserving Archaeological Remains in Situ: Proceedings of the 4th International Conference, Special issue of *Conservation and management of archaeological sites* 14(1-4).

Kars, H. and R.M. van Heeringen (eds). 2008. *Preserving archaeological remains in situ: proceedings of the 3rd conference, 7-9 December 2006, Amsterdam*. Amsterdam: Institute for Geo and Bioarchaeology.

Nixon, T. (ed.) 2004. Preserving archaeological remains in situ?: proceedings of the 2nd conference, 12-14th September 2001. London: Museum of London Archaeology Service.

Spennemann, D.H.R. 2011. 'Beyond "Preserving the Past for the Future": Contemporary Relevance and Historic Preservation', *CRM: the Journal of Heritage Stewardship* 8(1-2): 7-22.

Willems, W.J.H. 2008. 'Archaeological resource management and preservation', in H. Kars and R.M. van Heeringen (eds), *Preserving archaeological remains in situ: proceedings of the 3rd conference, 7-9 December 2006, Amsterdam*. Amsterdam: Institute for Geo and Bioarchaeology, 283-289.

Willems, W.J.H. 2012. 'Problems with preservation in situ', *Analecta Praehistorica Leidensia* 43/44: 1-8.

Willems, W.J.H. and M.H. van den Dries (eds). 2007. *Quality Management in Archaeology*. Oxford: Oxbow Books.

Williams, T. 2014. 'Archaeology: Reading the City through Time', in F. Bandarin and R. van Oers (eds), *Reconnecting the City: The Historic Urban Landscape Approach and the Future of Urban Heritage*. Oxford: Wiley-Blackwell, 19-45.

Making futures from the remains of the distant past

Archaeological heritage, connective knowledge, and the promotion of well-being

Timothy Darvill

Department of Archaeology, Anthropology & Forensic Science,
Bournemouth University, United Kingdom

Willem Willem's outstanding contribution to archaeological resource management over the past forty years is widely recognized and internationally celebrated. His interest in making the most of archaeological resources, both academically and in terms of their contribution to wider societally relevant agendas, was especially important and provided the prompt for this short paper. In a prescient comment on the future of archaeological resource management in the Netherlands he noted that in response to accumulating data from archaeological fieldwork 'the need will grow to convert this information into relevant knowledge about the past by critical analysis and syntheses' (Willems 1977: 13). Such a need is not confined to the Netherlands as commercial archaeology across Europe and the US creates data sets of unprecedented scale. All represent considerable investments of time, resources, and intellectual endeavour; archaeology as a discipline has a duty to make something useful from the resulting information.

Knowledge-building in archaeology needs to be creative. Constructing narrative accounts of the past is certainly one obvious, immediate, and important use of new data. But, as I have discussed elsewhere, this is only part of the picture. Narrative knowledge is just one of several equally valid kinds of knowledge that exists alongside, for example, strategic, indigenous/native, and contemplative knowledge (Darvill 2014a). In this short paper in appreciation of Willem's life and achievements I would like to explore another kind of archaeological knowledge which I identify here as 'connective knowledge'. It relates to the way that archaeologists help forge attachments between present-day communities and elements of the archaeological heritage, often by enhancing the power of place, in order to satisfy deep-seated human values such as identity, tradition, social solidarity, and the legitimation of action (see Darvill 2005: 28-32). In particular I would like to examine the link between connective knowledge and the wider understanding and promotion of well-being, happiness, and the quality of life.

Connective knowledge and well-being: philosophical considerations

Ontologically, connective knowledge can be identified as a distinct if slightly shadowy category of understanding or justification. It derives from an actual, constructed, or perceived chain of physical or experiential relationships extending geographically outwards and chronologically backwards in time from an individual's here-and-now state of being in the world. It is grounded in the idea that, once explained to individuals, the existence and nature of archaeological or historical features within a landscape, townscape, or seascape can yield the kind of experiences that trigger systematic neurobiological responses, including a sense of well-being and security. Why, we might ask, if not for hedonic reasons, do people in such large numbers return again and again to places such as Stonehenge (England), Avebury (England), Newgrange (Ireland), Carnac (France) or Maes Howe (Scotland) to name just a few amongst umpteen examples? For many people, standing inside such monuments equipped with a well-formed pre-knowledge of the place prompts powerful feelings that are almost impossible to describe, yet from the perspective of the observer, seem authentic, deep-rooted, and somehow resonant with the very DNA of their existence. Such things might, and often are, simply written off as 'spiritual' and considered of fringe interest and rather too 'New Age' for serious consideration. But archaeologists ignore this constituency at their peril; if we cannot provide the kind of insights that such communities desire based on real archaeology then we should not be surprised when they celebrate concocted edifices such as the 'Bosnian Pyramids' or 'The Holy Grail'. Dismissive views often focus only on the authenticity of the sites or objects rather than on such matters combined with the desires and responses of the subjects (or agents) in relation to the chain of inferences and associations linking the two. Consciously or not, creating narratives of historic landscapes, emphasizing the significance of authentic features and objects, and promoting the importance of the past for life in the present, archaeologists create powerful places. Bundled together, such information constitutes a connective knowledge as a route-map for the cognitive realization of pleasurable experiences in emotionally charged *locales*.

Epistemically, the starting point for creating well-structured connective knowledge relevant to the archaeological heritage lies in a phenomenological framework in which human experiences of familiar and unfamiliar materials, objects, and structures provide triggers for emotions and behavioural responses. Developing Heidegger's (1936) vision of how art is created we can ask what exactly the 'heritageyness' of heritage is all about? Is it a mental state, or a state of the world? How does the experience of heritage relate to belief-forming capacities and processes? And how, within western societies at least, can it be used to articulate and negotiate notions of identity and meaning? Inevitably, in starting to address these questions, the socio-political dimensions of knowledge creation come to the fore.

Political context

Archaeology and the pursuit of archaeological knowledge(s) is inextricably linked to politics and public policy. Since the early 1990s archaeological endeavour in Europe has found itself being asked to play a purposeful role within the prevailing political philosophy of 'instrumentalism': actions or activities undertaken not because they are useful or interesting in their own right but because they are tools or instruments of the state in the attainment of wider ambitions in the realm of human experience. In this perspective 'heritageyness' is seen in terms of the strong aesthetic, experiential, associative, and integrative dimensions of the historic environment. Heritage assets, literally 'our inheritance', are broadly defined in terms of archaeological remains, built structures, curated collections, and an assortment of traditions and events forming the intangible heritage. Taken together these create and facilitate engagements between past and present, enriching shared cultural values, and underpinning distinctiveness and identity.

Such instrumentalist thinking was first articulated in European legislation under Title IX (Culture), Article 128 of the Maastricht Treaty on European Union, signed by the 12 member states in 1993, which stated that 'The Community shall contribute to the flowering of the cultures of the Member States, while respecting their national and regional diversity and at the same time bringing the common cultural heritage to the fore.' This clause remains unchanged in the controversial Treaty of Lisbon signed by the 28 member states in 2007 where it appears as Article 167.

Similar intentions can be found fairly widely in other European agreements of various kinds, for example Article 1 of The Council of Europe's Framework Convention on the Value of Cultural Heritage for Society (opened for signature in Faro on 27 October 2005), emphasized that the conservation of cultural heritage and its sustainable use has a key role to play in human development and the quality of life. More recently, the communication document 'Towards an integrated approach to cultural heritage for Europe' adopted by the European Parliament on 22 July 2014, calls for member states to enhance the intrinsic value of heritage and take advantage of its economic and societal potential.

Heritage and well-being

A general link between heritage, environment, quality of life, and well-being as made implicit in the European agreements is widely accepted, but the detail and theoretical underpinnings are only just beginning to be explored. One key development was the concept of the 'Therapeutic Landscape' as expanded by Wil Gesler in the early 1990s as a framework for the analysis of natural, built, social, and symbolic environments which can contribute to physical and emotional healing and general well-being (Gesler 1993). Although some early work in this area included the study of traditional long-lived sites associated with health-giving (*e.g.* Asclepian Sanctuary at Epidauros, Greece; Lourdes, France) recent work has tended to focus on places relevant to particular sectors of the population and their special needs (*e.g.* Williams 2007). Other research suggests that taking museum objects into hospitals and other healthcare contexts has a positive impact on well-being (Ander *et al.* 2013).

On a different track, studies commissioned by English Heritage and reported in the 2014 edition of 'Heritage Counts' use data from a large sample of the UK population to consider the relationship between life satisfaction (a standard measure of well-being in academic and policy literature) and visits to heritage sites. Controlling for a range of socio-economic factors it was found that visiting heritage sites (especially historic towns and buildings) had a slightly higher impact on life satisfaction than participating in sport or the arts. And when a well-being

> 'Creating connective knowledge means building robust bonds of association between cultural heritage and present-day populations.'

valuation approach was used the amount of money that provides the same impact on well-being as visiting heritage was calculated as £1,646 per person per year, well above estimates of £993 as the value of sport in terms of its impact on well-being.

In practical terms, creating connective knowledge means building meaningful and robust bonds of association between recognized dimensions of cultural heritage and present-day populations. Such links may relate to known sites and landscapes or emblematic places demonstrably associated with particular people, events, or beliefs. Many archaeological fieldwork projects promote popular accounts of their work foregrounding exactly these kinds of insights; they represent a first step in building constructive knowledge and should be encouraged. The rising popularity of community archaeology shows another approach in which investigation provides the tool through which people connect themselves to elements of their past.

Another direct application of connective knowledge through heritage management is through culturally-driven regeneration. In 2005, the UK's Culture Secretary Tessa Jowell issued a policy discussion document on such matters under the title 'Better Places to Live'. This set out the case for strengthening the relationship between communities and the built environment in order to promote cultural identity and recognize that historic places still form part of peoples' lives. Making places matter is far from easy, but using both tangible and intangible heritage in place-production has already been successful in some areas (Darvill 2014b) and holds considerable potential for expansion into more archaeologically-based situations.

Looking forward

Diversifying the way archaeological data are used, especially in relation to resource management practices, increases the overall value of hard-won information and strengthens support for our endeavours. Across the sector there is considerable scope for expanding the kinds of knowledge that we create and recognizing their legitimacy and utility in support of public policy as well as academic interest. The idea of 'connective knowledge' outlined here certainly needs further development in respect to its philosophical underpinnings and practical applications, but it has considerable potential. By creating theoretically robust frameworks for the deployment of archaeological data in ways that are relevant to contemporary societal issues it should be possible to secure a bright future for archaeological resource management, meet some of the challenges thrown down by Willem and others, and make futures from the remains of a distant past.

References

Ander, E., L. Thomson, G. Noble, A. Lanceley, U. Menon and H. Chatterjee. 2013. 'Heritage, health and well-being: assessing the impact of a heritage focused intervention on health and well-being', *International Journal of Heritage Studies* 19(3): 229-42.

Darvill, T. 2005. 'Sorted for ease and whiz? Approaching value and importance in archaeological resource management', in C. Mathers, T. Darvill and B. Little (eds), *Heritage of value, Archaeology of renown. Reshaping archaeological assessment and significance*. Gainsville: University Press of Florida, 21-42.

Darvill, T. 2014a. 'Scientia, society and polydactyl knowledge: Archaeology as a creative science', in J. Bintliff and J. Turek (eds), *Paradigm found: archaeology theory – Present, Past and Future. Essays in Honour of Evžen Neustupný*. Oxford: Oxbow Books, 6-23.

Darvill, T. 2014b. 'Rock and soul: humanizing heritage, memorializing music and producing places', *World Archaeology* 46(3): 462-476.

Gesler, W. 1993. 'Therapeutic landscapes: Theory and a case study of Epidauros, Greece', *Environment and Planning,* D11: 171-189.

Heidegger, M. 1936. 'The Origin of the Work of Art', in A. Hofstadter (trans.) 1971, *Poetry, Language, Thought by Martin Heidegger*. London: Harper & Row, 17-87.

Willems, W.J.H. 1997. 'Archaeological Heritage Management in the Netherlands: past, present and future', in W.J.H Willems, H. Kars and D.P. Hallewas (eds), *Archaeological Heritage Management in the Netherlands. Fifty years state service for archaeological investigations*. Assen: Van Gorcum, 3-35.

Williams, A. (ed) 2007. *Therapeutic Landscapes*. Aldershot: Ashgate.

From the preservation of cultural heritage to critical heritage studies

Kristian Kristiansen

University of Gothenburg, Sweden

Public investment in heritage management originated in meeting the demands for conserving and restoring heritage loss in Europe following World War II, which generated large restoration and rebuilding programs. This was followed by urban and industrial expansion from the 1960s onwards, which spurred a new need to protect cultural heritage through planning and legislation. From the 1990s onward cultural tourism defined a new global economic sector and together with other new forms of heritage uses it expanded the job market, and new educational programs were introduced to meet these demands. However, today we witness another global 'obsession' with heritage, tangible and intangible, public and private, that redefines 'heritagisation' processes as an arena for the playing out of conflicts and ideologies of the present. Such 'heritagisation' processes have taken on new meanings and importance – politically and economically – during the past ten to fifteen years. UNESCO's expanding World Heritage Sites promote a universal concept of heritage while new individual and collective interests in vintage and reuse reflect lifestyle changes to support sustainable economies. Global re-urbanisation leads to similar conflicts over the re-use of public spaces or commons. At the same time, questions of cultural identities have resurfaced as new nationalist policies, which make selective use of cultural heritage to legitimize such claims. In other parts of the world similar claims are used to legitimize rights for underprivileged or indigenous groups. Finally, heritage as healing is yet another arena being explored from hospitals to refugee camps.

Heritage has become a selective, re-assembled past, a global domain for political struggles over national and local identities and lifestyle ideologies. This 'heritage from below' is met with the authorized 'heritage from above', and 'Critical Heritage Studies' represents a multi-disciplinary, global academic answer to these new encounters. Heritage – as elaborations of artefacts, practices and ideas of the past – constitutes a part of, and is used in, on-going political, economic, social and cultural processes traversing local, national and global scales. Heritage is re-assembled in numerous new ways in the present to define new futures.

The 'dark' and the 'bright' side of cultural heritage

The tremendous success of cultural heritage as a concept and formula for progress also in many developing countries (Meskell 2012) may easily cause us forget to ask the pertinent question: why? Why has the world witnessed this tremendous expansion of a selective reworked past, designated cultural heritage? Why have we been 'invaded by the past', rather than the future? Why are grass roots movements with both left and right wing political agendas mobilizing cultural and natural heritage now? The short answer is because reworked pasts have become powerful. They appeal to basic feelings of identity – or threatened identities, as some nationalist movements would have it. Sometimes I wonder if we have been too successful, and have forgotten to ask the right critical questions.

We need to stress the sometimes contradictory or dual nature of heritage, which we may term the 'Dark' and the 'Bright' side of cultural heritage. It is rooted in the dualism between exclusion/inclusion and raises important political as well as ethical issues about ownership, origins, belonging and identities, and how they

> 'We witness a global 'obsession' with heritage that redefines 'heritagisation' processes as an arena for the playing out of conflicts and ideologies.'

are constructed. Today we witness a global expansion of 'heritagisation' processes, and 'Authorized Heritage Discourse' as Laurajane Smith (2006) termed it, and we need to focus more critical attention on understanding these processes that represent a form of 'heritage from below'. Such 'heritagisation' processes cover a broad field of movements in which selective pasts are mobilized either from grass roots organisations or politicians, leading to new forms of identities and lifestyles at local and regional/national levels. They are responses to expanding urbanization and its effects on rural depopulation, consumerism, the environment, migration and its effects culture and identity to name an important few. All of these processes are contesting established values and leading to conflicts over identities, urban commons, and cultural canons – in short a restructuring of basic social and cultural values where a selective past is re-assembled and given new meaning. Several recent books demonstrate this engagement of Critical Heritage Studies with contemporary challenges in a globalized world (Biehl *et al.* 2014; Harrison 2013; MacDonald 2013; Meskell 2012; Smith 2012), but similar concerns were already presented by Willem Willems in his seminal 2009 World Archaeology article.

Bringing theory and practice together

While Critical Heritage Studies (CHS) has developed as an engaging academic response to these developments, and created a new discourse with a series of recent books, and also an Association of Critical Heritage Studies (http://criticalheritagestudies.org), which just held its second international conference in December 2014 in Canberra, Australia (the first being in Gothenburg in 2013, with 500 participants), I can also see an inherent danger in separating cultural heritage into practitioners with their hands in the dirt of practice and compromises, and critical academics with clean hands sitting in their ivory towers. There is a real risk that the two will drift further apart, although they need each other. To solve this inherent problem here in Gothenburg, we decided to create a Heritage Academy as a meeting place between the Academy and regional heritage institutions, mostly museums. This was done within the four-faculty Critical Heritage Studies-project (http://criticalheritagestudies.gu.se) financed by the Vice-Chancellor. All major museums in the region are now members, and a series of open seminars with participation from researchers, politicians and heritage/museum managers have created a new sense of collaboration between the university and museums/archives in the region. This cross-disciplinary activity, which also transcends the borders to museum institutions and the public, is considered to be productive among its stakeholders. It is an activity requested for many years, which is now up and running. We have had several one-day workshops on themes that the museums found burning and relevant, such as the future of collections, the role of heritage in rural areas of depopulation etc. My suggestion to every university conducting teaching and research in cultural heritage is to establish a heritage academy as a meeting place between theory and practice, and more importantly between people from these two fields, who will gradually develop a shared community.

Bringing people together

Willem has always been that kind of bridging personality: his life illustrates in an exemplary way how to build bridges: between people and between theory and practice; from his work in Dutch heritage to his position as Dean of the Faculty of Archaeology in Leiden, but always with an understanding of the international and global challenges that archaeology needs to confront to become successful. We met the first time some 30 years ago, when I lectured at the Rijksdienst Oudheidkundig Bodemonderzoek (ROB) in Amersfoort, where he was the new vice-director. Later we became close friends during our collaboration in the early years of the European Association of Archaeologists (EAA), which I remember fondly. Hard work and joy were the two sides of Willem, and in tandem with high personal integrity and loyalty to his friends, these personal characteristics go a long way to explain his achievements. We trod some of the same paths and fought some battles together, because we shared the same ideals of a European and international archaeology without borders, and without barriers between theory and practice. Grass never grows on a rolling stone, and Willem was always on his way travelling with great joy to all the corners of the world connecting with people, making friends. I am privileged to have been one of them.

References

Biehl, P.F., D.C. Comer, C. Prescott and H.A. Soderland (eds). 2014. Identity and Heritage. Contemporary Challenges in a Globalized World. New York: Springer (Springer Briefs in Archaeology).

Harrison, R. 2013. *Heritage: Critical Approaches*. London: Routledge.

MacDonald, S. 2013. *Memorylands: Heritage in Europe Today*. London: Routledge.

Meskell, L. 2012. *The nature of heritage: the new South Africa*. Malden, MA: Wiley-Blackwell.

Smith, L. 2012. 'Editorial: A critical heritage studies?', *International Journal of Heritage Studies* 18(6): 533-540.

Willems, W.J.H. 2009. 'European and world archaeologies', *World Archaeology* 41(4): 649-658.

Creative archaeology

Sjoerd J. van der Linde* and Monique H. van den Dries**

* CommonSites, The Netherlands
** Faculty of Archaeology, Leiden University, The Netherlands

Willem Willems was many things, but being traditional was not one of them. Ever since he exchanged his position of Chief Inspector for Archaeology at the State Inspectorate for Cultural Heritage in favour of becoming Dean of the Faculty of Archaeology at Leiden University, he passionately – and with childlike enthusiasm – criticized dogmas, traditional thinking and politically correct academic waffle. His latest and dearest enemy was the concept of 'preservation *in situ*' (Willems 2014), especially in the context of heritage discourses that centred upon unthinkingly preserving material remains for future generations, without any regard for present-day creative, commercial or local alternative values and uses. The fact that he himself had been so fundamental in setting up effective policies and implementing the principles of the European Convention on the Protection of the Archaeological Heritage (Malta Convention, 1992), including preservation *in situ*, did not prevent him from criticizing it. On the contrary, he was a strong advocate for exploring outside-the-box options and alternatives for a sustainable archaeological practice before former useful legislative concepts and tools would become political dogmas implemented by bureaucrats.

As colleagues within his chair-group on Archaeological Heritage Management, Willem always encouraged us to question the obvious and look for other directions. Accordingly, in this discussion paper we set out some possible directions to search for elements that embody a new form of archaeology, which may help to deal with present-day public, academic and political challenges. In our view, such an archaeology will be based foremost upon its *social values*, and upon a spirit that creates shared value, while actively exploring opportunities – an archaeology that is not primarily concerned with providing compliance and academic publications, but rather with creating narratives and public benefits. In contrast to prioritizing preservation and conservation values, we like to call this mode of practice and thinking 'creative archaeology'.

What is wrong with Malta?

In our view, the need for a 'creative archaeology' becomes quite apparent when looking closely at the results of a recent survey by the Europae Archaeologiae Consilium (EAC), one of Willem's cherished organizations, of which he had been the founding father. This survey on the implementation and perceived effectiveness of the different articles of the Malta Convention is based upon responses from representatives and officials of 34 European States (Olivier and Van Lindt 2014). When asked about the level of problems encountered during implementation of the different articles, respondents stated that especially articles 1-6 (dealing with legal and physical protection, integrated conservation and the financing of activities) were faced with moderate to serious challenges – in effect, this hints at problems encountered during implementing different forms of *in situ* preservation, preventive archaeology and the polluter-pays principle. When asked about the implementation of articles 7-12 (dealing with issues such as the dissemination of knowledge, exchange of skills, public awareness and outreach activities), the respondents stated that there were *no* significant problems encountered. If you look at the responses to the question of how effective the implementation of the different articles have been, we see a similar distinction in articles, albeit rather disturbing; whilst respondents stated that the implementation of articles 1-6 had yielded quite significant achievements, the implementation of articles 7-12 were said to have little to no significant achievements at all. There are probably many interrelated and good reasons for this, and we admit that the EAC survey only provides a very basic benchmark, but strengthened by our own experience, observations and analyses, for instance of the results of the Discovering the Archaeologists of Europe 2012-2014 project concerning the degree to which public engagement activities are embedded in the profession in Europe (Van den Dries 2015), we feel confident to say that this basically means the following: we have not encountered any problems in the Malta articles dealing with the implementation of public outreach, and dissemination and exchange of knowledge, simply because we have not bothered all too much with them in the first place.

We feel however that this is a serious problem, both from a moral perspective, as well as from a perspective about the sustainability of our profession. These days, our profession is faced with several serious challenges, especially where it concerns the workings of 'Malta archaeology'. Current critiques on the different forms of this type of archaeology include recurring statements about the poor level of knowledge production, a lack of quality and synthesis, the high costs involved in financing the polluter-pays principle, and the lack of real value for money and effective communication. Whilst the validity of some of these statements can be questioned (see Van den Dries and Van der Linde 2012), what matters here is that our profession is challenged with political and public critique that, in combination with a possible prolonged economic crisis, could form a serious threat to the survival of Malta archaeology as we know it – especially if we loose public and political support.

Co-creating social value

In order to tackle this, we feel that our profession needs to explore the opportunities that an implementation of articles 7-12 might yield – both academically, professionally and even commercially. We believe that an archaeology that focuses on creating output in the field of *social value* could offer a guideline – that is, if it sees valorisation not as an end or by-product, but rather as being at the core of our practice. Such a stance fits with the emphasis on public value being placed for example by the Council of Europe's Framework Convention on the Value of Cultural Heritage for Society (Faro, 2005), which the Netherlands has not yet signed, as well as with current European political and public trends that emphasise co-creation, transparency and demonstrable impact. What such a creative archaeology might entail, first of all, is that we start to see the public (and that includes developers and commercial parties other than clients only from the traditional development industry), as serious 'partners' or sometimes even as 'customers' of our work. This is because if we take their needs seriously, we might be able to turn the practice of 'delivering heritage compliance' in advance of development as our core product, into a practice that places creating 'social value' for society to the fore.

One example of this type of archaeology can be seen in current examples of archaeological practice that are being supported and funded not out of academic or commercial funds, but rather out of development and even aid funds. Our work with the Palestinian Authorities in Tell Balata (West Bank) for example (Van den

> 'We need to turn the practice of 'delivering heritage compliance' as our core product into a practice that places creating 'social value' to the fore.'

Dries and Van der Linde 2014), was supported by the Dutch Ministry of Foreign Affairs not because of the archaeological scientific knowledge and publications they would yield but because the proposed archaeological and heritage work could be seen as a *tool* towards creating social benefit for and with the Palestinian Department and with local communities, in the areas of tourism development, identity building, educational practice, and intercultural understanding. The *raison d'être* of archaeology here was to be found in the social value it would create – supported and fuelled by the narratives, stories and scientific interpretations (Taha and Van der Kooij 2014). Placing archaeology firmly within a discourse that sees cultural heritage as a human right, and demonstrating the social impact of the work, opens-up budget streams that would otherwise remain unavailable (Van der Linde 2012).

Another example of a possible form of creative archaeology that places social value at its core can be seen in a small public archaeology project that took place in Oss in The Netherlands. The inclusion of the neighbours in a typical development-led excavation revealed that both the participants and the local authorities expected and experienced all kinds of social benefits from the project. These varied from an increased social coherence in the neighbourhood to learning new skills and a feeling of happiness and well-being (Van den Dries, Boom and Van der Linde 2015).

A third opportunity worth exploring for a creative archaeology that is based on social value, lies in the fields of corporate social responsibility (CSR) and creating shared value (CSV). Traditionally, archaeologists and heritage professionals have been looking to the banking and development sectors for securing financial donations and support, but this in effect overlooks a huge base of potential CSR partners from other industries (Groot, forthcoming). While it is true that once cultural heritage (or access to cultural heritage and the freedom to interpret one's history) is recognized on a global scale as a human right, this might open up new streams of seeking CSR support, we should not forget that many policy discourses such as 'social inclusion', 'sustainable cities' and 'intergenerational equality' already provide many opportunities for finding support for our work. However, simply asking for philanthropic support is not 'creative' – rather, our discipline needs to think proactively about how we align our work in such a way that it creates shared value for commercial partners. Examples of creating such shared social values might well lie in providing companies and CSR agendas with the right stories, identities and engaging field practises that fit their brands, products and consumers' needs (Groot, forthcoming). This would not only create exciting new partnerships and, admittedly, challenges, but also new opportunities for alternative funding.

Playing to our strengths

The above just touches very generally on some opportunities that a creative archaeology, and an emphasis on social value, might yield. The simple fact of the matter however is that we do not know for sure if this is a direction worth following until we try, and until we support our archaeological work with research into the social impact that we have. We need more empirical data about the impact of our work, not only to gain public, commercial and political support, but also to improve our engagement with society in a way that goes beyond mere rhetoric and good intentions. It is in this context that we for instance aim to measure the social and economic impact and return on investment of various archaeological outreach and participation activities (www.nearch.eu).

It is important to state clearly that we do not believe that there is no value or place for sound, scientific archaeological research and fieldwork – on the contrary. We will never be able to create social value if we do not have archaeological research to draw from and be inspired by. However, our argument is that instead of focusing on creating academic publications, grey literature and policy compliance, we should think more creatively about what exactly archaeology can and should bring to society. We believe that the solution lies hidden somewhere in articles 7-12 of the Malta Convention, and that it has to do with valorising the narratives and enthusiasm of our work. Making these elements the core product of our discipline not only makes sense from a sustainable political, financial and moral sense, but also from a professional and personal sense – making the thrill and experience of archaeology the core product is simply more fun, and it allows us to start playing to our strengths again.

References

Groot, B.M. forthcoming. *Selling Culture. Private sector partnerships and the value of cultural heritage.* Leiden: Faculty of Archaeology, Leiden University (unpublished dissertation).

Olivier, A. and P. van Lindt. 2014. 'Valletta Convention perspectives: an EAC survey', in V.M. van der Haas and P.A.C. Schut (eds), *The Valletta Convention: Twenty Years After – Benefits, Problems, Challenges.* Brussels: Europae Archaeologiae Consilium (EAC Occasional Paper no. 9), 165-176.

Taha, H. and G. van der Kooij (eds). 2014. *Tell Balata: Changing Landscape*. Ramallah: Publications of the Tell Balata Archaeological Park Project.

Van den Dries, M.H. 2015. 'From Malta to Faro, how far have we come? Some facts and figures on public engagement in the archaeological heritage sector in Europe', in P.A.C. Schut, D. Scharff and L.C. de Wit (eds), *"Setting the Agenda": Giving new meaning to the European archaeological heritage*. Brussels: Europae Archaeologiae Consilium (EAC Occasional Paper no. 10), 45-55.

Van den Dries, M.H. and S.J. van der Linde. 2012. 'Twenty years after Malta: archaeological heritage as a source of collective memory and scientific study anno 2012', *Analecta Prehistorica Leidensia* 43/44: 9-19.

Van den Dries, M.H. and S.J. van der Linde. 2014. 'Introduction to the promotion, awareness raising and education strategy', in H. Taha and G. van der Kooij (eds), *Tell Balata: Changing Landscape*. Ramallah: Publications of the Tell Balata Archaeological Park Project, 127-132.

Van den Dries, M.H., K.H.J. Boom and S.J. van der Linde, 2015. 'Exploring archaeology's social values for present day society', in C.C. Bakels and H. Kamermans (eds), *Analecta Prehistorica Leidensia* 45: 221-234.

Van der Linde, S.J. 2012, *Digging holes abroad. An ethnography of Dutch Archaeological Research Projects Abroad*. Leiden: Leiden University Press (Archaeological Studies Leiden University 27).

Willems, W.J.H. 2014. 'Malta and its consequences: a mixed blessing', in V.M. van der Haas and P.A.C. Schut (eds) *The Valletta Convention: Twenty Years After – Benefits, Problems, Challenges*. Brussels: Europae Archaeologiae Consilium (EAC Occasional Paper No. 9), 151-156.

Sustainable archaeology in post-crisis scenarios

Felipe Criado-Boado, David Barreiro and Rocío Varela-Pousa

Institute of Heritage Sciences (INCIPIT),
Spanish National Research Council (CSIC), Spain

The aim of this contribution is to discuss the economic sustainability of archaeology in post-crisis scenarios. The text is rooted in two European-wide projects (Archaeology in Contemporary Europe, ACE; and New ways of Engaging audiences, Activating societal relations and Renewing practices in Cultural Heritage, NEARCH) in which the authors have been intensively engaged in collaboration with Willem Willems. His broad view of archaeology challenged any practice.

Heritage does not exist, but instead is a function of the social value added to it. The act of valuing comes before the act of appropriating, which is the very essence of any 'heritagization' process. Past and present 'do things' (either material or virtual), and some of these things are categorized by our culture as heritage because they are attributed a certain value (Robertson 2012; Sánchez-Carretero 2013). All societies have their own way of managing the past, memory, tradition and cultural products; but 'heritage' is a specific concept of European modernity. Other cultures do not have 'heritage' or similar concepts, although as a part of globalization, they have incorporated this concept and made use of it (see also Schlanger, this volume).

Many different actors are involved in the process of 'heritagization', producing different narratives, uses and claims in relation to heritage. All of these voices are legitimate, but the hegemonic spheres in these societies are the ones that study, manage and give name to heritage, shaping the Authorized Heritage Discourse (AHD) (Waterton and Smith 2009). AHD prevails over other voices arguing that their perspective is 'the correct' one because they know the 'real past', they use rigorous methodologies, etc. (Alonso 2011). From this perspective, society is reduced to playing the role of a passive spectator, a consumer who must be taught about how the past 'really' was (or what 'culture' is).

When archaeology just strengthens public outreach of heritage or applies unidirectional models of knowledge transfer, it supports the traditional paradigm and consolidates the divide between science and the world, between research and management, between experts and the public. Moreover, AHD is fully integrated into the capitalist system of production and circulation of commodities. In those areas with lower uptake of a heritage industry, interests linked to the exploitation of land and real estate speculation usually prevail. Where the heritage industry is more consolidated, it is the heritage itself that is reified and turned into a commodity ready to be consumed by tourists.

In this context, paradoxically, AHD must still act as a mediator between the different proposals of social participation in the process of 'heritagization', and as a warranty against the private interests that are also present in these processes (often as neoliberal practices). It must play the role of 'the public' in the processes of 'heritagization'. But this role is often questioned by those who defend the heritage *as a common*, because they identify 'the public' with the technocratic discourse that supports asymmetrical relations.

Beyond knowledge transfer: archaeology as social innovation

Today the balance between experts and the public is changing. In every field of experience (from politics to science) and also in heritage, the public demands active participation. In close connection to the very process of building a Public Science (Funtowicz *et al.* 2000; Criado *et al.* 2010), this demand for a 'public turn' in heritage management still waits to be theorized. So we need to shift towards a new paradigm for nesting a symmetrical transfer of knowledge between archaeology

> 'Heritage does not exist but is a function of the social value added to it.'

and society, which ranges from unveiling (in a critical sense) the social conditions for producing heritage, its discourses and its practices, to recognizing (in a positive, pragmatic sense) the intimate engagement between heritage and a public that consists of different types of publics, communities and actors. We focus on the notion that there can be no heritage without social links, considered as a close entanglement between the values assigned to heritage and the social context that assigns them. In the wake of the financial crisis and neoliberal policies in recent times, new practices are emerging: crowd funding, collaborative consumption, cooperatives, social currency, ethical finances, P2P loans or informal exchange networks, for instance. Despite their intrinsic diversity, all of these respond to the same demand: to deploy sustainable community projects that promote the value generated by and for the common, including heritage assets, and using increasingly inclusive and democratic tools.

This demand appeals to some research areas that can be useful for our objectives, mainly 'social innovation'. Aside from traditional studies of innovation with a focus on technological innovation, new concepts of innovation emerged during the 1980s, which resulted from an interactive process of exchanging know-how, experience and work to solve problems. This model has been named by Jensen *et al.* (2007) 'Doing, Using and Interacting', the DUI-model. The new understanding of innovation is associated with activities that are conducted by organizations which aim to meet social needs, through processes of mutual aid, community development, social care, etc. (Mulgan *et al.* 2007).

So some initiatives arise as an alternative to the political and economic hegemonic model. Although some attempts at co-optation by the dominant model (the contradictions of the *European Strategy for Social Innovation* are, for instance, quite obvious), demonstrate that its success seems unclear without a systemic change, the practice of 'social innovation' seems to fit and correspond to certain sociological trends in which new conditions for the development of culture emerge. These new conditions are related to 1. the network as a kernel of social organization that promotes participation and empowerment, communication and interaction (supported by the massive use of information and communication technology); 2. the blurring of boundaries between production and consumption; 3. the increase of collaborative and cooperative production, based on open and shared knowledge; 4. the acknowledgement of the active deployment of things and beings in the world; and 5. the growing role of more sustainable values as articulators of social life.

Beyond the public: 'prosumers' and innovation in archaeology

The old cultural heritage management scenario and archaeological practice does not help anymore. The socially innovative, open and inclusive, multi-vocal and communal (public empowered) character of heritage (desirable and utopian but rooted in tradition) is the starting point for new political and economic scenarios (of social change and sustainability). So we need to renew our vision of the horizon, for which we propose twenty concise points:

1. Replace the academic and linear concept of 'heritagization' with a participative and collaborative one.

2. Deconstruct policies that promote globalization in an uncritical way.

3. Create a new language for communication, an alternative vocabulary that considers new realities from a different perspective; we still lack a thesaurus of shared terms to talk about the new dimensions of heritage.

4. The new language mentioned in point 3 applies particularly to heritage management where we need concepts such as users, community, STS specialists, scientific activism, strong appropriation, *prosumers*, heritage as *commons* or heritage as a *cultural repository*.

5. Integrating other values in the production of knowledge: emotions, attitudes, experiences, creativity.

6. Involving other non-conventional disciplines in the core of our practice such as sociology, anthropology, economics, educational sciences, information and communication.

7. Including dialogue between different types of knowledge and interests, between researchers and managers, the authorities and the public, and between different communities.

8. Recognizing what or who the public is, and how it is identified and defined.

9. Thinking of the public not only as users of heritage, but also as producers in their own lives: the public becomes a heritage prosumer.
10. Assessing the social value of heritage by means of techniques for ethnographic, anthropological, sociological, economic and market inquiry.
11. Using advances in ICT and in reputation technologies applied to websites and social media to acknowledge the social valuing and reception of archaeological practices.
12. Negotiating in a positive manner the rising conflicts that affect heritage and condition attitudes towards it in increasingly multi-vocal and multi-cultural environments.
13. Promoting multi-agent practices and collaborative actions in archaeology.
14. Putting the public at the centre of the archaeological process, restating our role of experts as mediators of the demands by social actors in regard to the use of heritage in their daily lives.
15. Create transversal archaeological practice. Heritage is the subject of investigation and simultaneously the social context in which the scientific practice is applied.
16. Facilitate the strong appropriation of heritage by the public, instead of the weak appropriation that has been promoted up until now by academic and administrative spheres.
17. Root the projects in community-based settings to discover the engagement between the project and the community.
18. Link archaeology to social innovation processes, and thereby to the cultural and heritage industries, by incorporating them into the new models of open innovation that are based on active public engagement.
19. Transform heritage experience and practices into 'living labs' (a recent development in Europe). Heritage as a 'living lab' is a crucial case that facilitates exchange between formal and informal knowledge.
20. Avoid the temptation of *epistemic populism* (i.e., 'simply assuming that knowledge produced from the bottom up is automatically catalogued as subaltern epistemic knowledge' González-Ruibal 2012), recognizing that this is not self-generated but instead responds to power structures, wherever they are produced.

The integrative strategy outlined in this text is entangled with one major question: can archaeology contribute to the transformation of the hegemonic paradigm? We think we need allies from other disciplines and fields: not only for learning from/by them, but also to make a contribution from heritage and archaeology to the main ongoing 'intellectual war'.

The future of Europe is also played out on the grounds of heritage and archaeology. Not only because of their central position to negotiate present engagement with materiality, the past, memory and identity, but also because they create opportunities for bringing into existence new values and practices, to help materialize new forms of action and to design post-crisis scenarios. However, we cannot forget that these practices have little to do with hegemonic strategies. Therefore, the 'intellectual war' becomes a political guerrilla.

References

Alonso, P. 2011. 'Por una arqueología menor: de la producción de discursos a la producción de subjetividad', *Revista Arkeogazte* 1: 21-36.

Criado-Boado, F., A. Corsín and A. de Greiff. 2010. 'Definition of the Science and Society Field. CYTED', *Programa Iberoamericano de Ciencia y Tecnología para el Desarrollo (CYTED)*. Available at http://hdl.handle.net/10261/20961 (retrieved 20 July 2015).

Funtowicz, S., J. Ravetz, I. Shepherd and D. Wilkinson. 2000. 'Science and Governance in the European Union', *Science and Public Policy* 27: 327-336.

González-Ruibal, A. 2012. 'Hacia otra arqueología: diez propuestas', *Complutum* 23(2): 103-116.

Jensen, M.B., B. Johnson, E. Lorenz and B.A. Lundvall. 2007. 'Forms of knowledge and modes of innovation', *Research Policy* 36: 680-693.

Mulgan, G., S. Tucker, R. Ali and B. Sanders. 2007. 'Social Innovation, What is, why it matters and how it can be accelerated', *Skoll Centre for Social Entrepreneurship. Working Paper*. Oxford: Said Business School.

Robertson, J.M. (ed). 2012. *Heritage From Below*. London: Ashgate.

Sánchez-Carretero, C. 2013. 'Significance and Social Value of Cultural Heritage: Analyzing the Fractures of Heritage', in R. Candelera, M. Lazzari and E. Cano (eds), *Science and Technology for the Conservation of Cultural Heritage*. London: Taylor & Francis, 387-392.

Waterton, E. and L.J. Smith. 2009. 'There is No Such *Thing* as Heritage', in E. Waterton and L.J. Smith (eds), *Taking Archaeology out of Heritage*. Cambridge: Cambridge Scholars Publishing, 10-27.

Yours, mine, and ours

Relevance and application of heritage in contemporary society

Pei-Lin Yu*, Chen Shen** and George S. Smith***

* Boise State University, United States of America
** Royal Ontario Museum, Canada
*** Florida State University (courtesy professor), United States of America

It is critical that the relevance and application of heritage in contemporary society be clearly stated in order to be competitive at levels where policy crafting and revision, resource allocation, planning, and consultation take place. This is the best opportunity we have to promote the role of our collective heritage – yours, mine and ours – in a complex and ever changing world in a way that benefits individuals, communities, and nations.

Over the past two decades there has been progress in our ability to demonstrate the relevance and application of heritage with respect to major issues and concerns in contemporary society. This has required new adaptive strategies to ensure that heritage is broadly defined and fairly applied (*cf.* Smith *et al.* 2010; Messenger and Smith 2010; Smith 2012; Yu *et al.* 2011). Recent years have seen a wider application of heritage with respect to a variety of areas, including but not limited to, public education and presentation of the past, economic development, indigenous claims and rights, social and environmental justice, political agendas and ideologies, international agreements, collection management and museum exhibits, tourism, sustainable development, private land issues, religious and political issues, historic preservation, lobbying and advocacy, and the illegal international antiquities market. Yet much still remains to be done in ensuring the past has a place and role in modern society and that individuals, communities, and nations are able to connect to their past in a meaningful manner (Watkins *et al.* 2000; Clark 2006; Burke and Smith 2010; Willems 2010).

Wanted: inclusive heritage models

Incorporating a wide spectrum of stakeholders in the creation of new models, tools, and partnerships for protecting, managing, and enjoying our collective cultural patrimony, and demonstrating the place of heritage in the modern world, enhances the ability of heritage to compete successfully with other agendas for limited resources. This approach also allows different ways of viewing the past to coexist, furthering and appreciating differences and similarities among and between societies; an important concept in this era of exceptional cultural and geopolitical conflict. Recent changes in the ways that contemporary societies view, access, and value heritage are presenting new opportunities and challenges in efforts to present the past to the public in an accurate, balanced, and respectful way. This balanced approach has much to contribute to the future of political, economic, and educational policy, planning, and implementation. To this end we need to develop a broad and clear definition of heritage based on updated theoretical and applied concepts as an effective means to apply heritage to public policy, spending, management, and delivered services in a manner that demonstrates public accountability and is inclusive of all stakeholders. The definition should take into consideration the public perception of heritage; the politics of identity; heritage and human rights and social and environmental justice; uses and abuses of heritage; and how heritage is examined and presented. It is also critical to

> 'Much remains to be done in ensuring that individuals, communities, and nations are able to connect to their past in a meaningful manner.'

examine how heritage is applied to public policy, spending, management, and delivered services relating to a collective past in a manner that demonstrates public accountability as well as social and environmental justice arenas, while giving equal voice to our commonalities and differences, engaging the public in the decision making process. This can most effectively be achieved by:

- Developing a broad and clear definition of heritage and effective means for applying heritage to public policy, spending, management, and delivered services relating to a collective heritage in a manner that demonstrates public accountability.
- Examining and presenting heritage in such a way that captures individual experiences of heritage, social or economic aspects of heritage, and the processes and techniques used to understand heritage.
- Understanding that heritage gives equal voice to our commonalities and differences; applying heritage in social and environmental justice arenas.
- Developing workshops, national and international conferences, publications, grants, and collaborating with professional, governmental, and private organizations and sources of funding.
- Taking into account market forces and globalization's impact on heritage and how governments and policies deal with these issues.
- Developing methods to track data so that in a market-dominated world, a case can be made for enhanced efforts to protect and manage cultural heritage.
- Presenting heritage in terms of 'cultural capital', that is the stored and long-lasting value, as a method of achieving a quality that stands apart from financial worth while allowing economic principles to be applied to cultural heritage that are both measurable and applicable to heritage policy and long-term sustainability.

- Engaging the public and descendant communities in the discussion and decision-making process involving heritage and its application.

- Acknowledging that experts provide critical information to the public about the past based on rigorous research and peer review, while enabling the public to draw their own conclusions about their relationship to the past and what value they place on it.

- Promoting the teaching of heritage not only in our academic institutions at all levels but also in our communities as well.

- Dealing with conflicting heritage issues.

- Dealing with concerns of stakeholders.

Finding common ground with respect to the relevance and application of heritage in contemporary society is critical if we are to effectively develop best practices; be responsive to crisis or conflict situations on a global scale; ensure adequate funding at both the local, national, and international levels; and create new models, tools, and partnerships to help protect, manage, and enjoy our collective heritage.

References

Burke, H. and C. Smith. 2010. 'Vestiges of Colonialism: Manifestations of the Culture/Nature Divide in Australian Heritage Management', in P.M. Messenger and G.S. Smith (eds), *Cultural Heritage Management: A Global Perspective*. Gainesville, Florida: University Press of Florida, 21-37.

Clark, K. (ed). 2006. *Capturing the Public Value of Heritage: The Proceedings of the London Conference 25-26, January 2006*. Swindon, England: English Heritage.

Messenger, P.M. and G.S. Smith, (eds). 2010. *Cultural Heritage Management: A Global Perspective*. Gainesville, Florida: University Press of Florida.

Smith, G.S. 2012. 'The Role of Heritage Values in Protecting and Managing the Past for Individuals, Communities, and Nations', *Journal of Oriental Archaeology* 8: 23-28.

Smith, G.S., P.M. Messenger and H.A. Soderland (eds). 2010. *Heritage Values in Contemporary Society*. Walnut Creek, California: Left Coast Press.

Watkins, J., K.A. Pyburn and P. Cressey. 2000. 'Community Relations: What the Practicing Archaeologists Needs to Know to Work Effectively with Local and/or Descendant Communities', in S.J. Bender and G.S. Smith (eds), *Teaching Archaeology in the Twenty-First Century*. Washington DC: Society for American Archaeology, 73-82.

W.J.H. Willems. 2010. 'Laws, Language, and Learning: Managing Archaeological Heritage in Europe', in P.M. Messenger and G.S. Smith (eds). *Cultural Heritage Management: A Global Perspective*. Gainesville, Florida: University Press of Florida, 212-229.

Yu, P.-L., G.S. Smith, C. Shen and H. Fang. 2011. 'The International Conference Cultural Heritage Values in China: Identifying, Evaluating, and Treating Impacts to Cultural Relics, Shandong University, Jinan and Qufu, China, October 26-28, 2010', *Heritage & Society* 4(2): 261-264.

Mapping stakeholders in archaeological heritage management

Alicia Castillo

Department of Prehistory,
Universidad Complutense de Madrid, Spain

Stakeholders are often mentioned in discourses concerning cultural heritage management. The importance of engaging with various kinds of agents is rarely questioned, but the analysis of stakeholders as a detailed academic topic *per se* has been relatively neglected. In my opinion, this is probably because the understanding and consideration of stakeholders remains quite basic, and consequently deemed unnecessary to tackle in specialized publications. I started to rethink the role of agents in reaction to reading several recent management plans of World Heritage Sites. Often these documents mention the importance of involving stakeholders, but the degree and way in which this should be done often remained voluntary. I absolutely agree with this decision, as site managers have to decide for themselves the way in which to engage with stakeholders, depending on the main objectives of specific management concerns (I encourage people to consult these plans at the World Heritage Center website (www.unesco.whc.org)). Unfortunately, the management plans of World Heritage Sites are only examples of what is happening more broadly at other archaeological sites.

This article is based on a special session that I organized at the last international ICAHM meeting in Jishou (China), October 2014, which Willem Willems co-directed.

Reasons to improve dealing with stakeholders

There are many issues to improve in heritage management that could be analyzed from the perspective of stakeholders. I will deal here with the main problems that this topic presents. Probably the hardest issue to tackle within this topic is the difference of opinion concerning the content and meaning of cultural heritage for each person, or group of people – a clear issue for minorities in a country faced with dominant considerations of cultural heritage. In fact, personal reflections on marginal communities were the reason for questioning whether World Heritage archaeological sites or as I call them 'the archaeological dimension of cultural properties' have the same meaning for different stakeholders. Most people think that this is not true. However, it is clear that most of the efforts concerning the treatment of archaeological heritage have been decided by one minority: that is us, the experts.

In my opinion, there are two clear distinct groups: experts and lay people. Lay people recognize the relationship of archeology to the past, sometimes even just the legal category such as World Heritage, but this does not include an expert vision. On the other hand, the expert vision is very diverse too. It is evident that we can recognize several points of view and understandings of the past in each group. Because cultural heritage is not merely archaeology, which is one aspect of heritage, this means that archaeology contains just one of its possible meanings. And even inside the archaeological discipline itself, interpretations and meanings diverge. That is a relativist position, I know. But my aim is the opposite: accepting multi-vocality implies developing measures to identify all kinds of discourses in order to understand and interpret our past better. The totality might be false, but the recognition of the multiple options should not be overlooked.

From a pragmatic point of view, in order to improve communication among stakeholders we need to recognize their discourses and classify or organize the agents concerning them. In practice, we have observed that from a managerial point of view we are working with many kind of actors, but mostly with colleagues belonging to other professions or sciences, or people with political or administrative jobs, but rarely with lay people (even with visitors) – sometimes with tourists, but rarely with the population in general. This does not include a diffuse or educative perspective. There are very good projects from museums and archaeological sites dedicated to involving people who visit them, but normally we only change our actions or our discourse in reaction to their opinions slightly. Normally, outreach activities are directed mostly by us, and I confess that sometimes I think it is impossible to involve people in making decisions concerning heritage properties.

In my opinion, to involve local people meaningfully entails asking them questions such as whether they want to be part of a World Heritage Site? Would they like the site to be reconstructed at all? What do they think about the construction of roads close to cultural heritage? We need to listen more to citizens, but how can we avoid imposing a leading discourse? How can we include alternative heritage discourses and realize that what is important is not always the archaeological dimension? It is difficult, but in my opinion, we need to accept that the importance of cultural heritage lies within the connection and balance between different heritage dimensions. Discourses that people are faced with should include a transversal vision of the past, not solely the scientific vision. This might be the reality, but unfortunately it is sometimes very distorted because we often try to impose other ideas that are not shared by the majority of the public.

The traditional selection of actors

These days, one can often read a list of agents in reports or managerial plans for archaeological sites. In the best cases, they are organized by topic, public or private administration, and focus on aspects of archaeological heritage management (i.e. economic support agents, administration agents with competence for the sites, the research team, the restoration team and so on). These are mainly 'direct' agents, that is, organizations that are working with cultural heritage (such as archaeologists, site managers, or civil associations). Less frequently, they include the 'indirect' agents too. These would include organizations or persons who for several reasons have to act, or are affected by archaeological heritage management plans (such as property owners, environmental agencies, NGO's for cooperation, patrons and sponsors, urban planner enterprises, municipalities, and so). Finally, and very seldom, in specific actions, you can see the best example of how to deal with stakeholders: that is, a participatory process that expresses an interface with stakeholders – for example, to encourage inscribing a site such as World Heritage or inclusive actions with local communities or potential agents. These are the exception and are normally treated in the context of management or conservation actions (i.e., works concerning sites at risk by ICRROM could represent a good and exceptional example).

So far, I have never seen a list of stakeholders that includes 'negative' organizations. These are made up of agents that might boycott a project. The success of a project however depends on the consideration of all actors, not solely

> 'The success of a project depends on the consideration of all actors, not only those 'positive' organizations that agree with our management proposals.'

those 'positive' organizations that agree with our management proposals. Our attitude towards them so far has been either to ignore them or simply to identify them but not to include these kinds of actors. However they could be key in several situations. Consequently, we need to review the way in which we identify the stakeholders. Such a systematization of our methods could be very useful – to know our stakeholders well requires asking about our objectives as managers, as well as our past, present and future actions. We need to include more potential actors and negative people/agents for archaeological heritage.

Conflicting discourses

War conflicts are exceptional, although unfortunately more frequent than we would like, and obviously they form an extreme example of the lack of communication among actors. But I prefer to speak here about conflicts in ordinary contexts, where archaeological management problems can be very conflictive on several occasions. From my experience, it is easier to illustrate in the context of urban archaeology. The disconnection between values of owners, developers, archaeologists, politicians and organizations responsible for cultural heritage is the main reason for this.

Preventive archaeology in Spain forms a good example. Sometimes the use of legislation, relationships with land planning and the attitude of politicians and archaeologists has allowed for good solutions to archaeological heritage. But sometimes, with the same actors, the same laws and measures of protection, the result of archaeological heritage conservation or interpretation is very bad. The reason for this, in my opinion, is because the heritage articulations and wishes of actors have been ignored. Laws and measures facilitate archaeological works, but sometimes this is not enough and other kinds of actions are necessary so that social mediation can solve or prevent urban conflict. In order to do this we need to know the stakeholders well and understand that the same discourse, even the most correct legal discourse, could be poor and in need of revision depending on the people who you need to connect with.

Another important point here is how our stakeholders could be contacted. A list with contact data is clearly insufficient today. We need to keep actors updated about our activities via email, organize dedicated meetings, etc., but we then need to find a suitable way of reaching all actors, that is, mapping stakeholders effectively. In my opinion, we need to have a dynamic map of our stakeholders if we really want to strengthen their role and the possibilities of articulating their different discourses.

Conclusions

The following conclusions are informed not only by this specific essay. My colleagues and I have undertaken several studies on social perceptions of Spanish World Heritage cities and we have worked on mapping agents. This year we are starting social participatory processes in some World Heritage Sites with management objectives. The problems and topics that I deal with here will be different depending on their cultural, geopolitical, and economic contexts, but many of them could be approached with universal standards, such as the following:

1. Stakeholders are usually included as a list of organizations, generally directly involved, sometimes including representatives of communities, but these rarely include indirect agents and people (as individuals).

2. There are substantial problems with communication among stakeholders, even among groups of experts. This is sometimes due to the use of standard discourses and the lack of flexibility from interest groups.

3. Stakeholders cannot be considered and treated in the same way, depending on the subject matter of who works with them.

4. The mapping of stakeholders needs to take place prior to the implementation of activities – although this depends of course on the relative need.

Consequently, we need to work together to better value who should really be involved in cultural heritage management processes and go beyond the traditional list of actors; this means that we need to improve the models and techniques associated with this crucial part of management in our discipline.

Solving the puzzle
The characteristics of archaeological tourism

Annemarie Willems and Cynthia Dunning

ArchaeoConcept / ArchaeoTourism2012, Switzerland

Rien 'est plus ennuyeux qu'un paysage anonyme (Prosper Merimée).
[Nothing is more boring than an unnamed landscape]

Touristic activities at archaeological sites are often referred to as 'archaeotourism', but what exactly does this mean? In this paper the particularities of archaeological tourism will be defined in comparison to heritage or cultural tourism and we will argue that a better understanding and acknowledgement of the particularities of archaeological tourism will benefit the effectiveness of tourism management. We aim to build up a basic understanding of archaeology in relation to tourism because we believe this knowledge could be valuable to management plans for archaeological sites that are considered for touristic activity. We will specifically be speaking about the 'sites with little or no visible remains' as opposed to monumental archaeology.

Empty sites

According to Jonathan Culler (1990), empty [invisible] sites become sights through the attachment of markers. An archaeological site can be 'nothing' in tourist eyes until it is made visible with so-called 'markers', which exist in multiple forms like plaques, (written) guides or even visitor centres (Culler 1990). These markers represent the site, make the site recognizable and give information about its significance. A site can of course never be literally 'empty', but an archaeological site can easily go unnoticed to non-professionals without some pointers. This 'cloak of invisibility' protects the archaeological sites from bad intentions, but to make it suitable for visitors, markers are needed to provide the visitor with the right tools to visit the site in a respectful and sustainable way. Therefore, a management plan needs to be drawn up before the site is revealed to the visitor.

'Archaeological heritage' is that part of the material heritage which archaeological methods provide primary information on. It comprises all vestiges of human existence and consists of places relating to all manifestations of human activity, abandoned structures, and remains of all kinds (including subterranean and underwater sites), together with all the portable cultural material associated with them (ICAHM 1990). When dealing with archaeology and tourism one should always be aware that archaeology is a non-renewable source. When it is not excavated properly, or when it is destroyed or damaged it cannot be undone, thus also destroying all the information it could have given us and future generations about the past. This means that protecting the site and explaining the importance of protection to the visitor are essential to the preservation of knowledge in the future.

This vulnerability also applies to other forms of cultural heritage of course, but archaeological tourism differs from other cultural heritage in two ways. First, archaeological sites are embedded in the landscape, with elements above ground, below ground and/or under water. Second, archaeological methods used to obtain knowledge of the site, such as excavations, simultaneously destroy the anthropomorphic features in the landscape.

Special requirements for archaeological sites

From the 'archaeotourism' perspective, archaeological sites come in three stages: not-excavated, partially excavated and completely excavated. In the first stage the level of knowledge will be the lowest but the site will be completely intact. Visual aid is required to help the visitors see, experience and interpret the non-excavated site. The archaeologists depend on other sources to interpret the site (*e.g.* research results from similar sites in the region or further away, written sources if they exist, oral history and remote sensing techniques).

A site in its second stage provides more knowledge to the archaeologist. Where in the first stage the interpretation possibilities can be manifold, in this second stage the collected data from the excavation will point the interpretation in a more specific direction. The story of the site is still not complete and leaves room for the 'professional interpreters' to interpret the site and pass this information on to the visitor, thus becoming a marker himself.

In the third stage the site is completely excavated, which means that most of the data of the site has been collected and interpreted. The level of knowledge at this stage is the greatest, but there is often no material culture left *in situ*, and the features in the landscape will be gone.

Each of these three stages needs its own fitting presentation techniques and needs to be considered differently. Whereas in the first stage presentation techniques are needed to show what *may be*, in the third stage these techniques are needed to show what *has been*.

Another complicating factor for 'archaeotourism' is that archaeological sites are not always visible in their surrounding landscape. They can be concealed under the ground, under water or they may be invisible for laymen's eyes. This means that if and when a site is opened to visitors, they need help interpreting the site. Markers are essential to help visitors see, or as Copeland puts it: 'Making sense of the parts once the whole has been seen is often more effective than trying the build the whole from the parts. (…) There need to be panoramic views of the site and guided routes that enable the visitor to get an image of the whole site' (Copeland *et al.* 2006: 89). Nowadays there are many presentation and visualisation techniques, such as augmented reality, that help create this panoramic view.

The big puzzle

Markers are not just essential to help visitors see, but also to protect the site because it is easy to damage something you cannot see or do not understand. Therefore the development of a process for the visitor to better comprehend the site is essential for a long-term protection of any archaeological site.

Heritage interpretation is an educational activity that aims to reveal meanings and relationships through the use of original objects, by first-hand experience, and by illustrative media, rather than simply to communicate factual information (Tilden 1957). Archaeological sites are open to interpretation, because research can never provide the complete story of the site, there are always blank spots and the data are always subject to interpretation. An archaeological site can be considered a puzzle with many missing pieces. Through archaeology some of the pieces are

> 'The particularities of archaeological sites – their vulnerability, invisibility and potential for multiple interpretations – form the main pull factors for the visitor.'

found, but the puzzle and thus the story will never be complete. The expert interpretation may very well differ from the visitors' perception depending on the visitor's frame of reference. Visitors are curious about what is hidden and rely on the markers and their fantasy to interpret what they see. Visiting an archaeological site is therefore an emotional activity and a personal experience. The fact that part of the story is inaccessible provokes curiosity and stimulates fantasy. Shanks (1991) describes archaeology as being a vector of emotions and feelings, and stresses on the importance of the experiences it allows to convey. According to the American Institute of Archaeology (AIA) archaeological tourism combines a passion for the past with a sense of adventure and discovery: people are fascinated with ancient and historical remains. Archaeological tourism lets visitors experience the past and allows them to share in the thrill of discovery. The inaccessible nature of archaeological sites often adds to the sense of adventure.

From the above we can conclude that for empty or invisible archaeological sites the visitors will need markers to help them see, experience and interpret them. An archaeological site is not self-explanatory and is vulnerable since it is easy to damage something you cannot see, understand or are unaware of. Archaeological tourism has many resemblances with other forms of cultural tourism, especially heritage tourism, but the particularities can be summarized as vulnerability, invisibility and a potential for multiple interpretations. It is in particular these particularities that have a strong emotional appeal and they form the main pull factors for the visitor. They can be put to use when putting a site management plan into place and equipping the site or monument to become a 'touristic experience'.

Creating a new tourism brand?

A wide range of related activities, including archaeological tourism, heritage tourism, museum tourism, arts tourism and others all fall under the umbrella of cultural tourism and they all share common sets of resources, management issues, and desired aspirational outcomes (McKercher and Du Cros 2002). We do not believe it to be necessary to create a new brand named 'archaeotourism' and to communicate it as such to the visitor. We do, however, believe that the particularities of archaeological tourism should be acknowledged (Dunning and Willems 2013), because it will benefit all parties. The first step in preparing an archaeological site or monument for tourism is to understand what can turn an archaeological site into a touristic experience and what the motives and expectations are of the potential visitors. In this realm, there is still much to learn and do.

References

American Institute of Archaeology. *Guide to Best Practices for Archaeological Tourism*. Retrieved 12 March 2015 from https://www.archaeological.org/tourism_guidelines.

Copeland, T. 2006. 'Constructing Pasts: Interpreting the Historic Environment', in A. Hems and M. Blockley (eds), *Heritage Interpretation*. London: Routledge, 83-95.

Culler, J. 1990. *Framing the Sign: Criticism and Its Institutions*. Oklahoma: University of Oklahoma Press.

Dunning, C. and A. Willems (eds). 2013. *ArchaeoTourism. Archäologie und Tourismus in der Schweiz / Archéologie et tourisme en Suisse*. Biel/Bienne: ArchaeoTourism2012.

ICAHM. 1990. *Charter For The Protection And Management Of The Archaeological Heritage*. Available at http://www.international.icomos.org/charters/arch_e.pdf (retrieved 16 February 2015).

McKercher, B. and H. du Cros. 2002. *Cultural Tourism – The partnership between tourism and cultural heritage management*. London: Routledge.

Shanks, M. 1991. *Experiencing the Past – On the Character of Archaeology*. London: Routledge.

Tilden, F. 1957. *Interpreting our heritage*. North Carolina: University of North Carolina Press.

"Willem, give me an excuse to attend WAC!"

Reflections on social risk to archaeological world heritage

Nelly M. Robles Garcia

Instituto Nacional de Antropología e Historia (INAH), Mexico

In January 2008 Willem Willems and I found ourselves in a conversation trying to contextualize the social movement of 2006 that befell Oaxaca, particularly the historic centre and the archaeological zone of Monte Alban, inscribed in the UNESCO World Heritage List. The civil unrest originating in the resistance of radical groups to government decisions had reached the point of threatening the integrity of most iconic monuments of the site, important not only for their emblematic significance but as keystones of the local economy. As Oaxaca's economy depends heavily on tourism, local instability or damage to critical attractions puts the flow of national and international visitors at immediate risk.

As always the conversation was enlightening and productive; Willem's broad perspective enabled him to pinpoint with clarity the risk factor such civil unrest entailed for Oaxaca's heritage. "You should present the case at the World Archaeological Congress (WAC) in Dublin!" he advised me. Although the proposal was very attractive, it was difficult to imagine getting everything arranged in time to participate in an international congress at short notice, especially given the slow-moving bureaucracy most government archaeologists face in Mexico.

Civil unrest as a threat to cultural heritage

Nevertheless Willem's enthusiasm motivated me to collect the extensive reports in local, national, and international press on the consequences of the turbulence (The New York Times 2006). During the protest, the least of the damage included thousands of graffiti scrawls across the walls of historic structures; the use of stone with historic significance for the construction of barricades or as projectiles in street battles, vandalism of church atriums and colonial plazas, and fires left the city disfigured and in a deplorable condition. Although the destruction of the historic district was not among the objectives of the APPO (Asamblea Popular de los Pueblos de Oaxaca), the coordinating body for the opposition to Governor Ulises Ruiz, it was perhaps the most visible outcome of resistance to his rule.

The archaeological zone of Monte Alban, the other component of the World Heritage designation and the main tourist attraction in the state, was not directly affected. Workers at the site, though members of one of the unions confronting the governor, refused to permit access to the site by protestors seeking to include it as part of the arena of confrontation. However even a cursory review of visitor data demonstrated a dramatic reduction of tourist traffic as civil unrest grew. Not only did this mean a reduction in site income but a dramatic collapse of Oaxaca's economy, and with it grievous damage to the welfare of the city's inhabitants, the business sector, and surrounding communities dependent on commerce, services, and employment generated by their proximity to the city.

Convinced that the case merited international recognition I wrote to Willem "……just give me an opportunity to go to WAC!". Willem not only invited me but also named me co-organizer of a roundtable on social problems and their effects on World Heritage. This is how we became responsible for alerting the World Heritage community attending WAC to the threats civil unrest and government instability can represent to sites and monuments.

Beyond anthropogenic threats to heritage

As civil unrest is just one of many potential threats, its effects may be concealed by other social forces contributing to the degradation of cultural heritage. It is not 'war' as understood in professional discourse but as an incidental, unfortunate result of protest against governmental decisions or specific local circumstances. Such protests emerge from efforts by political figures or government programs to manipulate or mobilize groups through campaign platforms, patron-client relations, and promises of benefits or favors. Conversely those in authority may seek to extend control over, marginalize, or repress groups deemed to be adversaries or insignificant. When efforts at manipulation or marginalization break down the public response may be street demonstrations, mass meetings, or other forms of organized protest.

Such expressions of resistance or challenge may prove to be merely foreshadowing of more serious conflict. Protests in Oaxaca escalated to the point that for six months they essentially held the city hostage. Daytime demonstrations, nighttime violence, barricades and trenches, restricted access to public spaces, squads of irregular police and neighborhood vigilantes, sporadic fires, occasional gunfire, and calculated turbulence were all intended by the government and by protestors to intimidate the city's residents and make them more pliable. Oaxaca's status as a World Heritage Site was exploited by both sides for propaganda purposes, each claiming the other showed callous indifference to the conflict's visible damage to heritage values. Tangible heritage suffered physical damage as windows, doors, railings, balconies, and paving stones were used to build barricades. Graffiti covered every wall. Many of the historic buildings used by city or state government for bureaucratic purposes were sacked and burned.

But in some respects the worst damage to the historic city center were journalists' reports of extensive street violence and allegations of danger or death; reportedly the local population was afraid to walk in the streets. Through television, press, and electronic media the world observed Oaxaca's trauma and governments advised their citizens to avoid possible risk by deleting Oaxaca from their travel plans. Although the distress was real many reports exaggerated or sensationalized the situation, a posture made easier by visuals of burning buses, protest demonstrations, and street barricades. Tourism shrank to almost nothing and Oaxaca's economy began a dramatic free fall (Barthel-Boucher 2013: 157). Even Monte Alban saw visitation dwindle and on more than one occasion the daily visitor count was zero.

We do not need to remind the heritage community of the terrible effects open warfare has had on valued monuments and works considered the heritage of mankind but today civil unrest represents a new challenge. Not only may such forms of heritage suffer damage or destruction as a byproduct of such conflicts; they may become intended targets of violence as they command world attention in ways other properties cannot. As contending parties seek to mobilize opinion and resources in their favor, the value of heritage may lie not in its protection for future generations but in the threat to destroy it unless concessions are made or ransoms

> 'Civil unrest and social conflicts around the globe form the professional context of the next generation of archaeologists and heritage managers.'

paid. In this respect Oaxaca was fortunate its museums were not sacked of their valuable collections; religious art remained untouched in the churches, and other objects did not disappear. There is no guarantee Oaxaca or other places will be so fortunate in the future.

Civil unrest as a new challenge for heritage management

Oaxaca in 2006 represented a new kind of risk for cultural heritage in general and archaeology in particular. Although thanks to the dedication of its custodians, personnel, and nearby residents Monte Alban escaped the ravages of invasion or abuse, the clear and direct threat revealed a challenge previously unconsidered by heritage managers. Site conservation has long focused on preventing or recovering from natural disasters such as earthquakes or fires, or on dealing with long, slow processes such as erosion or deterioration of materials. But civil unrest can be described as a slow-moving earthquake, something developing and persisting across time. In the case of Monte Alban this slow-moving earthquake led to an unusual phenomenon as daily visitor counts fell below the number of staff employed there. Beyond the loss of revenue at the site, compounded by the economic losses to the guides, vendors, and others dependent on tourism, the absence of visitors due to travel alerts left the archaeological zone vulnerable in ways never contemplated.

The 2006 experience also underscored the critical importance of a positive relationship between site managers and the many stakeholders having an interest in Monte Alban. With the city of Oaxaca suffering upheaval and a lack of civil authority, with contending parties indifferent to cultural heritage dominating local politics, and with a lack of operational resources, Monte Alban was able to draw on social relationships with key actors nurtured over an extended period. It is not an exaggeration to argue that in large part Monte Alban escaped the damage to the historic center due the sense of mutual interest and support between the archaeological zone and its neighbors.

Of course this challenge is not unique to Oaxaca. One can look to the civil strife that affected Cairo, Egypt in 2011 (BBC 2011). In addition to the damage and disruption in the city itself, the civil unrest deterred visitors from traveling to sites such as Giza and Luxor, provoking the same kind of drastic reduction in tourism seen in Oaxaca. The tourist-dependent part of the economy has yet to recover, a burden on the cities and groups adversely affected. Whether site managers in Egypt have been successful in establishing the positive relationships with stakeholders as buffers against civil unrest is yet to be explored. Across the Middle East world heritage sites are under serious threat as civil unrest, sectarian conflict, and longstanding enmities spread across boundaries. In these circumstances not only are there few opportunities for stakeholders to come together but the destruction of cultural heritage itself may be viewed as a desirable goal or victory (Campbell 2015: 69).

A key aspect in quality management

This overview of what happened in Oaxaca in 2006 joins a list of outbreaks of civil unrest and social conflicts around the globe that form the professional context of the next generation of archaeologists and heritage managers. In this regard one can assert that heritage management is no longer the methodical application of formal principles and disciplinary techniques but also involves the capacity and flexibility to anticipate the implications of such outbreaks. In turn heritage management requires not only preparation for natural disasters but also for social disasters ranging from civil unrest to a sharp deterioration of the local or regional economy due to a reduction in visitation. This means taking proactive steps to promote what might be termed "site resilience" or the ability to deal with a traumatic event beyond a flood or earthquake. According to the World Heritage quality management general precepts (Willems and Van den Dries 2007, 8) that way it will be possible to manage in a more effective manner the effects and risks of conflict. Had social conflict been addressed in Oaxaca beforehand as a matter for risk prevention, it could have become an untouchable icon during the civil unrest instead of being its hostage.

References

Barthel-Boucher, D. 2013. *Cultural Heritage and the Challenge of Sustainability.* Walnut Creek, California: Left Coast Press.

BBC. 2011. *Egypt protests escalate in Cairo, Suez and other cities.* (www.bbc.com/news/world-middle-east-12303564)

Campbell, J.L. 2015. 'World Heritage and sites of conflict: how the war on terror is affecting heritage in Peshawar, Pakistan', in P.F. Biehl, D.C. Comer, C. Prescott and H. Soderland (eds), *Identity and Heritage. Contemporary Challenges in a Globalized World.* Springer Briefs in Archaeology. New York: Springer, 65-71.

The New York Times. 2006. *Violent Civil Unrest Tightens Hold on a Mexican city.* (www.nytimes.com/2006/08/24/world/americas/24mexico.html)

Willems, W.J.H. and M.H. van den Dries. 2007. 'The origins and development of quality assurance in archaeology', in W.J.H. Willems and M.H. van den Dries (eds), *Quality Management in Archaeology.* Oxford: Oxbow Books, 1-12.

Heritage from the heart

Pieter ter Keurs

National Museum of Antiquities / Institute of Cultural Anthropology, Leiden University, The Netherlands

In the beginning of the 21st century cultural heritage is high on the academic agenda. It is, however, not a new subject although in the past heritage often appeared in disguise. The anthropology of art as it developed in the 1970s was, of course, about heritage. Archaeology – classical archaeology, prehistory or whatever branch within the discipline – was mostly concerned with heritage, although we have to confess that site management and capacity building programmes for the local population were long overdue. Also, the erection and maintenance of monuments is hardly new. Emperors, kings, apostles, great men (rarely women) of science were honoured with statues that often survived the turbulences of the ages. And turbulences and heritage are two concepts that are closely related.

Heritage heist

An interest in guarding and maintaining heritage is often stimulated by crisis situations. The present destruction of statues and sites by *Islamic State* in the Near East has evoked many emotional reactions from Western countries, which cannot accept the barbarian practice of destroying valuable images from the past. However, we often do not realize that such practices are hardly new and unique. We are, rightly I believe, furious about the seemingly meaningless destruction of important heritage, but of course this destruction is not meaningless. The violent actions of Islamic extremists have sense in their own views. Whether passionately angry about the depiction of the human face or just looking for attention in the Western media, there is certainly a sense behind it all. There is, in fact, nothing strange about such aggressive behaviour against heritage. Of all people, heritage specialists should know this and try to comprehend the phenomenon. Apparently, attention to heritage is very often an emotional attention: something that is hard to measure and difficult to predict. It may help to look at examples from the past (European as well as Non-European) to comprehend why people sometimes behave aggressively towards heritage. Our own European past is certainly not without these incidents.

Before turning to Europe, I would like to cite an example from ancient North Africa. In the history of Carthage, the powerful metropolis on the coast of North Africa (present-day Tunisia), political violence and straight forward wars were regular, recurring phenomena. Most famous are the three Punic Wars in which Carthage and Rome fought over the dominance of Mediterranean trade networks. Finally Rome won, in 146 BC, but only after a long-lasting, fierce struggle. However, even before the famous Punic Wars the western Mediterranean was not often a peaceful region. In the beginning of the 4th century BC Carthaginian armies fought in Sicily, in fierce competition with local leaders and Greek trade settlements. During one of these conflicts the Carthaginians destroyed a temple dedicated to the Greek goddess Demeter. From that moment onwards the armies of Carthage were decimated by the plague and the wars started to go wrong. It was quickly decided that Carthage apparently did not pay enough attention to Demeter and a temple cult was founded in Carthage to honour the goddess who had, apparently, influenced Carthaginian warfare so negatively. Political conflicts

'Turbulences and heritage are two concepts that are closely related.'

and wars often had, and still have, religious connotations as well. Starting with the destruction of Demeter statues in Sicily, the Carthaginians quickly changed their policy. They imported Demeter statues from Greece, built a temple for them and honoured the goddess with rituals. People must have felt that their actions were effective because they continued to pay attention to Demeter for centuries. Even after the conquest by the Romans in 146 BC, Demeter statues continued to be seen as important in religious affairs and they were probably seen as being effective in household affairs as well. It was only later, when the first Christian sects started to dominate life in Carthage, that the Demeter studies disappeared. Fanatic Christian groups destroyed old statues and some owners decided to hide the marble images of Demeter under their houses. In the 20th century archaeologists found them back.

Here we see that Demeter, seen as a goddess who stimulated happiness in the family and the private sphere, was the victim of heritage destruction at least three times. In the 4th century BC in Sicily, in 146 BC during the destruction of Carthage by the Romans and again in the 3rd century AD with the rise of Christianity in the region. We really cannot say that the Demeter cult, with its peaceful and beautiful marble statues, has such a peaceful history. Violence and war threatened Demeter several times.

European history is of course no exception in the history of heritage destruction. A good example is the French Revolution (1789) and its aftermath. In an attempt to build a new society without a Christian religion (but with a religion of Reason) large amounts of statues and monuments that referred to the *ancient regime* were destroyed. The anger and emotional reactions of that period do resemble the anger and the emotions we see nowadays with the destruction of pre-Islamic heritage in some Near-Eastern countries. However, in the case of the French terror against heritage at the end of the 18th century, a counter-movement immediately became active. The failed painter Alexandre Lenoir (1761-1839) and his team rescued many statues from revolutionary violence and the authorities of Paris gave him an old monastery to store these treasures. It is a small miracle that this rescue operation occurred, for the terror of the French Revolution did not seem to have a lot of respect for the past. It is however justified to say that Lenoir was indeed one of the first state supported heritage protectors. His storerooms became the *Musée des monuments*, a museum that survived until after the Napoleonic era. And it was based on both the very personal and emotional reaction of Lenoir to stress the need for heritage protection as well as a deliberate state policy aimed at collecting and keeping heritage. Violence and war not only destroyed heritage, they also stimulated its protection.

Peaceful perils

Naturally, there are also many examples of heritage being threatened in more peaceful situations. Weather conditions may be important, but also the very human urge to modernize. Modernization has been the buzz word in many periods of human history and although modernity has brought us many good things, it is also inherently connected with loss. Let me again give an example from France. After the revolution of 1848 – the third in 60 years – a nephew of Emperor Napoleon, Louis Napoleon Bonaparte, became *Président de la République* and a few years later, in 1852, Emperor Napoleon III. One of the main interests in the period following the uncertain, and often violent, episodes of revolutions was to create a certain stability. The French state aimed at a stable society, if necessary under strict police control. The fear of a new revolution certainly determined many political decisions. One of the new Emperor's priorities was to restructure Paris in the name of modernity. He appointed Baron Haussmann as chief architect of this restructuring and the result was the Paris as we know it today, with its large Boulevards and impressive 19th century buildings. Practical reasons were certainly part of the story. For hygienic reasons the broad streets with the accompanying infrastructure of sewers were much more effective than the earlier medieval streets, but political and military reasons were also very important. It is easier for an army to move along broad streets from one *quartier* of the city to the other. The events of 1870, followed by the Parisian Commune, showed how effective the broad *boulevards* were for regaining State control. Naturally, during the Haussmannian renovation of Paris many medieval streets and building were demolished. The large-scale changes Haussmann realized forever changed Paris, but also destroyed an important part of Parisian heritage and therefore its history.

Heritage from the heart

The examples mentioned above show how heritage can be, and often is, a matter of politics and emotions. We can study heritage in a very clear, positivist manner (and I do not say that we should not do that), but in times of political pressure and straightforward war and violence heritage is mostly (by both competing parties involved in the conflict) seen as something political. The result can be protection or destruction, but in both cases it often involves personal, emotionally motivated actions. Heritage is something that comes from the heart. Professor Willem Willems understood this very well. Before his arrival at Leiden University, heritage was hardly part of the academic agenda. After his premature death in December 2014, the academic agenda can no longer do without heritage. A major change and a major achievement.

References

Clark, T.J. 1984. *The Painting of Modern Life. Paris in the Art of Manet and His Followers.* Princeton: Princeton University Press.

Docter, R., R. Boussoffara and P. ter Keurs (eds). 2015. *Carthage. Fact and myth.* Leiden: Sidestone Press.

Ter Keurs, P. 2010. *Materiële Cultuur en Vergankelijkheid.* Inaugural address. Leiden: Leiden University.

Crossing borders and boundaries
Global interactions in heritage management

'This is not Australia!'

Willem Willems and international heritage management

Ian Lilley

University of Queensland, Australia

Anyone involved in what Willem Willems (2014) called 'transnational heritage regimes' knows that there are often stark differences in approaches to heritage management between what some crudely characterise as 'the West and the rest'. At world heritage level, the need to accommodate such variation on an equitable basis sees us endeavouring to incorporate non-Western concepts of and approaches to heritage into a system based firmly on Western values and methods. To date we have had mixed results, but there is an expectation that we will succeed in the end, even if that end still lies some way ahead.

Most, if not all, archaeologists would know of World Heritage, at least superficially. In my experience though, far fewer are aware that other major global players such as international development banks and transnational corporations also have key roles in international heritage management and are facing the same issues as the World Heritage system in relation to non-Western approaches to heritage management. I worked with Willem across all three areas, as part of a snowballing collegial effort to ensure that archaeology remains a central element of the larger international cultural heritage mix along with architectural and art-historical heritage, but also (and increasingly) the intangible heritage of communities around the globe.

Regional differences colouring global thinking

While issues of 'the West and the rest' certainly loomed large in our thinking, Willem never hesitated to remind me – and indeed the rest of the global archaeological and broader cultural heritage communities – that there are also telling differences *within* 'the West' that continue to colour global thinking and action in the heritage field. I think most of us would take it for granted that 'the rest' (or, less crudely, the 'non-West') is far from an undifferentiated category, but rather a shorthand term encompassing an array of variation of greater or lesser magnitude amongst regions, countries, cultures and societies around the world. Fewer, though, would spend much time deconstructing the idea of 'the West' or contemplating the implications of any such decentring for international archaeological heritage management.

For present purposes, I define 'the West' as the historically non-communist countries of Europe and the Anglophone settler societies of North America and Australasia. There are all sorts of major and minor differences among these nations when it comes to heritage management, but Willem drew most attention to what he saw as a fundamental difference between the Anglophone nations (or what he called 'Anglo Saxon') nations – and specifically the settler societies – and the others. As one might expect from a Romanist who studied in the United States of America as well as in Europe, he did so owing to the fact that the Anglophone nations have closely-related and mutually-reinforcing common-law legal systems whereas the others have civil law traditions based in or heavily influenced by Roman law. The common law also applies in most other former British colonies, many of which remain loosely grouped as 'the Commonwealth'. Roman law is also influential in Russia and the old communist 'Eastern Bloc' of Europe (*e.g.* Hammer 1957), and indeed in Japan and both Chinas, as well as in most former colonies of continental European nations, such as those in Latin America, as Willem (2014: 109) recognised. This essay is too short to do anything more than note that much of what follows applies to some degree in all these countries.

Why should it matter that 'the West' is internally divided by its legal systems in this way? It is because this distinction lies behind the way global heritage management is developing, specifically in relation to engagement with local and descendent communities. This process is without question the most significant change in heritage management practice around the world since the field emerged as an area of professional activity. As Willem (2014: 109) put it:

> *'It is quite probable that the conscious involvement of local stakeholders in modern heritage resource management, and also the development of forms of community archaeology, where the local population participates in archaeological work, is to a large extent the result of a change induced by the regard and respect for other peoples' stakes in heritage resources. […] It is surely no coincidence that globally this started in countries with systems of Anglo-Saxon common law, where society is self-regulating, as opposed to the Roman law tradition where much depends on the State that regulates society. The latter system is more likely to adhere longer to exclusive stewardship of heritage resources to formal representatives of the state and asymmetrical power relations. This may in part explain striking differences in the role of native peoples in heritage management between most of Latin America and North America.'*

This matter came to the fore between Willem and me during a global teleconference when we were working on the Rio Tinto project 'why cultural heritage matters' (Willems 2014: 112). As project specialist advisor, I was blithely making what I thought was a well-agreed point to the international external advisory group of which Willem was a member when he interrupted to tell me forcefully 'Ian, this is not Australia!'. I was used to hearing that in relation to non-Western settings, including Latin America, but it caught me by surprise to realise Willem was referring to Europe and specifically the Netherlands. I had of course read his 2009 paper on 'European and world archaeologies' but until that telephone conference it had not really been brought home to me in any concrete way that we might not be entirely 'on the same page' about basic matters of community involvement.

What did he mean? He certainly did *not* mean that either the Netherlands nor Europe more generally did not agree with or undertake community engagement. Willem's caustic critique (2014: 120, endnote 2) of the attacks on 'Australian' heritage philosophy and practice made by Michael Petzet (in print in 2009 and in person during the 2011 ICOMOS General Assembly) leaves no doubt that he also dismissed out of hand the notion that 'Australian' approaches to engagement are fatally undermining the management of cultural heritage. Rather, he meant that it was wrong to think that Europe could follow an Australian model in any simple, straightforward way. This is because the way in which community engagement has evolved in Australia (and indeed the other Anglophone settler nations, despite differences within this group; Lilley 2000) has been profoundly influenced by the special dynamics of relations between settler and Indigenous populations in a common-law setting (for discussion of aspects of this situation see Lilley 2006). These conditions do not apply in Europe because in addition to it being composed almost entirely of civil rather than common law jurisdictions, 'In most of Europe', Willem noted, '…we are our own indigenes' (Willems 2014: 109).

From ICOMOS to IUCN

If in drawing this essay to a close we return to World Heritage, the arena in which Willem and I spent most time working together, we can see how the foregoing situation impacts on daily practice on the ground around the planet. As indicated at the outset, the World Heritage system is trying hard to adjust to the realities

> ' IUCN fills a void in community and especially Indigenous engagement that ICOMOS is not equipped […] to fill.'

of the postcolonial world, attempting to include more non-Western sites to help 'balance' the World Heritage List and to accommodate non-Western concepts of heritage and approaches to site management. Despite a great deal of effort and good will, this endeavour is still hampered by structural problems in the World Heritage framework.

One set of significant issues stems from differences between ICOMOS, the statutory Advisory Body to the UNESCO World Heritage Committee on cultural heritage, and IUCN (International Union for the Conservation of Nature), the Advisory Body on natural heritage. The former is a quintessentially 'European' organization in Willem's terms, heavily reliant on state intervention and with no formal mechanisms to deal with the various dimensions of indigenous or local community engagement despite a formally-recognised imperative to do so. The IUCN on the other hand has moved much more quickly and comprehensively, since the later decades of the 20th century, to shift from a Western- or Northern-dominated organisation focused on people-free 'fortress conservation' on the antiquated Yellowstone model, to a body with multiple intersecting formal and informal channels for community and especially indigenous engagement.

I am an active member of IUCN as well as ICOMOS and I am working on joint projects in different parts of the world to help bring the two organizations closer together in philosophy and practice. On that basis, I can say that IUCN has a much more postcolonial 'New World' feel to it than ICOMOS. This is despite the 'Australian' influence on ICOMOS that so concerns some colleagues and despite the fact that IUCN is based in a civil-law jurisdiction in Europe and has numbers of Europeans from civil-law countries in key positions as staff and members. A good indication of this difference was the strong and overwhelmingly positive Indigenous and wider community representation at the organisation's World Parks Congress in Sydney, Australia, in late 2014, in glaring contrast to the 2014 ICOMOS General Assembly held in Florence, Italy, in the same week. I was at the IUCN meeting, but anecdotal reports from colleagues who went to Florence despaired about its anachronistic content and atmosphere.

At the risk of over-simplifying, from what I have observed the profound difference evident at these two pivotal international meetings flows largely from the fact that people from common-law jurisdictions, including Britain as well as the Anglophone settler nations, play much more influential roles in IUCN than they do in ICOMOS. As a result, there is considerable – and inevitable – 'mission creep' on IUCN's part, as it fills a void in community and especially Indigenous engagement that ICOMOS is simply not equipped – and perhaps still fundamentally unwilling – to fill. Thus while I understand exactly what Willem meant when he told me so emphatically that Europe was not Australia, I also understand why he was so dismissive of Petzet's concerns about 'Australian' influence on global cultural heritage management. Far from being contradictory, these positions show that Willem could see the writing that is on the wall for ICOMOS and the 'transnational heritage regime' it represents if it fails to learn more quickly and comprehensively from the common-law 'Anglo-Saxon' world in the way that the IUCN (and the global development banks and international corporations) is doing to adapt to evolving circumstances. I think there is still time for ICOMOS to change successfully. I am just sorry Willem is no longer with us to help make it happen.

References

Hammer, D. 1957. 'Russia and the Roman Law', *American Slavic and East European Review* 16(1): 1-13.

Lilley, I. 2000. 'Native Title and the transformation of archaeology in the postcolonial world', in I. Lilley (ed.), *Native Title and the Transformation of Archaeology in the Postcolonial World*. Sydney: Oceania Monographs, 1-9.

Lilley, I. 2006. 'Archaeology, diaspora and decolonization', *Journal of Social Archaeology* 6(1): 28-47.

Willems, W.J.H. 2009. 'European and world archaeologies', *World Archaeology* 41(4): 649-658.

Willems, W.J.H. 2014. 'The Future of World Heritage and the Emergence of Transnational Heritage Regimes', *Heritage & Society* 7(2): 105-120.

A personal memoir of the early years of ICAHM

Henry Cleere

Council for British Archaeology (1974-1991) /
ICOMOS (1992-2002), United Kingdom

In 1975 I was invited to join the United Kingdom National Committee of the International Council on Monuments and Sites (ICOMOS). I was at that time Director of the Council for British Archaeology (CBA) and I was proposed by the Chief Inspector of Ancient Monuments and Buildings, the late Andrew Saunders, who wanted some support, since the rest of the Committee were all architects and planners. When I was in Paris shortly afterwards I called upon the Director of ICOMOS, Piers Rodgers, in the impressive historic Hôtel Saint-Aignan in the Marais district.

My first experience of ICOMOS in action on an international level was during the 5th General Assembly, which was held in Moscow in 1978. I was not greatly impressed by the organization at that time (and I cared even less for Moscow). One of my most abiding memories was the realisation that archaeology was barely represented within the membership of ICOMOS at all levels, as well as among the general members.

Shortly afterwards I was in Paris again, to give evidence to a parliamentary committee of the Council of Europe on metal detecting, since I was deeply involved in a campaign to reduce this wretched hobby in the UK. One of the others giving evidence was the new ICOMOS Director, François Leblanc, from Canada. Over lunch he told me that in his opinion and that of his Executive Committee, the UK National Committee was moribund and needed reactivating. In return I complained bitterly about the lack of archaeologists on the Executive Board. We agreed on joint action: I would do my best to shake up the UK Committee and he would encourage my candidacy for election to the Executive Committee at the next General Assembly in Rome in 1981.

We achieved both objectives. I invited the Chairman of ICOMOS-UK (The Duke of Grafton) and the Secretary (Marcus Binney) to lunch at The Athenaeum Club, and by the time we had finished our coffee and brandy they had both agreed to resign. I had previously taken the precaution of getting the agreement of Sir Bernard Feilden, who had recently retired from the post of Director General of ICCROM in Rome, and of Piers Rodgers, who had taken up the post of Secretary of the Royal Academy after leaving ICOMOS.

My electoral campaign went well in Rome, since Andrew Saunders had been obliged by minor mandarins in the Department of the Environment not to stand again by refusing to approve his expenses for attending meetings. I succeeded in talking to many ICOMOS members while I was in Rome and I was agreeably surprised to learn that many of them had begun as archaeologists but had felt obliged to keep quiet about this within their national monuments services. One of the points that I made was the need for an ICOMOS Charter specifically directed towards the archaeological heritage, something that was favourably received.

The run-up to ICAHM

At my first Executive Committee meeting I was firmly put down by the new President, Michel Parent, a French art historian who disliked 1. archaeologists, 2. left-wingers, and 3. Englishmen. Not long before I had been a member of an international working party set up by the Centre National de la Recherche Scientifique (CNRS) at the prompting of several far-left young archaeologists, all

> 'There was a need for an ICOMOS Charter specifically directed towards the archaeological heritage.'

of them *soixante-huitards*. The then head of French cultural heritage protection, a good friend of Parent who shared his prejudices, warned him about me. He therefore rigorously opposed any attempt that I made to introduce the concept of an archaeological heritage committee, leading to an eventual charter, into ICOMOS.

However, I took full advantage of the contacts that I had made via the CNRS working party with archaeologists from other countries, in particular Norway, Poland, Sweden, and The Netherlands, and these proved invaluable. I had also made some very good contacts during an eight-week Winston Churchill Travelling Fellowship in 1979, which took me to eight European countries (four on either side of the Iron Curtain). The redoubtable Margareta Biörnstad, head of *Riksantikvarämbetet* (Swedish Antiquities Service) convened a meeting in Stockholm with representatives from eleven or twelve countries which led to the preparation of a proposal for the establishment of an ICOMOS International Committee on Cultural Heritage Management. This proposal was presented formally to the President of ICOMOS, who met a delegation (consisting of Margareta, George F. MacDonald, Director of the National Museum of Canada, and myself) in Paris one weekend.

At our first meeting Parent was suspicious of what we were proposing. We went through our ideas point by point and he could find little to object to. However, the big problem came when we moved to the question of the eventual French text. We went into a number of questions of terminology, most of which George and I were able to deal with, but then we reached what appeared to be a stumbling block. He objected strongly to our use of the term 'cultural heritage management,' pointing out that *la gestion du patrimoine culturel* was meaningless in French. We then broke up, Parent reluctantly agreeing to continue the discussion the following day. We treated ourselves to a splendid Parisian dinner and tried out a number of alternatives. We had adopted 'cultural heritage management' because this term had been devised by the Americans in the 1970s and had become widely adopted (though I will admit that I had shared Parent's objections). We finally agreed upon 'archaeological heritage management,' against which Parent could find no argument.

Margareta Biörnstad then convened a small group to come up with a constitution for this new ICAHM, which would require Executive Committee approval and submission to the General Assembly for ratification. This group worked hard to come up with a structure and work plan that would meet with the approval of the next General Assembly, scheduled for Lausanne in 1990. Roberto di Stefano, the Italian architect who had succeeded Michel Parent, did not look favourably upon this proposal and made efforts to delay its presentation at the 8th General Assembly in Washington, DC, in 1987. His cynical attempt to delay the presentation until the 1990 General Assembly on legalistic grounds when the proposal was put by Margareta to the Executive Committee preceding the General Assembly was vigorously opposed by the Committee: he had to give way and ICAHM, the International Committee on Archaeological Heritage Management was born.

From committee to charter

Once the new committee had been validated by the General Assembly, work began to get ICAHM started. The Nordic countries (Denmark, Norway, and Sweden) cooperated in the provision of secretarial services for the new Committee. Two major objectives were identified at the first meeting of the provisional Committee for the first triennium in the life of ICAHM: 1. the drafting of a Charter for the Protection and Management of the Archaeological Heritage, and 2. the organization of the first international meeting on this subject.

The drafting of the Charter was initially in the hands of a member of the Danish monuments service, Carsten Lund, a lawyer by training, who worked with Léon Pressouyre from France and me in the finalization and harmonization of the English and French texts. These were distributed at the conference that marked the achievement of the second objective: it took place in Stockholm in September 1988 under the title 'Archaeology and Society – Large Scale Rescue Operations – Their Possibilities and Problems' (proceedings published in 1989 as ICAHM Report No 1). There were over a hundred archaeologists at this first-ever international meeting on archaeological heritage management, coming from 37 countries in all five continents. They warmly endorsed the structure, objectives, and recommendations of the Charter.

It may be relevant here to mention that this was not the first time that the international community became aware of ICAHM and its objectives. In 1986 Southampton hosted the first World Archaeological Congress, which replaced the XIth Congress of the International Union of Prehistoric and Protohistoric Sciences (IUPPS). The CBA had undertaken to organize a three-day symposium on 'Public archaeology and cultural resource management' as its contribution to the Congress, but its Council decided to withdraw this offer when the IUPPS Congress was cancelled, at a time when arrangements for the CBA symposium were well advanced. However, a telephone call to Stockholm resulted in the agreement of the fledgling ICAHM to serve as organizers. Margareta Biörnstad gave a spirited account of the genesis and programmes of the new body, which was well received by the large audience at the symposium (see Cleere 1989).

The ICAHM 'Charter for the Protection and Management of the Archaeological Heritage' was enthusiastically received by the new ICOMOS Executive Committee elected at the 10th General Assembly, which took place in Colombo, Sri Lanka, in 1993. This was very much due to the enthusiastic support of the President, Dr Roland Silva, trained in both archaeology and architecture, who was largely instrumental in the choice of topic for the scientific symposium in Colombo, 'Archaeological Heritage Management, Cultural Tourism, and Conservation Economics.' This event marked the end of the first phase in the life of ICAHM.

Envoi

The subsequent history of ICAHM has been a little chequered, with its management moving in succession to Sri Lanka, Canada, and Australia. Its programme of the last few years has been the most active and wide-ranging so far, under the enthusiastic joint presidency of Willem Willems of The Netherlands and Doug Comer of the USA.

References

Cleere, H.F. (ed). 1989. *Archaeological Heritage Management in the Modern World*. London: Unwin Hyman.

A view from the 'far side'

Margaret Gowen

Ireland

Recollection of thirty years practice in Irish commercial archaeology might not reveal any new 'wisdom in hindsight' but for the purposes of this short piece it has been an interesting personal reflection on commercial archaeology, some of the great concerns and developments that preoccupied the profession during that time and the immense influence of Willem Willems in both articulating and mediating them.

A rueful memory might be a good point at which to start this rather personal review. It goes back to a conference hosted by the Heritage Council in Ireland in the late 1990s that presented a review and audit of Irish urban archaeology. During discussion a colleague from our state heritage service stood up and declared (with reference to my company and our Temple Bar West excavation project, in particular, for which we received a 100 per cent audit rating) that Irish archaeological practice was 'being led from the bottom up'. I could only regard this statement as a compliment. However, it reflected the enduringly marginalised position of commercial sector archaeology within the professional in Ireland at the time.

Commercial archaeology – filling gaps

As in most other European jurisdictions archaeology was a very well-established state/museum and academic profession in Ireland prior to its rapid development-led growth after 1980. That growth accelerated beyond all expectation between the mid-1990s and 2005 after which the commercial sector of the profession all but collapsed following the financial crisis of 2007/8. What was unique about Irish commercial sector archaeology was that its early growth in the 1980s was left entirely to free market forces following a state embargo on recruitment. The professional status of commercial sector archaeology in Ireland in the 1980s can be (also somewhat ruefully) recalled as membership in the then Irish Association of Professional Archaeologists, which only opened up in 1989 for 'contract archaeologists' (a personally disliked term), following lengthy debate on what constituted a professional archaeologist (i.e. to be commercial sector or working on a contract basis was to suggest a status that was less than professional).

Unlike the United Kingdom and other jurisdictions in Europe, urban archaeology in particular had no structural precedents such as university, state service or trust-based excavation units (the National Museum had undertaken all the large Viking urban excavations in Dublin between the late 1960s and 1981 and trained a great many young archaeologists during that time). Urban and development-led 'rescue' archaeology had no framework for management, other than the Irish excavation licensing system, which licences every excavation undertaken, no matter what size. As in other European states, the Irish state heritage service had to develop a workable link between heritage protection and development control, which ultimately developed as an interface between the Planning and Development legislation and our National Monuments legislation. Accordingly, development led excavation, also called 'rescue archaeology' became more widespread. 'Rescue archaeology' became a term I grew to dislike as much as 'contract archaeology'. While the term described exactly what it was, it grew to be regarded as work of less integrity than research excavation. It has to be admitted that initial commercial sector development in Ireland and it standards were somewhat patchy as I found my professional 'feet' in a commercial sector context during the late 1980s and

> 'While only the commercial sector could address the rapid changes in archaeological heritage management, it was 'bashed' by the academic sector.'

early 1990s. Commercial sector work was necessarily development project focused but its management, standards and practice were entirely self-regulated by those engaged in the projects concerned at the time. Irish State policy and practice guidance was eventually formulated but was not published until 1999, following Ireland's ratification of the Valletta Convention in 1997 some five years after it was adopted. The Irish professional association also had to 'catch up' soon afterwards and did so under the guidance of Maurice Hurley then chairman, who steered its development into the Institute of Archaeologists of Ireland (IAI) in 2001.

A point that I still reflect on is the fact that Irish academic research regrettably remained disengaged with commercial sector activity during that very long time. In the early years that disengagement was compounded by distrust of archaeologists who worked for fees. From the perspective of the almost 'demonised' and certainly marginalised commercial sector, the criticism of standards of practice and the value of the work being undertaken was very often unfair and inaccurate even though the professional environment was so lightly regulated. It is important to clarify that the entire profession (state service, museum and commercial sector) was in 'fire-fighting' mode while the Celtic Tiger roared its way through the late 1990s and the first years of the new millennium.

Adding values

What did become quite clear as the years progressed, was that development-led activity was leading to a significant change in the character of archaeological heritage management. It also led to the emergence of a generation of highly motivated, well-trained, multi-skilled, professional archaeologists, all of whom 'learnt on the job', but were capable of archaeological and interdisciplinary research of a calibre that could match anything that was being undertaken in the university sector. It also became evident that some really significant results and important research findings were emerging that demanded review. What was singularly lacking was a focus on a more tangible return to a far more integrated up-to-date research knowledge base (University College Dublin 2006: 7-10). The lack of research engagement in professional development, with some notable exceptions, also reflected in the membership profile within the professional body (IAI) which became increasingly dominated by commercial sector members and their concerns. For me, membership of the IAI and participation in its work on professional development was of singular importance. It was informed by membership of the Irish ICOMOS Committee from 1992 and access to its international doctrinal texts and publications which reflected a welcome interdisciplinary and somewhat alternative, international conservation-focused heritage management environment. It informed my work in IAI which sought to steer the profession towards a greater focus on representation of all sectors and the development of guidance documents, standards of practice and the development of a continuing professional development (CPD) programme all of which have continued to this day.

International connections

My first encounter with the European Association of Archaeologists (EAA) and Willem was in 1995, following an invitation to present to an EAA session on 'Models of organisation in development-led archaeology' at Santiago de Compostela. Preparation of that paper highlighted that fact that, at the time, there was no easily modelled organisational structure in Ireland. It was a chastening realisation as definition on just how things 'worked' in Ireland was elusive. During the EAA annual business meeting the protection of the Cao Valley was discussed. I remember clearly the contributions of Henry Cleere and Willem which referred to the convention as their support (the year it was ratified in Ireland). I found much to interest me during those few days and four years later presented to a similar session in Bournmouth (1999) as a more well-established commercial sector practitioner, chair of the Irish ICOMOS Committee and a member of the IAI board, working on training and professional standards. Once again, at Bournmouth, Willem impressed as President of EAA and from that time onwards membership of EAA provided me with an important peer group of archaeologists and an opportunity for discourse with leaders in research and professional practice that I have valued immensely.

Membership of EAA meant that our paths continued to cross, informed by personal and professional concerns. These included (from our different perspectives) a focus on standards and the changing nature of archaeological heritage management across Europe. So in 2006, Willem was an obvious choice as keynote speaker for a day-long seminar hosted by the Royal Irish Academy (RIA) that sought to analyse the dysfunction within Irish archaeology and to define a future for the fractured Irish archaeological profession. In a memorably concise but wide-reaching presentation, Willem articulated just how much archaeological heritage management and practice had developed and changed in the European context since the adoption of the Convention (Willems 2007). This did not deter a significant degree of commercial sector archaeology 'bashing' by academic archaeologists during that long day, which failed to acknowledge the necessarily technical nature of heritage management research for impact assessment and management purposes. It also failed to acknowledge the amount of publication that had been achieved by commercial archaeology in an unregulated environment where publication was a matter of personal professional choice and was rarely funded by development projects. The discussion on the day missed the point of what ailed the profession at the time and it failed to reflect adequately on the findings of the foresight study, Archaeology 2020, which was initiated by the Department of Archaeology of University College Dublin (UCD) in 2004 and supported by the Heritage Council (University College Dublin 2006). It was a cathartic moment, however, for all who attended and Willem was a powerful advocate on the day, suggesting that 'a search for the guilty parties' was not helpful and that the profession needed to address the fact that the very nature of archaeology and modern archaeological heritage management had changed. Commercial sector activity, in many respects, simply reflected and addressed that change (Gowen 2007).

Work in progress

Ultimately both the UCD and RIA reviews gave rise to a renewed focus on how the university and research sectors of the profession might access the immense amount of critical new and wonderful information that was the product of more than two decades of intense excavation activity. Richard Bradley had already led the way in his synthetic research based on the UK and Irish 'grey literature' (2006; 2007). With both review reports in hand, lobbying with government was now possible and, in 2008, significant finance (€1 million) was made available to the Heritage Council to initiate the INSTAR (Irish National Strategic Archaeological Research) programme. To date this immensely successful synthetic research programme continues to be funded and has produced over 100 reports from 37 research projects based on hundreds of development-led excavation results and a huge record of dating information. All the reports are accessible on the Heritage Council website (http://www.heritagecouncil.ie/archaeology/our-initiatives/instar-web-archive-grant-programme/) and many of the projects have been published in a variety of forms. At the same time, the Irish National Roads Authority which began publishing in 2003, launched its project-specific series in 2007 and a research fellowship programme in 2006. Both of these initiatives continue to support new research endeavours.

While Willem was not engaged in these developments, his immense presence and overarching influence during 2005 and 2006 and on the profession generally was singularly influential and he supported and advised many Irish archaeologists prior to and after that important time through informal discussion and at relevant sessions during EAA Annual meetings.

References

Bradley, R. 2006. 'Bridging the two cultures. Commercial archaeology and the study of prehistorc Britain, *Antiquaries Journal* 86: 1-13.

Bradley, R. 2007. *The prehistory of Britain and Ireland*. Cambridge: Cambridge University Press.

Gowen, M. 2007. 'Quality management and Irish commercial sector archaeology', in W.J.H. Willems and M.H. van den Dries (eds), *Quality Management in Archaeology*. Oxford: Oxbow Books, 22-34.

University College Dublin. 2006. *Archaeology 2020: Repositioning Irish Archaeology in the Knowledge Society*. Dublin: University College Dublin.

Willems, W.J.H. 2007. 'The times they are a-changin': observations on archaeology in a European Context', in G. Cooney (ed.), *Archaeology in Ireland: A Vision for the Future*. Dublin: Royal Irish Academy, 5-23.

On translating the untranslatable, African heritage ... in African

Nathan Schlanger

Ecole nationale des chartes, France / UMR Trajectoires, France / RARI, University of the Witwatersrand, South Africa

Willem Willems' interest in African archaeological heritage was a sustained one, reflecting both his theoretical concerns with the nature and (under) representation of heritage from a global perspective, and his extremely pragmatic ambitions to do something about it, on the ground. On both counts, his towering presence was welcome at the 13th meeting of the Pan African Archaeological Association for Prehistory and Related Studies, held in Dakar in November 2010 (in conjunction with the Society of Africanist Archaeologists, SAfA). The venue was indeed ideal for launching ICAHM's (International Committee on Archaeological Heritage Management) 'Africa initiative' for archaeological heritage in Africa, including the identification and promotion of prospective World Heritage Sites. Together with ICAHM co-president Douglas Comer and other participants in the session, Willem singled out the issues involved (as reported in Willems and Comer 2011). Some challenges related to the wider under-representation of archaeological sites, in comparison with traditionally more visible (and visitable) monuments. Others, more specific to Africa, concerned the occidental origins of the notion of 'heritage', as well as the more specific administrative and conceptual difficulties surrounding the composition of a world heritage nomination dossier. While recognising the necessity of a top-down approach, Willems and Comer insisted on the importance of ensuring that proper heritage infrastructures – both material and intellectual – are developed across Africa. They also recalled, in line with UNESCO's operational guidelines, that 'Participation of local people in the nomination process is essential to enable them to have a shared responsibility with the State Party in the maintenance of the property' (cited in Willems and Comer 2011: 170).

The project

Although it developed quite independently, the initiative which I briefly present here (on behalf of all its participants) is well in tune with these ambitions. Launched in 2011, the 'untranslatable' project recently culminated in a book entitled 'Les Intraduisibles du patrimoine en Afrique Subsaharienne' (Heritage untranslatable in Sub-Saharan Africa), published integrally in French, English, Fulfulde and Bamanakan, under the direction of Barbara Cassin, a philologist and philosopher interested in issues of translation as a source of understanding, and Danièle Wozny, a former cultural *attaché* at various French embassies and more recently head of the World Heritage Department at the French Ministry for Foreign Affairs (Cassin and Wozny 2014). A series of workshops (held in Paris, Dakar, Gaborone, and the Fondation les Treilles) brought together core members of the project, mostly linguists and heritage specialists, including Hamady Bocum and Fary Silate Kâ (Sénégal), Moulaye Coulibaly (Mali), Herman Batibo (Tanzania and Botswana), Sozinho Matsinhe (Mozambique), as well as Vincent Négri and myself (France).

We took these challenges of translation head-on, as a means to provoke thought, highlight diversity and also empower action on ground, beyond dominant languages and discourses. Definitions of such concepts as 'heritage' and 'museum' were long derived from UNESCO and European bodies without really considering alternative traditions, or thinking through the complex and fluid relationships between heritage, territory, history, memory and identity. In reality, conceptions of 'heritage' and 'museums' vary depending on the place, time, and linguistic universe in which they take shape. There is therefore scope for a pluralist and comparative exploration of language difference based on 'untranslatables' – not in the sense of what does *not* get translated, but rather of what is always *in the process* of being translated – with languages considered as ways of *making* as well as seeing the world.

Hence the project's particular emphasis on words: much as heritage is made of objects, monuments and forests, as well as a wealth of animals, plants, traditions and narratives, it is primarily expressed in 'words'. What tethers a heritage to its culture are the words of its particular language. However, words – in this case UNESCO's – also define the criteria (outstanding, universal, symbolic, integrity, authenticity, identity, immaterial, nature, culture, etc.) used for the international recognition of heritage properties and their promotion as instruments of economic, social, and cultural development.

Giving the words 'museum' and 'heritage' the attention they deserve, we have chosen to address their translation in several African languages. In coordination with the African Academy of Languages, five vehicular cross-border languages were chosen (in addition to French and English, themselves African languages through their colonial fate): 1. Fulda (Fulfulde), spoken by over 30 million people in West Africa, from Senegal to Nigeria; 2. Bambara (Bamanakan), spoken specifically across Mali but part of a linguistic Mande continuum including Burkina Faso and Ivory Coast; 3. Swahili (Kiswahili), spoken by some 80 people across Central Africa, mainly as a second, international language; 4. Sukuma (Shisukuma) spoken from Tanzania to Lake Victoria; and 5. Tsonga (Xitsonga), located in Zimbabwe, Mozambique and Southern Africa.

So, how do the words 'museum' and 'heritage' come up in these languages?

Saying 'museum'

The chapter on 'museum' includes a discussion of the following headings: official definitions (including UNESCO, ICOM, etc.), a history of the word and the reality it describes, discussions on 'colonial museums', 'site museums', 'community museums', 'culture banks', and some propositions regarding exhibitions and self-contemplation, museums and inventiveness, and dialogues between African and the 'West' around the museum. In addition, a major part looks at equivalents to *musée* and museum in the African languages we had identified. After all, when the target language does not have a concept, word, or term for the thing to be named, a neologism must be created or a term is borrowed from the source language. Here are a couple of examples.

In Fulfulde: *resorde pinal* ('culture conservatory'). The basic semantic characteristics we identified to the term 'museum' are: the notion of place or locale; the notion of conservation (as in keeping things and objects); the notion of culture or civilisation: cultural elements are preserved in this place so they may be visited and examined; contact with these artefacts simultaneously allows people to develop their culture – the notions, therefore, of observation, admiration, information and delectation. We came up with, and rejected, a large number of proposed terms, either because they tended to be limited to the notion of admiring observation (as in *yeeɓirde*, 'the place where one admires things'), or because they were not

> 'Switching between languages enables us to gain an outsider's perspective on how different languages can enrich each other's perceptions on heritage.'

specific enough and could have been used in other senses (as in *galle pinal*, 'house of culture', or *suudu pinal*, 'room/hall of culture', which was coined by analogy with *suudu defte*, 'library', but was even more reductive). We also rejected the idea of borrowing the original French word, phonetically adapted as *miisee*, since this word was unknown to, and meaningless for, the local population.

Working with the natural lexical creativity of the language, and taking into account the first three basic semantic characteristics of place, conservation, and culture, we came up with a very clear neologism: *resorde pinal*, a term composed of two substantives: *resorde*, 'reservation and preservation place' and *pinal*, 'culture', leading to 'a *place/locale* for the conservation of [things related to] *culture*'.

In Bamanakan: *fɛnkɔrɔmarayɔrɔ* ('place where ancient things are conserved'). In the Bambara tradition, the place where ancient and extremely important things are conserved is generally sacred and consecrates fetishes, *gris-gris*, and other things related to the physical and spiritual protection of human beings against evil spirits and ill-intentioned people. These sacred objects may be preserved in a hut, bag, *canari* (pottery vessel) or calabash and may belong to a man, woman, or youth. Access to it is private, and it is therefore out of bounds for the public. In the Bambara language, this 'man hut' is called *cɛ* ('man') *-so* ('hut', 'house').

The equivalent to a 'museum' for the Bambara people might be a place for the conservation of things that have been deconsecrated, either because there are no officiating priests, guides, or teachers to initiate the new generations into the rituals (sacrifices, libations, offerings), or because the rituals have been transgressed. Losing their historical and socio-cultural value, 'sacred' things may thus be shared and known by all. The neologism *fɔnkɔrɔmarayɔrɔ* (*fɛn*: thing, object; *kɔrɔ*: ancient; *mara*: to conserve; *yɔrɔ*: place) which we ended up settling on to translate the notion of 'museum' literally means 'the place where ancient things are conserved'.

In Swahili, just to mention another example, museum comes up as *Makumbusho*, 'a site of collective memory' and as *nyumba za makumbusho*, 'houses of memory'.

Talking about 'heritage'

Following the same pattern, the chapter on heritage or patrimony begins with definitions in European languages, including in legal contexts, and then discusses the basic terminology used in the World Heritage Convention, criteria for world heritage nomination, the notions of cultural landscape and intangible heritage, and then moves to a discussion of the equivalents to heritage in Sub-Saharan Africa. Here again are some examples.

In Fulfulde: *ndonaandi*. The notion of patrimony exists and is well-understood in the Fula language and culture. The Fula concept of 'patrimony' does not have exactly the same definition as the French word '*patrimoine*', but it comes very close to it. It is expressed through the couplet *ndonaandi* /*ron – aa – ndi*/ 'tangible, concrete heritage', inherited from one's ascendants, particularly ancestors and *ndonaagu* / *ron – aa – gu*/ 'intangible heritage'. *Ndonaandi* is formed from: *ron* ('heir') – *aa* – [PASSIVE] *ndi* [the NDI class for masses, a generic total, and connotes a whole, a weight, etc.), and means 'the whole of the visible, concrete, material ancestral heritage'. Everything pertaining to sites, buildings, symbols, objects, etc. belongs to this category. *Ndonaagu* is formed from: *ron* ('to inherit') – *aa* – [PASSIVE] *gu* [the NGU class for abstractions, qualities and characteristics, relationships, etc.), and means 'the whole of the ancestral heritage which is transmitted in the form of ideas, characteristics, or qualities'. Everything pertaining to ways of thinking, rites, traditional ceremonies, socio-cultural practices, individual or collective character, etc. belongs to this category.

In Bamanakan: *forobaciyɛn* ('common heritage'). This heritage can pertain to several categories. The movable heritage is translated as 'movable valuable object' (*Forobadɔnnikofɛn tataw*). The immovable heritage chiefly refers to a place or locale, and is translated as 'place or site of community knowledge' (*forobadɔnni yɔrɔ*). This translation shows that the Bamanakan understanding of the immovable cultural heritage is problematic, since 'immovable' refers to the place or locale where a property is situated, rather than to the notion of immovability. In *Bamanakan*, the word for 'intangible' is *farintan*, which means 'disembodied', in the sense of something that is not solid. This designation is very appropriate since what is intangible is immaterial and impalpable (…). It is rather difficult to translate the word 'natural' in *Bamanakan* without a specific context. 'Natural' can be translated as anything related to the forest (*kungo*) or at least anything that is not in an inhabited zone. However, the natural heritage has another connotation. It can also be translated as 'environmental community heritage' (*sigida forobaciyɛn*). In this case too, the meaning of the word 'environment' is not limited to the forest, and to its flora and fauna. In Bamanakan, the word 'cultural' means 'what is known or knowable' (*dɔnko*). In this translation, 'cultural' refers to knowledge, experience, know-how, and learning and the search for knowledge, as well as anything that is integral to culture and humanism – in the Bambara social conscience, the latter refers to both the process and the state of realization of a social being.

Other discussions of 'heritage' are worth mentioning: In Swahili *urithi*, and in Sukuma *bulisi*. Generally, these speakers define the natural heritage as divinely created and the cultural heritage as man-made. The word *urithi* refers to familial inheritance and to properties inherited from the family, and, by extension, to patrimony. This word was borrowed from Arabic, which has been spoken in Tanzania since the ninth century and has exerted a strong influence on Tanzanian languages, especially *Swahili*. Speakers of Sukuma use a phonetic variant of the same word: *bulisi*. Recently, this word has started to be used in a broader sense, to refer to the common and shared heritage: *urithi wa Tanzania* (Tanzania's heritage) and *urithi wetu* (our national heritage).

Conclusions – gained in translation

The Untranslatables-project is still ongoing, and we hope to expand further the scope of our work, both in terms of the languages concerned (in Africa and also beyond) and the terms debated (including those of 'restitution', 'reparation', 'repatriation', 'authenticity'). Already now, it is possible to see that the benefits of the exercise are both practical and conceptual, and fully convergent with Willem's interests. For one, the project makes accessible occidental conceptions of 'museum' and 'heritage' to African-language populations. Likewise, operationally, it will serve heritage and museum administrators to explain to local communities on the ground what 'heritage' and 'museums' are about, in both occidental and African conceptions. Last but not least, the imperatives of translation have expanded our understanding of the concepts themselves. Switching between languages, as we have seen, enables us to gain an outsider's perspective on what there is in a language, and how different languages can enrich each other's perceptions. Transfers, interactions, and borrowings between discourses and texts, together with mistranslations, cross-meanings, betrayals, shortcuts and detours, are central to the operation of language and thought. So, now that we can consider European and African languages together – and, even more so, now that Bamanakan readers can appreciate in their own language the ways Fulfulde speakers conceive their heritage (and vice versa) – there is clearly scope for us to capitalize and build further on these cultural meanings, gained in translation.

References

Willems, W.J.H. and D. Comer. 2011. 'Africa, Archaeology, and World Heritage', *Conservation and Management of Archaeological Sites* 13(2-3): 160-173.

Cassin, B. and D. Wozny, with H. Batibo, H. Bocum, M. Coulibaly, F.S. Kâ, S. Matsinho, V. Négri and N. Schlanger. 2014. *Les intraduisibles du patrimoine en Afrique Sub-Saharienne* (Heritage untranslatable in Sub-Saharan Africa). Paris: Demopolis.

The Oyu Tolgoi cultural heritage program, Mongolia

Jeffrey H. Altschul* and Gerry Wait**

* Nexus Heritage, United Kingdom /
Statistical Research Inc., United States of America

** Nexus Heritage, United Kingdom

Sometimes you know a project is going to be an adventure from the outset. Not often perhaps, and not reliably, but sometimes you do just know it is going to be fun. Only in retrospect can you see that it was also transformational. Mongolia– the name conjures up images of nomads, Chinggis Khan, dinosaur bones, vast landscapes, and mystery. Few people live in Mongolia (less than 3 million) and fewer visit. Yet, it is under attack, not by the Russians or the Chinese, but by the world, attracted to its minerals and natural resources. It is not the first time; Mongolia's minerals have been exploited by foreigners since the Bronze Age, but this time it is different. Multinational companies armed with cash, sure as any missionaries of the past in the righteousness of their mission to bring the country into the 21st century.

The only thing standing in their way is the Mongolian people. At public meetings, at the ballot box, in the local *soums*, the public is clear; yes, they want satellite dishes, cell phones, cars, MTV, and Coca Cola, but they are also fiercely determined to remain Mongolian, speaking their own language, clothed in their traditional dress, eating their foods, protecting their ancestral sites, and allowing a place in a developed world for nomads.

A big challenge

In 2010, we were part of the Mongolian International Heritage Team (MIHT) which had been charged with developing a Cultural Heritage Program (CHP) for Mongolia's South Gobi province (Ömnögovi *aimag*). The South Gobi is under intense pressure from mining and one mine in particular, Oyu Tolgoi, is so large and so complex that the government required the company to complete a CHP not simply for the mine but for the whole province, which could serve as a model for the nation. The MIHT was led by one of the authors (Altschul), along with John Olsen of the University of Arizona (USA), and B. Gunchinsuren of the Mongolian Academy of Sciences (MAS), Institute of Archaeology (MASIA). For each category of cultural heritage we paired international experts with Mongolian specialists in ways to allow cross-fertilization. For archaeology and paleontology we paired Jeff Homburg (USA) and Diane Douglas (USA) with Ch. Amartuvshin (MASIA) and Kh. Tsogtbaatar (MAS Center of Paleontology). For museums and heritage tourism, we had Chen Shen (Canada) and Hilary du Cros (Hong Kong) working with J. Gerelbadrakh (Mongolian State University of Education), and for intangible heritage and public education, the other author (Wait) worked with Chuluun Sampildondov and Lham Purevjav from the MAS Institute of History.

Willem Willems (Netherlands) served as senior advisor and peer reviewer. As the only one on the team that had helped devise a national heritage management program as well as international conventions and charters protecting cultural heritage, Willem had all the right credentials. But it was not only his knowledge and experience that was needed; we needed his presence. Willem commanded attention with his endless supply of jokes – scurrilous, in dodgy taste, delivered with impunity and good humour. Together with Hardrock, our 20-something translator and lead singer of Mongolia's best known Death Metal band (yes, there is more than one!), Willem would belt out tunes in time with music from his iPhone to the great amusement of our Mongolian team members, instantly winning them over. Walking into a room with his instant coffee in one pocket and his precious bottle of *'oude jenever'* in the other, Willem signaled that he was ready for anything and so the rest of us were too.

And, that was a good thing. In ten days we had to come up with a CHP for an area the size of Greece in a country as rich in heritage. We dashed all over the south Gobi in our 4x4s, getting a crash course in the size and scope of the problem. No roads, vast landscapes, and cultural heritage ranging from Jurassic Park-like fossils at the 'flaming cliff' of Bayanzag, Paleolithic sites strung along long extinct rivers and lakes, the ruined Buddhist monasteries of Galbyn, and the attempt to recapture their Buddhist heritage at Demchog. Every day we met with the public– herders, elders, teachers, monks, *soum* and *aimag* governors, and mining officials. We heard the need to preserve paleontological remains, archaeological ruins, traditional festivals, games, foods, dresses, silversmiths, nomads, Mongolian long-songs – the *urtyn duu* – and the *uvt gazruud* or sacred places.

But how? The real problem was not how to record and preserve south Gobi long-songs – as important as that was – the real problem was systemic. Everything had to go – the Soviet-style committees in control of cultural heritage that never met; the laws that could not be enforced; the registered monuments that were not protected; and the cultural heritage personnel that were not trained. It all needed to be replaced with a cultural heritage system that could function in the face of rampant development.

A reformative approach

From an early age, Willem had the innate ability to get in a car and immediately fall asleep. In a land where there are no roads and one bounces from one rut to another, such an ability inspires awe and jealousy. Exasperated one day, the senior author woke Willem up and said they had to work on the heritage management structure. Jeff showed Willem a piece of paper on which he had drawn an organizational scheme, complete with boxes and arrows all arranged in a very complicated array of chaos. Willem took one look at it, said 'no, no, no,' and then proceeded to rearrange the boxes and arrows into a simple, yet elegant, structure; said 'here' and promptly fell back to sleep. And so, Mongolia's cultural heritage structure was born.

Well, not really. What happened was that we took the pencil and paper drawing back to our Mongolian colleagues, who then rearranged the boxes and the arrows yet again in line with Mongolian political and economic realities. After all, it is their structure. Our job was to open a discussion, which we did, that ultimately led to a comprehensive reconfiguration of the legislative and regulatory framework of cultural heritage management in Mongolia as well as a tax-based revenue stream to provide financial support to conserve and manage all forms of cultural heritage in

> 'We opened up a discussion that ultimately led to a reconfiguration of the legislative and regulatory framework of cultural heritage management in Mongolia.'

the Gobi in the face of an unprecedented mining boom. The resulting CHP covers public policy, stakeholder and community involvement, tangible and intangible heritage programs, regulatory compliance, public education, heritage tourism, museums, and capacity building and training. The Oyu Tolgoi CHP was published (Gunchinsuren *et al.* 2011a) as was the year-long baseline study that underlies the CHP (Gunchinsuren *et al.* 2011b). Both the Oyu Tolgoi CHP and the baseline study are publically available on the internet (see references).

Within Mongolia, the MIHT has influenced everything from site forms to amendments to the national law on cultural heritage. After years of wrangling between the government and the private partners involved in Oyu Tolgoi, the Mongolians are taking the first steps in implementing the CHP. It will be a long process, full of twists and turns. But it will be the Mongolian's process, who set off on it having thought through many of the issues every country faces when balancing cultural heritage preservation with economic development. Outside Mongolia, the CHP continues to be studied as a model for developing countries to incorporate cultural heritage management with economic development. Rio Tinto incorporated the CHP as a case study in its cultural heritage guidance (Rio Tinto 2011). The CHP has been discussed at numerous national and international conferences (see, for example, Wait and Altschul 2014).

Willem was proud of his participation in the MIHT, which he highlighted on his personal website. We, too, are proud; not just of our work, but of our association with a man whose greatest accomplishment was not his intellect or his personal triumphs, which were legion, but his ability to bring the best out in others, even us.

References

Gunchinsuren, B., J. H. Altschul and J.W. Olsen (eds). 2011a. *The Oyu Tolgoi Cultural Heritage Program*. Ulaanbaatar: Oyu Tolgoi, LLC. Available at http://ot.mn/en/communities/land-and-cultural-resources (retrieved 27 February 2015).

Gunchinsuren, B., J. H. Altschul and J.W. Olsen (eds). 2011b. *Protecting the Past, Preserving the Present: Report on Phase 1 Activities of the Oyu Tolgoi Cultural Heritage Program Design for Ömnögovi Aimag*. Ulaanbaatar: Oyu Tolgoi, LLC. Available at http://ot.mn/en/communities/land-and-cultural-resources (retrieved 27 February 2015).

Rio Tinto. 2011. *Why Cultural Heritage Matters: A Resource Guide for Integrating Cultural Heritage Management into Communities Work at Rio Tinto*. London: Rio Tinto. Available at http://www.riotinto.com/documents/ReportsPublications/Rio_Tinto_Cultural_Heritage_Guide.pdf (retrieved 27 February 2015).

Wait, G. and J.H. Altschul. 2014. 'Cultural Heritage Management and Economic Development Programmes: Perspectives from the Desert Fringes Where IGOs and NGOs Have No Locus', *Public Archaeology* 13(1-3): 151-163.

The Caribbean challenge
Archaeological heritage management in a varied geopolitical and cultural landscape

Corinne L. Hofman

Faculty of Archaeology, Leiden University /
ERC-synergy project NEXUS1492, The Netherlands

The indigenous history of the Caribbean started around 7500 years ago. This archipelagic region comprises more than 7000 islands, islets and cays of which many were once occupied by Amerindian communities who migrated from various parts of the surrounding mainland(s). By AD 1000 regionally and culturally diverse societies had developed throughout the Caribbean, and by 1492 a web of interlocking networks of human mobility and exchange of goods and ideas spread over the Caribbean Sea, crossing local, regional, and pan-Caribbean boundaries (Curet and Hauser 2011; Hofman and Bright 2010). These networks undoubtedly affected the manner in which the Spanish dispersed throughout the region and the Americas as a whole, following Columbus' landfall on Guanahani or San Salvador in 1492 (Hofman 2014). The Caribbean is the NEXUS of the first encounters between the New World and the Old that changed history forever. Indigenous resistance, European colonization, and the influx of enslaved Africans, beginning in the 16th century, led to the mixing of biological ancestries and the formation of new identities and social as well as material worlds (*e.g.* Deagan 2003; Valcárcel Rojas 2013). These processes ultimately contributed to the formation of present-day Caribbean society. Apart from the rich indigenous archaeological record, and the fact that Amerindian biological and cultural continuity is evident amongst the various descendant communities throughout the Caribbean, in contemporary oral traditions as well as in cultural and religious practices, indigenous contributions are disregarded in current discourse and global history (Hofman 2014). The indigenous side of the encounters is poorly known, underrepresented and overshadowed by the European version of the narrative. The impact of the colonization processes and colonial interactions is felt in common daily life throughout the region and worldwide to this day.

Caribbean heritage under siege

Today the Caribbean is composed of a multi-ethnic and multi-cultural society shaped by a long and complicated history of indigenous, enslaved African, Asian and European encroachment. The current geopolitical division with Spanish-, French-, English-, and Dutch-speaking islands reflects this diversity for policy making with implications for archaeological heritage management (Hofman 2014; Hofman and Haviser 2015; Siegel and Righter 2010; Siegel *et al.* 2013). The geopolitical and cultural diversity, the general lack of awareness of the complex island histories, and the multiple stakeholders involved in the preservation process of archaeological heritage, have in many cases slowed down the effective enforcement of regulations and heritage legislation.

The region's archaeological record is threatened by natural catastrophes and risks but also increasingly by economic developments, often resulting from the tourist industry. Next to the threat of tropical storms, hurricanes or extreme wave events, rising sea level, volcanic eruptions, and earthquakes, the continuous construction of mega-resorts, golf courses and other tourist development projects as well as looting and sand mining have had serious impacts on the region's archaeological sites (*e.g.* Hofman and Haviser 2015; Siegel *et al.* 2013). Many Amerindian sites have already been completely destroyed or heavily damaged (*e.g.* Fitzpatrick 2012;

> ' Indigenous Caribbean contributions are disregarded in current discourse and global history.'

Hofman and Hoogland 2012; Hofman *et al.* 2012). Natural and human factors are rapidly destroying the heritage landscapes of the Caribbean and erasing its multi-facetted histories. Immediate attention to and protection of the islands' heritage is urgent as there is an evident danger of losing an essential part and a forgotten chapter of global heritage and world history.

In many Caribbean islands archaeological heritage management is in a state of transformation as most have developed some form of heritage legislation on the basis of national and international standards (Siegel and Righter 2011). A wide range of stakeholders is often involved in the heritage preservation process and the implementation of laws is dealt with at the local level. These laws and regulations are often not adequately enforced, and government agencies in charge with protecting heritage resources do not have the means to do so (Hofman and Haviser 2015; Siegel *et al.* 2013). Many islands do not have the trained personnel to warrant that developers, public-works departments, and multinational corporations comply with the existing legislation (see chapters in Siegel and Righter 2010 for an extensive overview of heritage legislation in the various islands). Often difficult choices have to be made between the preservation of archaeological sites and the promotion of economic development (Siegel *et al.* 2013). On the smaller islands, non-governmental organisations (NGOs), interested individuals and vocational archaeologists are often the driving force in heritage protection.

Successful joint initiatives

The protection of the islands' cultural heritage is a concern of the entire Caribbean region and everybody would agree that the rich archaeological record needs to be properly documented, interpreted, where possible preserved, and widely promoted (Hofman and Haviser 2015; Siegel *et al.* 2013). Governmental cooperation and joint initiatives are essential, including local private/public sector co-funding, which should serve to highlight, preserve and maintain the archaeological heritage of the islands. Examples of successful initiatives include the proposition of a code of ethics for cultural heritage management by the Organisation of Eastern Caribbean States (OECS) to be applied in all of the associated islands (Eric Branford, personal communication 2010). Then there is the development of National Parks in several Caribbean countries which has been shown to contribute directly to people's awareness of their past, while at the same time creating jobs and education programs (*e.g.* Virgin Islands National Park Service, http://www.nps.gov/archeology/sites/npSites/stJohn.htm). Another example is the promotion of cultural tourism which has become a flourishing fact of life in the Caribbean, and which has been identified recently as the most significant developing aspect of tourism world-wide. Many islands increasingly promote their unique historical legacy to attract visitors from all over the globe (http://kalinagoterritory.com; Siegel *et al.* 2013). Finally, there are more and more large archaeological projects that are financed by private investors and construction companies carrying out extensive building activities in the islands. In Puerto Rico and the US Virgin Islands this is done according to US laws and in the French and Dutch Caribbean these projects are in compliance with the Valletta Convention (Hofman and Haviser 2015; Siegel and Righter 2011). But also on other islands such projects become increasingly commonplace, although these are still very much dependent upon individual initiatives, goodwill and contacts.

Projects that are carried out in such contexts should be conducted in close collaboration with specialized research organisations, whereby the cooperation and engagement with local governments, communities, and cultural heritage institutes is fundamental. Over the last decade, Leiden University has been involved in a number of such projects across the Caribbean (*e.g.* Hofman and Haviser 2015; Hofman and Hoogland 2012). These projects encouraged the participation of local Caribbean researchers and students who are considered to be critical for the communication of the achieved scientific results to the resident public and to raise awareness of the importance of the archaeological heritage that would otherwise be lost in these large scale operations.

At that time, Willem Willems, then Dean of the Faculty of Archaeology, visited two of such projects. The first was the Spanish Water project in Curaçao in 2008, where rescue excavations were carried out in the spirit of the Valetta Convention prior to the construction of a golf course. The project was conducted following an agreement between Leiden University, the *Dienst Ruimtelijke Ordening en Volkshuisvesting* (DROV), the National Archaeological Anthropological Memory Management (NAAM) and the Santa Barbara Plantation (Hofman and Haviser 2015). The investigations uncovered twelve shell middens dating to between 2500 BC and AD 1500. In 2010 Willem also visited the Argyle rescue project in St. Vincent. This project was carried out preceding the construction of the Argyle International Airport as a form of collaboration between Leiden, the St. Vincent and The Grenadines National Trust and the St. Vincent and The Grenadines International Airport Construction Company Ltd. The excavations revealed the unique remnants of an early colonial *Kalinago* settlement (Hofman and Hoogland 2012). A model of the reconstructed village at Argyle has recently been donated to the National Library in Kingstown.

NEXUS 1492

As a champion of archaeological heritage management, Willem Willems was asked to participate as one the four Principal Investigators in the Synergy Project 'NEXUS1492: New World Encounters in a Globalizing World', financed by the European Research Council (www.nexus1492.eu). We started the project in 2013 and we very much enjoyed working together with our colleagues Prof. dr. Gareth Davies of the Free University (VU), Amsterdam (Faculty of Earth and Life Sciences, Deep Earth and Planetary Science Cluster), Prof. dr. Ulrik Brandes of the University of Konstanz, Germany (Department of Computer and Information Science), and the team of approximately thirty international PhD students and postdocs, including many from the Caribbean. NEXUS1492 is a uniquely devised trans-disciplinary research programme using multiple temporal and spatial scales in the context of intercultural Amerindian-European-African dynamics at play across the historical divide. The primary temporal focus is the period between AD 1000 and 1800, which encompasses the consolidation of complex indigenous pre-colonial Caribbean societies until the last phase of Amerindian resistance against the colonial powers. Despite significant scholarly effort, Amerindian Caribbean histories and legacies are still considerably underrepresented in the local and global discourse due to theoretical, methodological, and societal concerns. NEXUS1492 aims to rectify these imbalances by bringing to light the immediate and lasting effects of the colonial encounters and colonization processes on indigenous Caribbean cultures and societies. It also aims to contribute to a more nuanced historical awareness and to the design of a heritage programme with local, regional and global implications, including local communities, island nations, and the pan-Caribbean region.

NEXUS1492 comprises four interconnected projects combining archaeology, geochemistry (provenance studies), network sciences and heritage studies. The choice for the combination of these four disciplines is based on the currently unexploited, but high complementarity of theories, methods, techniques and data, to address the main research questions of the programme, evolving around the complex intercultural interactions across the historical divide and the ensuing centuries. Willem was responsible for the heritage project, which aims to understand the varying relationships of the communities to diverse heritages and at the same aims to create tools to improve regulatory frameworks and build capacity for sustainable heritage management. In order for this to be locally embedded, the program is designed to enhance collaborative research, education and museum practice, and to promote public outreach and community engagement. In NEXUS1492 Willem was supervising three postdocs and three PhD students. He leaves a great void in the NEXUS1492 project.

References

Curet, L.A. and M.W. Hauser (eds). 2011. *Islands at the Crossroads*. Tuscaloosa: University of Alabama Press.

Deagan, K.A. 2003. 'Colonial origins and colonial transformations in Spanish America', *Historical Archaeology* 37(3): 3-14.

Fitzpatrick, S.M. 2012. 'One of the shoals of giants: Natural catastrophes and the overall destruction of the Caribbean's archaeological record', *Journal of Coastal Conservation* 14(1): 1-14.

Hofman, C.L. 2014. *The future of the past: Intercultural dynamics and diversity in a globalising world*. (439th Dies lecture) Leiden: Leiden University.

Hofman, C.L. and A.J. Bright (eds). 2010. Mobility and exchange from a pan-Caribbean perspective. *Journal of Caribbean archaeology*, Special Publication No. 3.

Hofman, C.L. and J.B. Haviser (eds). 2015. *Managing Our Past Into the Future: Archaeological Heritage Management in the Dutch Caribbean*. Leiden: Sidestone Press (Taboui no. 3).

Hofman, C.L. and M.L.P. Hoogland. 2012. 'Caribbean Encounters: Rescue Excavations at the Early Colonial Island Carib Site of Argyle, St. Vincent', in C.C. Bakels and H. Kamermans (eds), *The fifth decade, Analecta Praehistorica Leidensia* 43/44, 63-76.

Hofman, C.L., M.L.P. Hoogland, D.A. Weston, L.E. Laffoon, H.L. Mickleburgh and M.H. Field. 2012. 'Life and death at Pre-colonial Lavoutte, Saint Lucia', *Journal of Field Archaeology* 37(3): 209-225.

Siegel, P.E. and E. Righter (eds). 2011. *Protecting heritage in the Caribbean*. Tuscaloosa: University of Alabama Press.

Siegel, P.E., C.L. Hofman, B. Bérard, R. Murphy, J. Ulloa Hung, R. Valcárcel Rojas and C. White. 2013. 'Confronting Caribbean heritage in an archipelago of diversity: Politics, stakeholders, climate change, natural disasters, tourism and development', *Journal of Field Archaeology* 38(4): 376-390.

Valcárcel Rojas, R. 2013. 'Contacto y Colonialismo. Escenarios de interacción hispano-indígena en las Antillas Mayores', in I. Hernandez Mora (ed.), *Cultura material e Historia. Encuentro arqueológico II*. Camagüey: Ediciones El Lugareño, 37-56.

The organic nature of monuments' use

Jay B. Haviser

Sint Maarten Archaeological Center (SIMARC), Sint Maarten

Willem Willems and I were professional colleagues and good friends for decades. As our friendship endured, it primarily consisted of sporadic and often spontaneous encounters. Regularly we would meet during my annual lectures at Leiden University, or at various international professional conferences. Yet most often, our discussions about work, life and humanity would occur while he was passing through Sint Maarten, the Dutch Caribbean island where I work and reside. Sometimes for a day, sometimes for a few days, we would meet on Sint Maarten and enjoy each other's company over good food, drinks and engaging conversation. Often we would go out to experience the island life, and depending on the season our excursions included a variety of adventures. Once while having drinks in Philipsburg during Carnival, a costumed parade was marching past, and we spontaneously jumped from our chairs and joined the parade. That is the kind of friendship that Willem and I always knew.

One of the key elements in our ongoing professional discussions evolved around a concept we referred to as 'the organic nature of monuments use'. How humanity's historical features in the world have a life of their own, from birth and original use, to abandonment, to re-configuration, to re-use, to re-interpretation, to re-abandonment, etc., culminating in eventual physical disintegration, yet with frequent intangible cultural re-integration (Willems 2012; Haviser 2005). We would talk for hours on these concepts, and at each new meeting we would present recent personal experiences that demonstrated elements of our theory. At our last meeting, here on Sint Maarten in early 2014, I related to Willem a recent experience I had had which very precisely exemplified our continuing theoretical discussion. This is a summary of that discussion we had under a warm Caribbean sun, with cool drinks and delicious creole food.

Cultural reflections

In 2014 I was to give a lecture for the EUROTAST Marie Curie program (Exploring the History, Archaeology and New Genetics of the Transatlantic Slave Trade) on the small Senegalese island of Gorée, situated on the West African coast. The theme of this international symposium was the Trans-Atlantic Slave Trade, and the delegates for the event including myself, spent a week on the island which had only a few hundred inhabitants surviving on a couple of hectares of rocky land, isolated from the Senegalese coast. My presentation was entitled 'The Caribbean as a Mirror to Africa; with the steel-pan drum as mirror metaphor', in which I was stressing the dynamic reformation of African cultural traditions into new and unique Caribbean forms (Haviser 2014). The shining silver face of a steel-pan drum has many reflections, not just one, thus my point was that Caribbean cultural manifestations were reflective of many facets of cultural traditions, including African, however none of which are truly a pure reflection of the original source cultures, as they have become new creolized creations. I was indeed presenting a hard concept for my Caribbean colleagues to accept, the lack of pure African traditional transmissions in the West, and the general ignorance of what are authentic African cultures, displayed by most African Diaspora groups in the region. Yet as expected, my African colleagues readily understood and agreed to the concept that most African Diaspora cultures in the west actually know very little about authentic African cultures and thus manifest symbolic or superficial forms of 'Africanism' expression. The overall conclusion of my paper was that we should not be promoting Caribbean Cultures as pure images of African origins, but rather we should highlight pride in the unique, multi-faceted, and dynamic cultural creolizations we have created from many cultural origins.

Being an 'island man' myself, in my personal time on Gorée Island, I would explore the tiny island and meet its folk, with a clear empathy for small island life and nuances. From leaders to workers, from shop owners to religious authorities, I tried to meet as many as I could. One of the groups on the island that immediately caught my attention, being from the Caribbean, was a colony of Rastafarians residing there. Thus I set out to embed myself as far as possible into the local Rastafarian community, to learn about them at all levels of their society. My initial entrance came through a man named Bobo, who sold healthy natural food and teas in a tiny shed called 'Bobo Best Tea', situated on the path that led to the old fort atop the highest point of Gorée Island. After two days of visiting Bobo for tea, discussing life in general, his life, and life on Gorée, I asked if I could meet the leader of the Rastafarian community on Gorée. He agreed to request a visit to Ras Makha Diop, for which I waited another day to get a positive response and an appointment to meet.

Before telling of my meeting with Ras Makha, I must first provide some background of the physical setting in which the Rastafarians live on Gorée Island. Strategically located off the coast of Senegal, Gorée Island played a vital role in the military protection of the key trading city of Dakar, which was at the cross-roads of the interior Saharan and west coast transportation routes. From the 18th century, the French had built a fortification atop this tiny island, part of which still stands today. Even more important for this story was the strategic position of Dakar in World War II, as a primary control point for French West Africa. During World War II, on the entire top of the island of Gorée, the French constructed concrete bunkers and cannon placements, riddling the hilltop with dozens of underground chambers and tunnels. These massive concrete features were abandoned after the war, and remained forgotten and unattended until the 1970s, when Ras Makha Diop arrived from Dakar and took residence in them. Ras Makha Diop was a social activist in Dakar, who had decided to leave the mainland and establish a Rastafarian community in the abandoned concrete bunkers and tunnels of Gorée Island. Today, all of these bunkers and tunnels are resided in, and the hilltop is a bastion of Rastafarian culture, with a small art-market economy, selling unique local artistic creations to visitors who come to the island daily.

With Bobo as escort we arrived at Ras Makha's house, the best preserved and largest of the hilltop concrete bunkers. I was introduced and formally received to sit and talk with Ras Makha at his reception area and educational center about the faith. When I mentioned that I was lecturing there on an African-Caribbean mirror metaphor of steel-pan drums, he smiled and said that he had one. Calling out to his daughter to go get it from a storage area, he explained that a Trinidadian man had given it to him many years before. His daughter then brought out the old heavily rusted metal drum, which had rarely, if ever, been used. He made an awkward plunk at the face of the drum, obviously not knowing how to play, nor having much knowledge about the Caribbean at all. Then I gave him a CD with steel-pan

> 'All of humanities monuments have an organic nature to viably live again.'

music, which we listened to, and he then took the drum and placed it prominently in the education area, to be now kept there, he said. I was witnessing a full circle of the mirror metaphor, this uniquely Caribbean musical instrument with African roots had found its way back to Africa, just as the Rastafarian movement followers in the Caribbean had always dreamed to do. Ras Makha had little knowledge of the steel-pan as a symbol of Caribbean culture, just as the Caribbean people have little knowledge of the cultural symbols that represent authentic African traditions, yet each feel the connection of mutual cultural dynamics.

Ras Makha invited me back the next day for lunch with his family. It was a very personal and open gesture that he did not extend to many, and we discussed deeper concepts regarding the colonization of the concrete historic structures his community inhabited. I asked how Rastafarianism could be relevant in Africa itself, such that the roots of the religion were from those in the Diaspora with hope of returning to Africa (Haviser and MacDonald 2006). His response was clear and confident; Rastafarian faith was not about where you are from, it is about where you are going, and how you chose to live your life, with love, harmony and self-respect, which has no continental boundaries. Yet, he was also fully aware that 'Babylon' was out there in the world, ready to oppress his faith and people. And for that he was preparing, so his community had intentionally taken refuge among the concrete bunkers and tunnels as a stronghold against attack, both spiritual and physical, from those enforcing the degradations of 'Babylon'.

Living monuments

As Willem and I discussed this case over more cool drinks, I came to a conclusion that the symbolic and often distorted representations that Caribbean folk of the African Diaspora have towards Africa, have three key elements. Firstly, the root contradictions between Continental Africa versus African Diaspora foundations of identification with Africa. The former have long and dynamic ethnic histories, of which the slavery era is merely one part. Whereas the latter has as the very basis of their existence the trans-Atlantic slave trade, it is a central and dominant element in the African Diaspora identity. Secondly, although both groups endured European colonial pressures, the vastly dispersed populations of Continental Africans were far more isolated from direct contact with the Europeans and European domination of their daily cultural matters. The Caribbean Diaspora folk on the islands however were in daily and intimate contact with the Europeans, including a significant domination by the Europeans of their cultural matters. This crucial difference in personal contact relations allowed for a greater degree of European influenced cultural foundations in the multi-faceted Caribbean contexts of identity formation (Haviser in press). Thirdly, the identity formation variations between Continental African and Caribbean Diaspora folk is further complicated by the historical omissions and distortions of the role of Africans in understanding their own histories. The more isolated populations of the continent were able to maintain historical recollections for themselves, outside the control of European interpretations. However the constraints of a small island geography and close personal contexts in the Caribbean provided the Europeans more influence in historical representations of the broader society, thus imposing themselves, not the African descendants, as more central to history and society – a society in which the Africans and their descendants were forced to participate and survive (Haviser 2013).

Just as Ras Makha is preparing his community for the challenges of the coming age, so too are we, as heritage preservation and culture specialists, preparing our intellectual communities for an uncertain future. Monuments, like culture, are a living and vital ether, which must change and adapt to survive. They must constantly re-create themselves, just as the Rastafarians of Gorée Island are re-vitalizing life into abandoned concrete monuments. So too have all of humanities monuments an organic nature to viably live again.

References

Haviser, J. 2005. 'Slaveryland: A new genre of African Heritage Abuse', *Public Archaeology* 4(2): 27-34.

Haviser, J. 2013. *Truth and Reconciliation: Public Archaeology in the Caribbean*. EUROTAST Symposium, Archaeology of Slavery: Reclaiming History from Africa to the Americas. St Maarten: University of St. Martin.

Haviser, J. 2014. *The Caribbean as a Mirror to Africa*. EUROTAST Symposium, Reflections on Origins and Trans-Atlantic Connections. Dakar: Lycee Mariama Ba, Gorée Island.

Haviser, J. in press. 'Syncretism and Cognition apparent with African and European Religious and Aesthetic Expressions in the Caribbean', in T. Clack (ed.), *Archaeology, Syncretism and Creolization*. Oxford: Oxford University Press.

Haviser, J. and K.C. MacDonald (eds). 2006. *African Re-Genesis: Confronting Social Issues in the Diaspora*. One World Archaeology Series 23. London: University College London Press.

Willems, W.J.H. 2012. 'Tourism and Archaeological Heritage. Driver to development or Destruction?', in C. Gottfried and S. Hidalgo Sánchez (eds), *Heritage, a driver of development*. Proceedings of the 17th ICOMOS General Assembly Symposium. Paris: ICOMOS.

Why history (still) matters
Museum collections and the politics of heritage

Mariana de Campos Françozo

Faculty of Archaeology, Leiden University /
ERC-synergy project NEXUS1492, The Netherlands

In April 1914, shortly before the outbreak of the First World War, a fleet of circa seventy German and Austrian merchant ships anchored in Portuguese harbors to avoid the risk of being captured by the British navy. The ships remained untouched at Portuguese ports for almost two years when in February 1916 Portugal succumbed to diplomatic and economic pressures from Great Britain and impounded the ships. By doing so Portugal joined the war as an ally of Britain and the ships and their cargo were thus considered to be part of the patrimony of the Portuguese state (Bouquet and Freitas Branco 1988: 61-62).

One of the ships, the *Cheruskia*, a steamboat of over 3,000 tons, carried a very special cargo. It had left Basra, in present-day Iraq, loaded with a share of the material results of over a decade of German excavations at the Assyrian site of Assur, led by the notorious Walter Andrae (1875-1956). The ship was destined for Berlin and its contents, to the Berlin City Museums; however, it would be the subject of a long diplomatic battle and would not reach its destination until late in the 1920s.

Objects following people

The *Cheruskia* was renamed *Leixões* and incorporated first into the Transportes Maritimos do Estado and subsequently ceded to England; soon thereafter, in 1918, it was torpedoed by a German submarine 200 miles from the American shore, when *en route* from Hull to Boston (Wrecksite.eu, 2014). Its archaeological cargo had been stored in Lisbon Customs and there the Assyrian collection remained until the end of the war. In 1921 it was transferred to the University of Oporto upon the creation, on paper, of a Museum of Ancient Archaeology – a decree by the Minister of Education, who happened to also be the Vice-Chancellor of Oporto University. Yet, there were no specialists at Oporto – nor elsewhere in Portugal – who could examine the contents of the collections, so two French Assyriologists were brought to Oporto to evaluate part of the collection (Andrae 1927: 2).

In the meantime, Walter Andrae tried to lobby the Portuguese government and intellectual circles to have the collection sent to Germany. Perhaps an early case of repatriation claims, Andrae's efforts included an offer to exchange the Assyrian material for collections from German museums belonging to the Staatliche Museen Preussischer Kulturbesitz. Two changes of government in Lisbon and the military *coup d'état* of May 1926 that eventually led to the creation of the *Estado Novo* put a stop to the transaction until finally in that same year a new military cabinet, sympathetic to the pleas of Walter Andrea, agreed to the return of the Near Eastern collection to Berlin (Andrae 1927: 4; Bouquet and Freitas Branco 1988: 65). The objects finally made their way to the Pergamon Museum in Berlin in 1927, and were shown to the public from 1930, soon after the return of the seized collections (Klengel-Brandt 1995: 65). A counter-collection was assembled hastily, including ethnographic and archaeological material available from Berlin museums, and was sent to Oporto early in 1927. It contained sets of exactly 50 archaeological and ethnographic objects from the Berlin museum departments of China, Japan and Korea; East Asia; Africa; Oceania; North and Middle America; South America; and Pre-History.

In 2015, as this paper is being written, the site of Assur (Ashur) is a UNESCO World Heritage Site and belongs in the List of World Heritage in Danger (http://whc.unesco.org/en/list/1130). The Pergamon Museum in Berlin is undergoing major reconstructions until 2019 and the Assyrian collection is only partially on display. The counter-gift collection sent to Portugal is spread throughout different Portuguese museums and has only been partially identified and studied: Mary Bouquet and Jorge Freitas Branco have researched the Melanesian collection now kept at the Museu de Etnologia in Lisbon (Bouquet and Freitas Branco 1988) and I have been working on 86 Pre-Columbian pieces at the Museu de História Natural da Faculdade de Ciências at Oporto, as part of a larger project of identifying Caribbean collections in European museums within the research project 'NEXUS1492: New World Encounters in a Globalizing World'.

People following objects

Research on the Oporto collection is still ongoing – it includes the identification of the pieces, the reconstruction of their trajectories from the Americas to the Berlin museums, and a critical look into their significance today. Much more than describing yet another curious history in the world of museums, however, this case-study highlights some of the possibilities of research into museum collections and archaeological heritage in its broadest sense. The history of the German-Portuguese exchange of archaeological pieces sheds light on the mobility of collections and their circulation from the late nineteenth to the early twentieth century – a formative period of the anthropological and archaeological sciences. Evidently, this was also a time of political consolidation for nation states, when museums and their collections were instrumental in creating and disseminating ideas and representations about the nation and their people, frequently in opposition to what the nation was thought *not* to be (Bennett 1995). Collections were then assembled and often defined in terms of national property. From the German museum's perspective, the power and possibilities inscribed in the Ashur collection, not to mention its value, far outweighed the sub-sets that composed the gift to Portugal: perhaps duplicates, replicas, or simply uninteresting objects, these 'leftovers' from the Asian, African, Oceanic and American collections in Berlin were sent to Portugal, where they remain unstudied and stored away from public view until today.

While the history of museums and collections is not exactly a new discipline, studies into the dynamics and politics of object collecting and display gained momentum in the first half of the 1980s, marked particularly by the publication of the seminal *The Origins of Museums* in 1985 (Impey and MacGregor 1985) and the subsequent launch of the *Journal of the History of Collections*. Now, about three decades later, we witness a renewed engagement with private and public museum collections, involving curators, conservators, museum management and education staff, as well as academics and stakeholder groups such as indigenous peoples, diasporic communities, artists, and transnational audiences, among others (Van Broekhoven *et al.* 2010; Golding and Modest 2013).

Recently, major research projects have been launched to identify the whereabouts of specific ethnographic and archaeological non-European collections in European museums – for instance, the projects *Artefacts of Encounter* and *Pacific Presences*

> 'Studies into collection history address the present just as much as they address the past.'

based in the United Kingdom, and the *NEXUS1492* 'Caribbean Collections in European Museums'-project. By focusing on the history of collections, these projects show that in their trajectory to and within museums, objects materialize the relationships between imperial and scientific practice and the historical processes of identity construction and knowledge-making. Furthermore, research into collection history proves that the scientific or academic categories we use and operate with are not self-evident – *heritage* included. Rather, they are related to historical processes that have the power to shape the types of science, the types of archaeology and heritage studies that were and are possible, in the past as well as today. By looking at processes of de- and re-contextualization of collections, we have the chance to gain a closer insight into the development and limitations of our own discipline.

Heritage values

Likewise, studies into collection history address the present just as much as they address the past. Taking the past as a starting point, not an end in itself, opens up the possibility for (re)documenting local histories and helping make sense of contested pasts: material culture thus becomes a medium to connect peoples, histories and values. Collection history re-contextualizes objects so as to help determine what can and what should be done with them in the present. While indigenous peoples all over the world – and particularly in the Americas – have been reviving their traditional knowledge, museum storages function as repositories of this knowledge in material form. Hence, a fruitful approach to working with museum collections is allowing the histories of objects to come to light and be reinterpreted in contemporary contexts. Moreover, such an approach enables us to recognize indigenous and local agencies and political acumen even when these are limited by the strings of unequal power relations.

The history and the politics of museum collections, objects, and displays can help to counterbalance static, fixed notions of culture and identity, as well as problematize traditional narratives about the past and the nation. That is the work of heritage – other than a fixed past, an ever-reinvented present.

References

Andrae, W. 1927. 'Der Rückwerb der Assur-Funde aus Portugal', *Mitteilungen der Deutschen Orient-Gesellschaft* 65: 1-6.

Bennett, T. 1995. *The Birth of the Museum: History, Theory, Politics*. London and New York: Routledge.

Bouquet, M. and J. Freitas Branco. 1988. *Artefactos Melanésios. Reflexões pós-modernistas. Melanesian Artefacts. Postmodernist reflections*. Lisbon: Museu de Etnologia.

Golding, V. and W. Modest (eds). 2013. *Museums and Communities. Curators, Collections and Collaboration*. London: Bloomsbury.

Gonçalves Guimarães, J.A. 2005. 'Espólio arqueológico da América pré-colombiana em Portugal', *O Arqueólogo Português* IV (23): 451-466.

Impey, O. and A. MacGregor (eds). 1985. *The Origins of Museums. The Cabinets of Curiosities in Sixteenth- and Seventeenth-Century Europe*. Oxford: Clarendon Press.

Klengel-Brandt, E. 1995. 'The History of the Excavations at Ashur and of the Vorderasiatisches Museum', in P.O. Harper, E. Klengel-Brandt, J. Aruz and K. Benzel (eds), *Discoveries at Ashur on the Tigris. Assyrian origins*. New York: The Metropolitan Museum, 17-20.

Van Broekhoven, L., C. Buijs and P. Hovens (eds). 2010. *Sharing knowledge and cultural heritage*. Leiden: Sidestone Press.

***

Research presented in this paper is part of the ERC-Synergy project *NEXUS1492: New World Encounters in a Globalizing World,* directed by Prof. dr. Corinne L. Hofman at Leiden University and funded by the European Union's Seventh Framework Programme.

The problem of landscape protection

Amy Strecker

Faculty of Archaeology, Leiden University /
ERC-synergy project NEXUS1492, The Netherlands

One of the first conversations Willem Willems and I had upon starting my position at Leiden University in 2014 concerned Tara and the M3 motorway in Ireland. The case concerned the approval by the Irish government, in 2003, of a motorway through the Tara-Skryne valley, one of Ireland's foremost archaeological landscapes. In latter years Willem had become notoriously critical of the *in-situ* approach to archaeological heritage espoused in the Malta Convention (Council of Europe 1992) and of the designation of landscapes as discrete cultural heritage sites more generally. While I agree with Willem's conviction that cultural landscapes and their designation in law are inherently problematic, I argue that in certain special cases, the protection of cultural landscapes is desirable and indeed required by law, as the case of Tara illustrates. This does not mean the freezing of certain areas – a dubious notion – but it does mean the sensitive consideration of development appropriate to areas that are important for people also beyond their archaeological value. The term 'people' is central here, as the problem arises when we ask who decides what is appropriate. In most cases, this decision is one of public policy, whether a preservation order or planning permission; it results in the official landscape. The recent linking of landscape with human rights attempts to counter this, by emphasizing the right of communities to participate in landscape and cultural heritage policies. This short essay charts this development and assesses it in terms of implications for legal practice. In doing so, I hope to continue the dialogue with Willem and to pick up on allusions in his later writings to the human rights-based approaches to cultural heritage.

The 'democratisation' of landscape

In 1992, when the World Heritage categories were broadened to include 'cultural landscapes' within the scope of the World Heritage Convention (WHC), the proposed rationale was to give recognition to the intangible and associative values attached to landscapes, to sustainable agricultural practices and to 'people and communities' (Rössler 2006). However, more than twenty years on, it is clear that attaching universal importance to landscapes can have negative consequences for the communities who live in those areas and imply restrictions on land use and socio-cultural development. The desired humanisation of landscape was difficult with such a state-centred instrument as the WHC. Lowenthal's remark on the incompatibility of simultaneously commending national patrimony, regional and ethnic legacies and a global heritage sheltered in common (Lowenthal 1997: 227) rings true in the case of landscapes, which are in a constant flux and more problematic to manage than discrete monuments and sites. The European

Landscape Convention (ELC) diverged considerably from previous instruments by espousing a more democratic approach to landscape. Adopted in 2000 under the auspices of the Council of Europe, it provides for the active participation of the public in the formulation of landscape plans and polices (Articles 5 and 6) and not only focuses on outstanding landscapes, but also on the everyday and degraded landscapes where most people live and work. Unlike the WHC, there is no list of landscapes of outstanding importance, and in contrast to the WHC (and indeed the Malta Convention), the European Landscape Convention (ELC) not only focuses on conservation but also on the rehabilitation and planning of landscapes, and thus the creation of new spaces. The underlying rationale is that a purely conservationist policy helps deflect attention from the forces leading to change elsewhere, and thus neglects those areas not afforded protection. The definition of landscape provided in the text is all encompassing: 'landscape is an area, as perceived by people, the result of action/and or interaction with natural and cultural factors.' Landscape can be anything and everything then, which is why the ELC has been so well received by so many disciplines.

Legal application

The approach of the European Landscape Convention is arguably one of sustainable development and good landscape planning. However, as pointed out by Antrop, landscapes change continuously in a more or less chaotic way as a reflection of society's social and economic needs at a given moment, and thus the concept of sustainable landscapes could be viewed as a utopian goal (Antrop 2006). For this reason the implementation of the European Landscape Convention has been for the most part an awareness-raising and educational project, and a challenge for political sensitisation at the local and regional level. The convention is not designed as an instrument to access justice or challenge the abuse of power in planning decisions. While the ELC has been of enormous importance for shifting the paradigm of landscape discourse and linking it with democracy, legally speaking, it is ambiguous for practical application. If we take the case of Tara discussed here at the beginning, the fact that Ireland had signed and ratified the ELC before the case unfolded made no difference to the outcome of the proceedings, as no implementing legislation had been drafted. However, even if domestic legislation had been drafted to comply with the ELC's provisions, including the 'recognition of landscapes in law', this may not necessarily have led to the safeguarding of the Tara landscape and the re-routing of the motorway. Ireland was already found to be in breach of the Environmental Impact Assessment directive for failure to properly assess sites along the motorway route, and despite the overwhelming expert advice strongly urging the government to reconsider (including from the statutory consultation body under the National Monuments Act), the government chose to proceed with the contentious route nonetheless. In terms of the participation of the public, submissions were made at the oral hearing stage from a broad spectrum of local and national groups and individuals in favour of re-routing the motorway. But participation does not always equal meaningful involvement and without its two complementary pillars – access to information and access to justice – it is significantly weakened as a legal mechanism. What does this mean for landscapes such as Tara and major infrastructural projects, then?

In the case of Tara, the lack of proper designation at national level was crucial to the case. During the judicial challenge at the High Court, the judge stated that the buffer zone placed around the Hill of Tara was intended as planning guideline and not a legal designation. The case was dismissed on the grounds that the applicant, among other things, did not have 'sufficient interest' or *locus standi* in the case at hand, i.e. he was not personally affected by the decision as he was not a resident or

> 'In landscape protection, the question of 'whose landscape' we are talking about has not been resolved.'

land owner in the vicinity of the motorway. The judge stated that there are certain cases where a cogent theoretical argument could be made regardless of personal interest, but that this was not the case here, as he could not see how an 'abstract landscape theory' was one such exception.

Discussion

Despite the procedural and substantive weaknesses in the case, the major limitation was the lack of proper designation of the landscape of Tara beyond the archaeological monuments on the hill itself. It is important to note at this point that although Tara was predominantly classified as an archaeological area, it is in fact a cultural landscape with importance far beyond its archaeological components. As stated by the Director of the National Museum at the time:

> *'Tara is a unique cultural landscape which has significance for our national heritage that extends beyond the sum of its individual components [...] It is one of a small number of complexes that are of more than usual cultural importance from the standpoint not only of archaeology, but also of history, mythology, folklore, language, placenames study, and even of national identity'* (Wallace 2005).

It is the cultural, historical and associative values attached to Tara which made it unique and worthy of an elevated level of care in the consideration of planning applications. It is worth recalling here the text of the Framework Convention on the Value of Cultural Heritage for Society (Council of Europe 2005), which provides that states 'recognise that rights relating to cultural heritage are inherent to the right to participate in cultural life, as defined in the Universal Declaration of Human Rights (Article 1a). A heritage community, as defined by the Convention, 'consists of people who value specific aspects of cultural heritage which they wish, within the framework of public action, to sustain and transmit to future generations.' (Article 2b). Importantly, it provides that states recognise the public interest associated with elements of the cultural heritage in accordance with their importance to society (Article 5a). The notion of public interest proceedings is well established in some jurisdictions and widens the 'sufficient interest' test beyond the consideration of individual interests, such as property, to also consider collective issues, such as the environment and cultural heritage.

However, despite these developments at the level of regional international law, a number of problems remain for the protection of landscapes beyond discrete monuments and sites. First, the governance of landscape is still within the realm of public administration. Second, it is not an enforceable legal right (Strecker 2012); and third, ultimately the question of 'whose landscape' we are talking about has not been resolved. For these reasons, carefully selected legal designation for unique landscapes such as Tara is required.

References

Antrop, M. 2006. 'Sustainable Landscapes: Contradiction, Fiction or Utopia', *Landscape and Urban Planning* 75, 187-197.

Council of Europe. 1992. *European Convention on the Protection of the Archaeological Heritage (Revised)* Valletta, 16 January 1992. CETS no. 143.

Council of Europe. 2000. *European Landscape Convention*, Florence, 20 October 2000. CETS no. 176.

Council of Europe. 2005. *Framework Convention on the Value of Cultural Heritage for Society*, Faro, 27 October 2005. CETS no. 199.

Lowenthal, D. 1997. *The Heritage Crusade and the Spoils of History*. London: Viking.

Rössler M. 2006. 'World Heritage Cultural Landscapes, A UNESCO flagship Programme 1992-2006', *Landscape Research* 31, 333-335.

Strecker, A. 2012. 'The Human Dimension to Landscape Protection in International Law', in S. Borelli and F. Lenzerini (eds), *Cultural Heritage, Cultural Rights, Cultural Diversity: New Developments in International Law*. Leiden: M. Nijhoff, 327-347.

UNESCO. 1972. *Convention Concerning the Protection of the World Cultural and Natural Heritage*, Paris, 16 November 1972. 1037 UNTS 151.

Wallace, P. 2005. *Report to the Minister of the Environment, Heritage and Local Government on the Archaeological Excavations along the M3 Navan-Dunshaughlin Route*, March 2005.

Scientific illiteracy
What is the reality, what are the pitfalls?

Sander van der Leeuw

ASU-SFI Center for Biosocial Complex Systems,
Arizona State University, United States of America

Scientific illiteracy is an important phenomenon in western countries, and nowhere as widely spread as in the USA, where almost a third of the population – about 100 million people – close their eyes and ears as soon as science, or things scientific, are broached. Contrary to what many scientists believe, from an anthropological perspective this is not due to a lack of understanding or scientific education. Rather, it is a different, unscientific, way by which people explain for themselves their personal experiences, making them understandable and acceptable.

Perception and cognition together constitute the only interface between human beings and the outside world. All our experiences pass through a cognitive filter that limits the number of dimensions of any phenomena that we can simultaneously know to around 7 ± 2; the capacity of our Short-Term Working Memory (Read and Van der Leeuw 2015). Moreover, our ideas are under-determined by our observations (Atlan 1992). A very large number of theories could in principle be conceived in order to explain even relatively simple systems, and the lack of a sufficient number of observations prevents us from conclusively evaluating them all. As a result, an overwhelming majority of our ideas are in effect over-determined by prior experiences. Such worldviews are acquired very early in life, in the context of the family, the school and the social networks of children. That implies that science is only one way among others to explain the world around us.

STEM losing voice

Our society is presently confronted with a conjunction of social, environmental, economic, financial and other crises. We could view the situation as one in which our society is (temporarily?) incapable of processing simultaneously all the information necessary to successfully deal with the different kinds of dynamics with which it is confronted. Hence, we deal with only one or two aspects of the crisis at a time, and that prevents us from adopting a shared culture and vision that would enable us to manage the crisis in all its many guises.

Maintaining a sufficiently dense flow of information to enable a society to organize itself and to respond in a coherent manner to the challenges that it encounters, requires a wide and deep participation of the population in its shared culture. Without that participation, society is riddled with misunderstandings, or even open conflicts, and after a certain time it loses its coherence.

Much of the West's social and cultural interaction rests upon the language of the sciences, technology, engineering and mathematics (STEM) and other scientific disciplines. As a universalist language it has enabled the spread of a world-view that generated many material benefits. Our capacity to overcome the current crisis may therefore be closely related to the proportion of our population that is able to communicate in STEM terms.

But the STEM disciplines, according to many, no longer respond very effectively to our social expectations. Science has been 'oversold', so that our society's expectations of the sciences are no longer very realistic, while the unintended

> 'Science is only one way among others to explain the world around us.'

consequences of our actions have rapidly spread to all sectors of life, leading some to adopt a dystopic vision of the future. Our society seems therefore to be losing its faith in STEM, as evidenced by reductions in research funding and scientific illiteracy.

From an anthropological perspective, scientific activity is structured questioning, observation, and organization of knowledge and insights. That process is implemented and developed by a social community of researchers belonging to different disciplines. The society of which they are part determines the context in which that process unfolds, impacting on the questions posed, the means chosen for observation and the values against which the results are interpreted. 'Facts' that have been obtained 'objectively' answer questions that have been negotiated inter-subjectively and auto-referentially. Science should therefore not decide between absolute or abstract 'true' or 'false', but determine the degree of validity of observations with respect to the questions asked and their context. Though the knowledge that we produce is generally trustworthy and helps us construct our society, it is profoundly anchored and integrated in the social dynamics of the society involved.

The role of science has changed

Since about two centuries ago, the STEM disciplines have progressively been institutionalized as the main source of innovations for industry; more recently, science has been called upon to provide a 'rational' basis for political decisions. This institutionalization has changed the sciences themselves. Epistemological relations have become ontological ones, and our vision of the world has been fragmented into disciplines in the process. The relationship between the sciences and society has also been transformed: the STEM disciplines are now part of the political domain and have therefore become contestable by all.

The difference between science and policy is important to understand the impact of this transformation. The political domain is openly subjective. It is the arena in which the 'irrational' foundations of society are confronted, in order to negotiate non-rational but emotionally satisfactory solutions; in that arena, one looks toward the future and tries to predict. In the process, one confronts the hidden dimensions of complex issues. But in the scientific domain one identifies many 'objective' ideas: one inquires into the 'irrational' bases that originate in the social domain in order to identify 'rational' responses. Science focuses on clarifying the present by reducing the number of dimensions taken into account. Moreover, science often changes topics and disciplinary perspectives.

The public does not experience STEM in a purely intellectual, 'detached' manner. Scientific activities and opinions are always perceived and judged as expressions of substantive social relations, interactions and interests. The main factor governing the role and the perception of the sciences is the public's confidence in the scientific institutions and the scientists, and that confidence is subject to the vagaries of opinions circulating in social networks. Understanding, whether scientific or other, is, I repeat, a social construction that is part of the identity of individuals and communities.

In order to discern some other dimensions of this theme – the social construction of 'the truth' by both scientific and other actors, I will use as an example Brian Wynne's (1989) study on the way the impact of the Chernobyl disaster was perceived among sheep farmers in the North of England, near the (highly controversial) nuclear installation of Sellafield. After the Chernobyl incident, the British scientists that were in charge of measuring the radioactivity in the area made two major mistakes: 1. they had too much confidence in their science and their personal expertise, and 2. their scientific communication did not take into account the fundamental uncertainty and the surprises that the population was used to dealing with in daily life. The sheep farmers' trust in the sciences was thus greatly diminished, leading to a breakdown in the legitimacy of the scientists in the eyes of the sheep farmers. As a result, the following hypothetical dialogue between a sheep farmer and a scientist is typical, in which both protagonists legitimate their ideas as a function of their social identities, rather than with respect to the applicability of the ideas to the local realities of the terrain and the environment:

Scientist: 'I can assure you that my approach is the right one – it is justified by the fact that I bring an objective perspective to bear on these questions because I am a stranger to these parts, and have been educated in a university …'

Farmer: 'No, you are wrong, - my approach is the correct one because I have been born here, I know the soils and what grows on them in minute detail, and therefore also know how to manipulate them successfully …'

Once the confidence of the sheep farmers in the scientists had been lost, they concluded that they were dangerous to the cohesion of their local society and herdsmen's way of life. They saw the scientists sent by the government as liars trying to hide the dangers of the Sellafield nuclear establishment, rather than to help them overcome the dangers of the Chernobyl radioactive cloud.

Multiple perspectives instead of a single truth

A first lesson to draw from this episode concerns the relationship between phenomena and ideas. Any phenomenon (object, relationship, process) manifests itself in an infinite number of dimensions, and is therefore essentially poly-interpretable.

Because of the limitations of our cognitive system, our ideas are limited to very few dimensions, and are much less poly-interpretable. This impacted the ways in which scientists and local farmers looked at the future. Because they admitted the poly-interpretability of all aspects of their daily life, the world-view of the sheep farmers was one of doubt, unpredictability and risks, gathered over a lifetime of needing to manage the unintended consequences of their actions in the face of many types of unpredictability. But the scientific perspective, which reduces the dimensionality of phenomena in order to gain clarity, focused on certainty or its absence, intellectually limiting the predictive value of the science.

Hence, scientists accept uncertainty as a limitation to what they can say and do, but do not depend for their livelihood and daily activities on dealing with it, and have not found ways to discuss it that are helpful to practitioners. This in turn explains the fact that in the scientific domain one contrasts the 'unanticipated consequences' of our actions (explained below) with the 'expected outcomes' of scientific reasoning, while in the public domain, all consequences of actions are part-expected and part-unexpected.

Ambiguity has a special role in this discussion. Because science aims to remove contradictions and ambiguities by reducing the number of known dimensions of the real world to a minimum, it creates a reduced and unreal vision of the world. Sheep farmers cannot dodge the unpredictability of the world they must manage. They accept the complexity of the world in which they live, the contradictions they cannot solve, and their incapacity to control events. Ambivalence and ambiguity play a major role in their worldview.

Each side expects the other to understand it, because neither side has thought about these issues. The absence of understanding then creates mistrust. The researchers search for knowledge, while the public searches for understanding and experience. The association of researchers with governmental institutions and corporations aggravates public distrust of the scientists. The sheep farmers felt trapped in a web that marries science with bureaucracy, negating the foundations of their own identity and society.

Reconsidering scientific practice

Two questions now arise. Is the degradation of trust in science near a point where the crucial role of science in advancing human well-being may be compromised? And if that is the case, what could be the cause and what could we do to counter this trend?

The scientific community has – wrongly – tried to become the best example of the modern skeptical institution. In its wake, all kinds of other institutions have adopted the same attitude and a rationalist logic, hiding the political and emotional aspects of their decisions and actions. This has led to alienation and extra-institutional forms of politics - the 'crisis of late modernity'. An institutional reform of the organization, the control, and the social relations in science is therefore necessary, including a renegotiation of our 'scientific' and 'social' roles as scientists, in order to counter the emergence of inappropriate power structures.

It will be indispensable to work towards a reflexive recognition of the conditionality of science, in the hope that it will lead to a critical examination of our fundamental – pre-analytical – assumptions that constitute the context of our scientific visions and knowledge. In that process, we need to better connect the dynamics of the scientific communities with those of the non-scientific ones, so that we are better able to take the social context of scientific constructs into account. Reasoning and understanding are indeed contextual and cannot be controlled in science – or elsewhere for that matter.

References

Atlan, H. 1992. 'Self-organizing networks: weak, strong and intentional. The role of their underdetermination', *La Nuova Critica* 19-20: 51-70.

Read, D.W. and S.E. van der Leeuw. 2015. 'The Extension of Social Relations in Time and Space during the Palaeolithic', in F. Coward, R. Hosfield, M. Pope and F. Wenban-Smith (eds), *Settlement, Society and Cognition in Human Evolution*. Cambridge: Cambridge University Press, 31-53.

Wynne, B. 1989. 'Sheepfarming after Chernobyl: a case study in communicating scientific information', *Environment* 31(2): 10-15, 33-39.

Home sweet home
Managing archaeological resources in the Netherlands

Veni, vidi, vici

Calling for a professional register for Dutch archaeology

Leonard de Wit

Cultural Heritage Agency, The Netherlands

Willem Willems must have been overjoyed when he returned from Valletta in 1992. I would not be surprised if the signing of the Convention giving better protection to Europe's archaeological heritage left him feeling rather cocky. '*Veni, vidi, vici*', he would have thought to himself, before returning to earth rather quickly. Euphoria never lasts long and all the hard work still lay ahead. In fact, it was not until 2007 that the Netherlands ratified and implemented the Convention.

The Netherlands has seen major changes to archaeological heritage management as a result of the Valletta Convention: it is now embedded in spatial planning, control is lodged with local authorities and market forces have been introduced. We are now at the start of a new chapter, with a new Heritage Act coming into force in 2016. The most fundamental change to the legal system concerns quality assurance in archaeology. An evaluation of the system has identified its flaws and the new Act will make provision for mandatory certification of contractors, which replaces admission to the excavation market via the Minister. This is a fairly major change, one which contains an apparent contradiction: government control through self-regulation. For the first time in over three decades a profound change to Dutch archaeological heritage management will occur without the direct involvement of Willem Willems.

Market and government

In about 2000 the Dutch government decided that the implementation of the Valletta Convention should be accompanied by the introduction of market forces. We can say in retrospect that the implications of this decision were not fully appreciated at the time. One aspect – assuring the quality of research – was given a prominent place on the agenda. As long as archaeological research was the sole preserve of government agencies and research institutions, there was no pressing need (an incorrect assumption, as it happens) for fundamental reflection on a system of quality assurance. Until that time the various institutions within the sector had enjoyed complete freedom to manage the archaeological process as they saw fit. Even the most basic principles, such as the obligation to document, deposit and report, were not laid down. It was the impending arrival of market forces that gave this discussion an enormous boost.

Willem Willems had mixed feelings about the political decision to introduce competition. He had greater confidence in the French system, in which an archaeology tax made funds available for research that was managed by government agencies. But if market forces were going to be introduced, he wanted the necessary safeguards in place. There needed to be a discussion about quality within the archaeological process. He was very well aware that archaeological companies would be operating in an environment where some commissioning bodies were not at all interested in high-quality research. The advent of competition therefore needed to be accompanied by a good deal of government direction. Standards and principles for sound research had to be adopted.

The battle for quality

This understanding coincided with a new direction in Willem Willems' career. As research director of the National Service for Archaeological Heritage (ROB) he had been given too little scope to do what he felt was important. It must have been a difficult decision for him to leave the National Service, into which he had put his

> 'If market forces were going to be introduced, Willem wanted the necessary safeguards in place.'

heart and soul since 1977. He accepted the task of setting up a quality assurance system for Dutch archaeology within the new rules. Anyone meeting him at that time at the Ministry of Education, Culture and Science in Zoetermeer (near The Hague) will agree with me that he was a 'displaced person'. That bureaucratic environment was clearly not his natural habitat – you could say he was *ex situ*.

And yet it was extremely important that it was precisely this man – with his commitment, expertise and pioneering spirit – who should tackle that particular mandate, at that time and in that place. We continue to enjoy the benefits of his work to this day. It was not a bureaucratic exercise, but a process centred on archaeologists. Like no other in his field, Willem Willems was able to prevent opposing views (of which there were plenty) from escalating and to work towards a result that was acceptable to everyone. And the results were indeed promising: the Dutch Archaeology Quality Standard (KNA) was drawn up, and standards and processes were laid down and made mandatory for contracting parties. The State Inspectorate for Archaeology was also set up to monitor compliance with these standards. The name of the first director will come as no surprise to anybody: Willem Willems.

But the system was not yet complete. It is all very well to establish processes and standards, but if the actors who work with them do not have the right qualifications, things can still go wrong. Despite years of hard work and negotiation, attempts to create a professional register for Dutch archaeology failed. Although Willems was chair of an evaluation committee, there was no great rush of registrations. 'It was an error of judgement on our part,' Willems admitted. 'We should have had registration fully organised before all the positions of interest were taken up'.

The ensuing discussion about which criteria should be used can be traced back to individual people and business interests.

Déjà vu

Now it is a question of repeating ourselves. The legislator will set out guidelines and encourage the archaeological sector to make a success of the certification system. There seems to be support among the key players. But at the same time there continues to be – as always – a lot of disagreement among interest groups about principles and the scope of the certification requirement. In my view, it won't be long before we once again come up against a need for professional registration. When we talk about quality, this first and foremost involves good people doing the work. Do the actors who carry out the research have the right qualifications? There is no point having a certification system that ignores this issue. For this to succeed, the archaeological sector must demonstrate greater unity than it has done until now.

Hence my appeal to the archaeological community: have another go at professional registration but don't persist endlessly. Remember that 'the better is the enemy of the good' and hold back in terms of representing sectional interests. If this succeeds, we will spare a fleeting thought for Willem Willems – veni, vidi, vici – before getting back to business as usual. When it comes to sound archaeological research, complacency is a poor counsellor.

Paving the way

The Malta Convention as a blessing for the place of cultural heritage in the new environmental planning act

Monique Krauwer

Department of Arts and Heritage, Ministry of
Education, Culture and Science, The Netherlands

In recent years Willem Willems sometimes appeared rather sceptical about the success of the Council of Europe's Malta Convention in the Netherlands. Much can be said about the Malta Convention and its impact on archaeological heritage management and archaeological research, but just as important is the fact that the Convention sparked a process that has led to archaeological heritage being successfully integrated into today's environmental policy. Malta's significance therefore extends far beyond archaeological heritage alone.

In his article 'Malta and its consequences: a mixed blessing', Willem referred to this in a roundabout way as one of Malta's positive outcomes (Willems 2014). He stated that archaeological research is better integrated into spatial planning, and he pointed to the major advances in the internal integration of cultural historic disciplines such as archaeology, historical geography and architectural history. But he was too modest. With the policy document Modernising Heritage Management (Ministry of Education, Culture and Science 2009) and the new Environmental Planning Act (*Omgevingswet*), it is clear that Malta paved the way for cultural heritage management to be embedded in legislation as a matter of course.

Looking back on my own career, making the transition from municipal and provincial archaeologist in the 1980s and 1990s to policy advisor on cultural heritage at the Ministry of Education, Culture and Science (OCW), I can see with increasing clarity just how crucial Malta has been for the development of cultural heritage policy in a broad sense, and how it has slowly and almost imperceptibly found its way into regulations. Its firm position in the new Environmental Planning Act marks the culmination of the work that Willem began when he accompanied Hedy D'Ancona, the then Minister of Culture, to the signing of the Malta Convention in 1992.

From Malta to modernising heritage management

Although the Convention was signed by the Netherlands in 1992, it was 2007 before the Archaeological Heritage Management Act came into force. However, the spirit of Malta could be felt from 1992 onwards. The knowledge that 'Malta was on its way', and that the law would require spatial developments to take account of archaeological values, slowly filtered through to the different levels of government. The provinces were vital to this process. In the 1990s it was the provinces that incorporated archaeology into their regional plans, demanding in turn that local authorities demonstrate in their zoning plans how they were managing the known and as yet unknown archaeological values. The aim was to preserve as much as possible in the soil.

The provinces and the state made agreements: the provinces appointed provincial archaeologists and the state and provinces took care of archaeological monument maps. A growing number of local authorities developed their own

> 'Signing the Malta Convention paved the way for cultural heritage to be embedded in Dutch legislation as a matter of course.'

archaeology policies and saw the benefits of considering archaeology at the start of spatial processes. It meant no more unpleasant surprises midway through the construction process, and considerable goodwill among local residents, who saw their heritage being treated with due care.

Whereas Malta was still primarily a matter for the Ministry of Education, Culture and Science, the proposed safeguards within spatial planning undoubtedly helped to inspire the Belvedere policy paper, issued in 1999 by four ministries of the time: Housing, Spatial Planning and the Environment; Agriculture, Nature and Food Quality; Transport, Public Works and Water Management; and Education, Culture and Science. The paper's key points were an integrated approach to archaeology, built heritage and landscape, and greater priority given to cultural heritage in the shaping and planning of the Netherlands. This commitment on the part of other ministries was important for awareness at national level of the value of cultural heritage. The programme on Protecting and Developing the Archaeological-Historical Landscape (2000-2008) of the Netherlands Organisation for Scientific Research (NWO), which was also supported by other ministries, encouraged research that would promote the integration of cultural historical values into spatial planning.

By the time that Malta was finally implemented, in 2007, all levels of government were so accustomed to working in the spirit of Malta that the transition to the new archaeological policy went fairly smoothly. Changes to legislation (the Monuments and Historic Buildings Act 1988 and several other acts) simply confirmed existing practice. The Spatial Planning Decree was one of the general administrative orders (*Algemene maatregelen van bestuur*) under the national Planning Act that was amended. From then on, local authorities had to take archaeological aspects into account in their zoning plans. This proved an important step in the coming of age of archaeological interests.

Built heritage: the Granada Convention

Surprisingly, the signing of the Council of Europe's Granada Convention (1985) did not affect such changes to legislation. In 1994 the Netherlands ratified the Convention, which stipulates that the protection of architectural heritage is an essential spatial planning objective. Architectural heritage must be taken into account at all stages of the process, from the drawing up of development plans to procedures for authorising work (Article 10, Granada Convention).

The state did designate protected urban or village areas from the 1960s onwards and in such instances local authorities were tasked with producing a protective zoning plan. But until the 2009 policy paper on Modernising Heritage Management, implemented in 2012, there was no general directive to municipalities to take account of architectural heritage in their spatial policies.

As well as simplifying regulations, one of the main aims of Modernising Heritage Management was to secure culture historical interests in spatial planning. The policy on archaeology served as a model here. It was therefore a relatively easy step to extend the provision in the Spatial Planning Decree that local authorities should consider archaeological heritage to include cultural heritage in a broader sense – archaeology, built heritage and cultural landscape. In fact, it was not until this step was taken in 2012 that the Granada Convention was truly implemented.

A new legal framework for cultural heritage

The Netherlands has about forty statutes, a hundred and twenty general administrative orders (*Algemene Maatregelen van Bestuur*, AMVBs), and several hundred ministerial regulations relating to the environment. There are rules governing spatial planning, soil protection and water management, the natural environment and historical monuments, ecosystems, noise, buildings and infrastructure. Each of these regulations focuses on an individual issue and has its own rationale and terminology. As a result, they frequently contradict one another, which frustrates new developments. This is one of the main reasons why the Dutch government has drafted a new Environmental Planning Act (due for 2018) – a single statute unifying and simplifying all the environmental rules and regulations (Ministry of Infrastructure and Environment 2014).

This large-scale legislative operation by the Ministry of Infrastructure and Environment began in 2011. The purpose of the new Act is twofold: to achieve and maintain both a safe and healthy physical environment and a high-quality living environment. The idea is to simplify and improve existing regulations. This will mean lower research costs, shorter procedures, a flexible and transparent system, more decision room for provincial and local authorities, fewer rules, an integrated approach, and room for sustainable development. Zoning plans and permits will be replaced by integrated environmental plans and permits. The new act will replace several existing ones and large sections of other ones, such as the provisions in the 1988 Monuments Act relating to the environment. What is left of the Monuments and Historic Buildings Act (the designation of listed monuments and provisions on archaeology and archaeological depots) will be combined with some smaller acts on movable cultural heritage and a new section on museum funding, to create a new Heritage Act (due for 2016).

While it is understandable that cultural heritage makes up only a small part of the vast scope of the new Environmental Planning Act, the new act is nevertheless essential for the protection and preservation of cultural heritage. That is why the Ministry of Education, Culture and Science has devoted considerable energy to safeguarding cultural heritage within the act. The results so far are promising. Protection levels will be about the same or even stronger, and the requirement that local authorities should indicate how they will manage cultural heritage is now included in the act itself, not only in the general administrative orders. International conventions such as Malta and Granada have been most helpful. Within a few years cultural heritage protection will be firmly enshrined within the new Heritage Act and the Environmental Planning Act.

While the impact of the Malta Convention on fundamental archaeological research may be open to discussion, it is an undeniable fact that Malta was a blessing for the preservation of cultural heritage in a broader sense. In my work coordinating this fundamental issue on behalf of the Ministry of Education, Culture and Science, I am grateful to Willem for guiding us to Malta.

References

Ministry of Education, Culture and Science. 2009. *Beleidsbrief Modernisering Monumentenzorg*. The Hague: Ministerie van Onderwijs, Cultuur en Wetenschap.

Ministry of Infrastructure and Environment. 2014. *The Environmental Planning Act in brief: scope for development, safeguard for quality*. The Hague: Ministerie van Infrastructuur en Milieu.

Willems, W.J.H. 2014. 'Malta and its consequences: a mixed blessing', in V.M. van der Haas and P.A.C. Schut (eds), *The Valletta Convention: Twenty Years After. Benefits, Problems, Challenges*. EAC Occasional Paper No. 9. Brussels: Europae Archaeologiae Consilium, 151-156.

Visualizing the unknown

On the making and use of predictive maps in archaeological heritage management

Jos Deeben and Bjørn Smit

Cultural Heritage Agency, The Netherlands

Willem Willems' quest to understand the social organisation of pre- and protohistoric societies on the basis of burial analysis (Willems 1978) and his analysis of the Roman (colonial) occupation of the Netherlands using the geographical model of the Rank-Size Rule (Willems 1983) made him part of a select group of researchers in the Netherlands who introduced and applied the principles of processual archaeology in the late 1970s and early 1980s. This signified a major change for at least three facets of archaeological research: the emphasis on human behaviour, research into the formation of the archaeological record and the 'scientification' of archaeology, with its attempts to define concepts and theories. Archaeology as a social science, which not only described the past, but also explained it and could even make predictions based on the 'laws' and regular patterns identified. The empirical cycle became the accepted way of generating and verifying knowledge.

Processual archaeology and the development of modern archaeological heritage management

Processual archaeology became an important seedbed for modern archaeological heritage management in the Netherlands, which began to develop in the 1980s. Until then, heritage management had been limited to the selection of monuments and historic buildings for protection based on the expert knowledge of provincial archaeologists, with a clear preference for visible monuments such as dwelling mounds (terps) and barrows. Modern heritage management developed at the State Service for Archaeological Investigations (ROB) under the directorship of Willem Willems (1989-1999) (Deeben *et al.* 2006: 54-60). He regarded archaeological heritage management (AHM) as a cyclical process based on: 1. documentation and registration of archaeological values; followed by 2. inventorisation; 3. value assessment; 4. selection for protection or excavation or deselection; 5. interpretation/synthesis; and 6. interaction. The latter provided the necessary feedback in the cycle (Willems 1997).

In the inventorisation phase, it is not only known archaeological values that are important. In a country such as the Netherlands, where a large proportion of archaeological values are covered by sediments or water, unknown archaeological values are important as well. Given the notion in processual archaeology that human behaviour displays regular patterns, it was assumed feasible to predict the location of archaeological sites on the basis of those patterns. Since around 1990 several hundred predictive maps have been produced in the Netherlands using this principle.

A national comprehensive predictive archaeological map

A predictive model attempts to pinpoint where unknown archaeological remains might be located; the outcome can be shown in the form of a predictive archaeological map (in our case an *Indicatieve Kaart Archeologische Waarden*, IKAW). Such models are used both in archaeology concerned with occupation history ('academic archaeology') and archaeology that focuses on the preservation of archaeological remains. Only the goals the models serve differ. In AHM, it is

> 'Modern heritage management developed at the State Service for Archaeological Investigations (ROB) under the directorship of Willem Willems.'

important to know where remains are likely to lie for the purpose of inventorisation, so the model has a descriptive function. In archaeology concerned with recounting our history, the key concern is why archaeological remains are located where they are located, and in the processual sense the model has an explanatory or, as is known nowadays, interpretive function. These different goals have led to extensive debates in the Netherlands between two groups (Van Leusen and Kamermans 2005; Verhagen *et al.* 2010). The debate on the AHM models focused among other things on the emphasis on variables from the natural environment and the absence of cultural variables in the models; the bias in the spatial distribution and quality of archaeological information that can impact on the outcome of the model when inductive methods are applied; the statistical methods used; and the lack of verification of the model. The critics of our approach however have never offered an alternative in the form of an alternative predictive model that integrates the two goals, although new theoretical approaches have recently been formulated (Verhagen and Whitley 2012).

Predicting the location of archaeological remains is the key focus of AHM predictive models. This was also the goal of the three generations of the Indicative Map of Archaeological Values, which indicates where archaeological remains are likely to be situated, irrespective of their nature or age (see *inter alia* Deeben *et al.* 2002). The map was intended as a source of inspiration to be used during desk-based surveys and in recommendations for further investigation. The results of these further investigations, generally a field survey, would serve as input for more detailed predictive models that would for example provide information on the nature and age of the remains. The purpose essentially remained descriptive, focusing on an initial inventory.

Despite four and a half pages of notes on the limitations of using the IKAW (Deeben et al. 2002: 47-51), the map took on a life of its own in AHM practice. Further investigations focused largely on areas of high and/or moderate indicative value. Zones with low indicative value were generally excluded from any further investigation for motives largely unconnected with archaeology, such as social and economic interests. Although the map had been produced at a scale of 1:50,000, it was used at a scale of 1:10,000, serving for example as a basis for local authority policy maps.

Predictive maps now and in the future

As a result of the decentralisation of heritage management in the Netherlands, most local authorities now have a predictive archaeological map of their area. In the absence of a uniform picture and standards for predictive archaeological maps, and because they were all produced on the basis of individual initiatives, many maps exist, with a large variety of symbols, methodology, data and scale. It is therefore possible that, for example, similar zones on either side of a municipal boundary may have different predictive values. This alone gives sufficient reason to produce a uniform national predictive map. However, this is not regarded as desirable by several of the parties involved because, given its level of detail, a national map could never do justice to the local variation in subsurface archaeology. The local authority level allows a more detailed map to be produced for a smaller region. In theory, these maps should be able to more adequately reflect the variation in occupation. This does not however mean that no models or maps are being developed at national level. The Cultural Heritage Agency is in fact currently working on a national map depicting the spatial aspects of housing, burial, infrastructure and ritual for various modes of existence or levels of social organisation (hunter, fisher and gatherers; early farming societies; late farming societies; state societies) to allow predictions to be made. The expert knowledge of archaeologists is used for modelling. The goal is to indicate what activities (associated with the themes listed) took place in the past in various landscape zones. One advantage of using these themes is that it produces more differentiated predictions. These models will eventually be reflected in a national map. The likely density of archaeological remains will play no role in this and the map will not show zones with a higher or lower density of expected archaeological remains. The maps will be useful in the first phase of AHM, including in desk-based surveys for the purpose of drawing up a specified prediction for a research area.

The predictive models shortly to become available may potentially be better, as more geological data and public datasets are available on the physical environment, including a 3D model of the subsurface in the Netherlands (Stafleu et al. 2011), a detailed palaeogeographical dataset of the Rhine-Meuse delta (Cohen et al. 2012) and the digital elevation map of the Netherlands (AHN). These datasets allow the depth of geomorphological units and geological deposits to be modelled. One important goal of the new national predictive archaeological maps is to survey the depth of expected archaeological remains, as well as the differentiation by theme and mode of existence. Using a combination of these geological datasets and the archaeological data that have become available since the publication of the first IKAW, we can obtain a better understanding of the nature, depth and age of the unknown archaeological resource in the Holocene area of the Netherlands.

Discussion

Since 1997 the translation of the three generations of the IKAW into some form of archaeological policy and the consecutive formulation of regional and local predictive AHM maps have led to a huge quantity of new archaeological data, despite the maps' limitations and their targeted use in zones of high and medium value. We can therefore say that the comprehensive national predictive map has certainly proved its worth. We acknowledge that insufficient research has been performed over this period in zones of low value, as a result of which they have not been 'verified'. The new generation of predictive models and maps could be significantly improved by incorporating the hugely increased quantity of geological data into the models, and by 3D modelling, use of expert knowledge and independent verification of the models using data on the known resource. However, if AHM had waited for more sophisticated models, as proposed by the critics, many archaeological remains would have been silently lost because there was no comprehensive national overview of the unknown resource that could provide guidance for further assessment of potential sites.

References

Cohen, K.M, E. Stouthamer, H.J. Pierik and A.H. Geurts. 2012. *Digitaal Basisbestand Paleogeografie van de Rijn-Maas Delta*. Utrecht: Departement Fysische Geografie, Universiteit Utrecht.

Deeben, J., D.P. Hallewas and Th.J. Maarleveld. 2002. *Predictive modelling in Archaeological Heritage Management of the Netherlands: the Indicative Map of Archaeological Values (2nd generation)*. Amersfoort: Rijksdienst voor het oudheidkundig Bodemonderzoek (Berichten van de Rijksdienst voor het Oudheidkundig Bodemonderzoek 45), 9-56.

Deeben, J., J. van Doesburg and F. van Kregten. 2006. 'Hoe de archeologie uit de romantiek verdween: enkele ontwikkelingen in de methoden en technieken van het Nederlandse archeologische veldwerk sinds 1970', in O. Brinkkemper, J. Deeben, J. van Doesburg, D.P. Hallewas, E.M. Theunissen and A.D. Verlinde (eds), *Vakken in vlakken. Archeologische kennis in lagen*. Amersfoort (Nederlandse Archeologische Rapporten 32), 41-72.

Stafleu, J., D. Maljers, J.L., Gunnink, A. Menkovic and F.S. Busschers. 2011. '3D-modelling of the shallow subsurface of Zeeland, the Netherlands', *Netherlands Journal of Geosciences* 90, 293-310.

Van Leusen, M., and H. Kamermans (eds). 2005. 'Predictive modelling for Archaeological Heritage Manangement: A research agenda', *Nederlandse Archeologische Rapporten* 29, 25-92.

Verhagen, P., H. Kamermans, M. van Leusen and B. Ducke. 2010. 'New developments in archaeological predictive modelling', in T. Bloemers, H. Kars, A. van der Valk and M. Wijnen (eds), *The Cultural Landscape & Heritage Paradox. Protection and Development of the Dutch Archaeological-Historical Landscape and its European Dimensions*. Amsterdam: Amsterdam University Press, 431-444.

Verhagen, P. and T.G. Whitley. 2012. 'Integrating Archaeological Theory and Predictive Modeling: a Live Report from the Scene', *Journal of Archaeological Method and Theory* 19, 49-100.

Willems, W.J.H. 1978. 'Burial analysis: a new approach to an old problem', *Berichten van de Rijksdienst voor het Oudheidkundig Bodemonderzoek* 28, 81-98.

Willems, W.J.H. 1983. 'Romans and Batavians: regional development at the imperial frontier', in R. Brandt and J. Slofstra (eds), *Roman and Native in the Low Countries, Spheres of Interaction*. Oxford: British Archaeological Reports International Series 148, 105-128.

Willems, W.J.H. 1997. 'Archaeological heritage management in the Netherlands: past, present and future', in W.J.H. Willems, H. Kars and D.P. Hallewas (eds), *Archaeological Heritage Management in the Netherlands. Fifty Years State Service for Archaeological Investigations*. Assen/Amersfoort: Van Gorcum, 3-34.

***

At the time this book went to print the editors learnt of the untimely and sad loss of our colleague Jos Deeben.

A plea for ethics

Reflecting on sustainability and preservation *in situ* of archaeological resources in the Netherlands

Tom Bloemers

University of Amsterdam (Emeritus professor),
The Netherlands

In early November 2014 I received the 42nd issue of The European Archaeologist, the newsletter of the European Association of Archaeologists (EAA). On page 39-40 it contained the summary of a session on 'Preservation *in situ* or excavation?' organized during the EAA conference in Istanbul (2014) by C. Andersson, D. de Jager, E. Kars and V. Vandrup Martens. Reading about Willem's contribution to the session (see also Willems 2014) motivated me to discuss it with him, and we agreed that same month to do so, as we frequently had such discussions over the past 40 years. Unfortunately this time it was not to be. Instead, I will discuss it here.

Starting from Willem's statement: 'preservation in situ sucks'

What triggered me most were some quotes from the session, such as 'Willem used to be an advocate for preserving *in situ* but now considers it to be a dogma for western archaeological heritage management…Today the bulk of money spent in archaeology [in the Netherlands] goes to evaluation work. Fewer and fewer sites are excavated, which leads to less knowledge which in turn leads to fewer stories to be told and in the end the public is going to lose its interest in archaeology'. Willem continued in his article on the same topic (Willems 2014) by supporting the importance of knowledge production. He referred to the statement of the American heritage expert Bill Lipe saying '[…] the social benefit that archaeology can provide to society … is primarily …knowledge about the past … In situ preservation … of archaeological resources is a **tool** [Willem's bold typing] for optimizing that benefit' and that 'Long-term, frugal consumption of the archaeological record by well-justified research – both problem-oriented and mitigation-driven – must be an accepted and integrated part of the preservation program …' (Willems 2014: 152-153).

Willem based his change of opinion on observations in Dutch development-led archaeology. In particular some recent figures on preservation *in situ* are relevant in this respect, such as a recent analysis of 6000 archaeological site reports, produced between 2007 and 2011. It shows that 32 percent of 426 sites that were considered 'worth preserving' were indeed preserved *in situ*. For nature development and industrial areas the percentages were 67 and 46 percent, for building schemes only 19 percent (Schute *et al.* 2013: 55-58).

For the time being these figures offer the best benchmark we have. They show that two out of three sites nowadays have to be preserved *ex situ* by excavation or watching brief. But what does this mean for the argumentation in favour or against preservation *in situ*? It shows that preservation *in situ* is possible in the Dutch context, but does it mean that it should be intensified since the percentage of preserved sites is rather low? Or does it show that this approach has no future and that excavations – under good research conditions – are the only way forward? The answer surely deserves to be discussed further. In both cases, is there room for research and excavation-based story telling?

Reflecting on sustainability

From my perspective, the discussion on preservation *in situ* should also include aspects of sustainability and ethics. Sustainability is described by Achterberg (1994) as activities, processes and structures that for an indefinite period continue or have to exist. My interpretation of this in relation to archaeological resources, is that these are essentially so valuable that sustainable management is necessary. The prime reason is their importance for the quality of the knowledge about the human past, and of the present well-being of our society and environment. According to Achterberg, sustainable management is also aimed at doing justice to present and future generations, since they all are entitled to enjoy cultural history (Achterberg 1994: 36-40; Bloemers 2005: 80-83).

In dealing with 'Valletta', European archaeologists operate within a field of interaction with four dimensions: 1. Society takes a central position where politicians, professionals and citizens decide how to act following their perception of the value of the archaeological resources and the stories archaeologists tell. 2. The stock of archaeological resources is larger than we know at present because of its inherent invisibility, but it is certainly not infinite. To evaluate its significance, refined assessment systems have been developed. 3. Knowledge is usually defined as knowledge about the past, as in Willem's statement. 4. Ethics are sometimes mentioned, but generally not explored in-depth. How archaeologists implement the aims of the Valletta Convention is determined by their perception of these four dimensions in the context of the society in which they work or belong to. And this perception in turn reflects the paradigm(s) that are dominant in the discipline.

The stock embodies the primary and authentic sources of archaeological qualities, which can only in a limited way be known. For the whole of the Netherlands, the number of (highly) valuable archaeological sites was about 13,000 by the end of 2007; they covered about 66,000 hectares (Beukers 2009: 26-38 and 74-77). This can be considered as the known stock of archaeological resources *in situ*. About 65 percent of this stock is covered by sediments or deposits, 10 percent is in danger of erosion, 20 percent is situated in areas with a high ground water level. Historic towns and villages and the maritime heritage are not included, a crucial omission to be repaired as soon as possible! As a primary source for the known and the unknown, this stock is the gateway to knowledge about the human past. But at the same time, it is the gateway to knowledge about heritage preservation. This raises the question of why historic knowledge should be given priority over heritage knowledge, since one is a condition for the other and vice versa. Should their ranking not be *ex aequo*?

Discussions and actions about the aims and effects of the Valletta Convention, within archaeology and between archaeology and society, have to be framed by ethics in order to justify high impact decisions ranging from preservation to renewing the Convention. In this context ethics are more than codes of conduct; they describe the attitude, the set of views and assumptions a group of actors has

> 'Why should historic knowledge be given priority over heritage knowledge?'

about an object or a situation (Achterberg 1994: 144-147). But such ethics are not yet well-developed in (European) archaeology. Maybe we can learn something from disciplines with more developed pragmatic ethics dealing *e.g.* with environment, nature or health? We need to elaborate on the significance of ideas such as the precautionary principle to cope with uncertainty, stewardship entrusted to our generation, intergenerational justice, the ownership of archaeological resources as a common and/or private good. And what is the meaning of a '(sustainable) future' in archaeological (heritage) thinking given human generations and past and present time as disciplinarian core issues?

Epilogue

The perception that preservation *in situ* has become a 'dogma' that frustrates archaeology clearly needs further reflection. By reflecting on it the dogma can be disposed of its rigid and polarizing connotations and transformed into a legitimate view to be seriously questioned. For me, the result of such a reflection is that only a deepening of the ethical framework for acting in the present will create a constructive way forward towards a sustainable future for archaeological resources, not only 'for ourselves' (Willems 2014: 155) but hopefully also for next generations. This is what I would have loved to discuss with Willem.

References

Achterberg, W. 1994. *Samenleving, Natuur en Duurzaamheid. Een inleiding in de milieufilosofie*. Assen: Van Gorcum.

Beukers, E. (ed.). 2009. *Erfgoedbalans 2009. Archeologie, monumenten en cultuurlandschap in Nederland*, Amersfoort: Rijksdienst voor het Cultureel Erfgoed.

Bloemers, J.H.F. 2005. 'Archaeological-historical landscapes in the Netherlands: management by sustainable development in planning', in M. Ruiz del Árbol and A. Orejas (eds), *Landscapes as Cultural Heritage in the European Research. Proceedings of the Open Workshop Madrid, 29th October 2004*. Madrid: Consejo Superior de Investigaciones Científicas, 69-85.

Schute, I.A., M.E. Lobbes and M. Verbruggen. 2013. *Archeologie voor de toekomst. Kwantitatieve analyse van het behoud van archeologische waarden (2007-2011)*. RAAP-rapport 2618. Weesp: RAAP Archeologisch Adviesbureau.

Willems, W.J.H. 2014. 'Malta and its consequences: a mixed blessing', in V.M. van der Haas and P.A.C. Schut (eds), *The Valletta Convention: Twenty Years After. Benefits, Problems, Challenges*. Brussels: Europae Archaeologiae Consilium (EAC Occasional Paper no. 9), 151-156.

Preservation *in situ* at Almere, the downside of our success

Dick de Jager

Department of Urban Development,
Municipality of Almere, The Netherlands

Willem Willems had a big personality. His commitment to heritage management was sometimes expressed in a provocative, in-your-face style. However, being blunt and wearing your heart on your sleeve are not always the best qualities for the manager of a supervisory body. When, in 2002, Willem became inspector-general for the Dutch State Inspectorate for Archaeology (later integrated into the State Inspectorate for Cultural Heritage) he knew he had to hire staff that would complement him in this regard. He always had a knack for surrounding himself with people who would contribute to a positive team effort and that's why, when my colleagues and I were hired, we were told to contradict him whenever possible. This usually led to spirited discussions and, eventually, to a joint opinion on key aspects of the emerging archaeological quality system in the Netherlands. In this way, our reports and evaluations (*e.g.* Aten *et al.* 2003) made a difference.

Years later, when I was one of the organizers of a session on the pros and cons of preservation *in situ* at the EAA conference in Istanbul, I knew I had to invite Willem to guarantee a good discussion (Andersson *et al.* 2014). He didn't disappoint and boldly stated that 'preservation *in situ* sucks'. As always, he followed up such a statement with facts and figures. He argued that the Valletta Convention of 1992 had led to fewer excavations in the Netherlands and to many sites being nominally preserved *in situ* only to be slowly deteriorating, thus never contributing to research. According to Willem, the main drives behind this change were bureaucratization and commercialization. In his view, those in charge of heritage management, the municipalities, lacked adequate knowledge and claimed that archaeological research was a matter for the universities. His main point was that preservation *in situ* should not be a goal in itself, but only the means for optimizing research and the dissemination of knowledge of the past.

In the spirit of tradition I would like to contradict Willem and argue that preservation *in situ* can be implemented successfully by a municipality, without losing sight of scientific research and the moral duty to share our knowledge of the past. For this I will use my current working environment, the city of Almere, as an example.

Almere: a new town with an old history

The city of Almere is a new town on reclaimed land in the Flevopolder of the Netherlands, a drained segment of an inland sea. It is located just east of Amsterdam. The first inhabitants arrived in 1976 and now there are about 200,000 people living there. In the perception of most outsiders, Almere has little or no history. What they do not realise is that Almere actually has a long history; below the city lies a vast, very well preserved, Stone Age landscape sculpted around the ancient river Eem. Before the land was drowned as a result of the melting polar icecaps (what's new!), it had been an attractive living space for thousands of years. The Stone Age sites of Almere are mostly Mesolithic, but some are late-Palaeolithic and some are Neolithic. They differ in size from 400 to 40,000 square meters. The ancient remains are remarkably well preserved because they were submerged

> 'It is increasingly difficult to convince politicians and developers that yet another site has to be preserved because it is so unique.'

and covered with peat and clay. Additionally, many shipwrecks from the former Zuiderzee are scattered over the reclaimed land. Because of the city's young age, the municipal archaeologists were able to implement a Valletta-proof policy of *in-situ* preservation.

Unlike the rest of the Netherlands, archaeological prediction models are not used in Almere. Lack of sufficient data about the prehistoric landscape has led to another approach. In order to align the urban growth and the care of archaeological remains in the best possible manner, the municipality has opted to identify and preserve only a representative sample of the archaeological remains. There is no selection up front; every part of the municipality has an equal examination requirement. But after the exploratory phase of each borehole survey only 45 per cent of the undisturbed area is mapped. Choosing this 45 per cent ensures that every type of old landscape within the area is represented (high, low, near water etc.), apart from that the chosen area is random. In contrast to the 'old land', possible sites that are found in this way are valued with core probes instead of trail trenches. This is due to technical and financial reasons; the sites are simply lying too deep in the underground and there is substantial water pressure from all sides.

The municipality has opted to preserve all the undisturbed sites, and mould the new city around them. No buildings or roads are allowed over the sites, unless it can be proven that there is no negative impact on the archaeological record. So far, no one has been able to do so. Almere is the only city in The Netherlands to do so on this scale and in this way significantly influences national statistics on preservation in situ. This is called the 'Almere-effect' (Schute *et al.* 2013: 85).

The importance that the people of Almere attach to the prehistoric sites in their city is remarkably high. On the one hand, they explicitly want to know what they entail, and on the other hand they want them preserved for future generations. Following up on this, it has been decided to shape and structure these locations in a way that they are recognizable and can be experienced (Gemeente Almere 2012). By now, more than eighty in situ preserved Mesolithic sites are visible as open areas within the growing urban area. Information is transferred to visitors on site, via websites and by means of an educational programme. In this way, the sites strengthen and enhance the identity of the city and they become places where people like to meet each other.

All boxes ticked

After fourteen years of policy and research, Almere can tick almost all the boxes of the Valletta Treaty: non-destructive methods of investigation are applied wherever possible (art. 3), the sites have been preserved *in situ* (art. 4), archaeology is integrated in the spatial process (art. 5), research is developer-driven and -paid (art. 6), survey-methods are constantly improved upon (art. 7) and we have engaged the public and facilitated public access to archaeological sites (art. 9). On top of this the archaeologists of Almere have improved on the statistical analysis of core probe data, learned a lot about the landscape development and the dating of the sites and have provided the new town with a history, identity and a new public image. All in all, this shows that *in situ* preservation can be applied successfully. Nothing needs to change for Almere. Or does it?

There is however a downside to the success of the Almere policy. Because of the highly specialized prospection methods, we only have limited information about the sites. Lack of opportunity and money prevents us from creating added scientific information and individualized archaeological stories. There is no differentiation between the sites, although they differ over a period of 5000 years and may represent many different types of settlements, burial sites or locations of hunting, fishing and gathering. We do not find everything by core probing (no additional shipwrecks, no off-site) and because we do not excavate, we do not have impressive, appealing finds to display to the public. We are forced to tell the same story over and over again because there are no location specific tales. As a consequence, it is increasingly difficult to convince politicians and developers that yet another site has to be preserved because it is so unique.

Conclusion of the discussion

In the final discussion of the EAA session in Istanbul we came to the conclusion that while sites such as those in Almere can certainly be preserved, there are many others that need to be excavated. Even if safeguarded, sites are often abandoned and if no scientific (protective) measures are taken, this results in a potential loss of the valuable archaeological heritage. We always have to be aware what we are saving and for whom. As usual, I now personally also have to come to the conclusion that Willem was (partly) right after all … Saving sites for the future can mean stagnancy. Not just in a scientific way, but also seen from a communication standpoint. Because the general opinion during the session was that preservation *in situ* is not always the preferred solution, it was implied that the Valletta Convention ought to be rewritten. However, this should not happen in the near future because the present text is a very important foundation for the work of many archaeologists who are only starting to implement the Valletta principles. For a good future heritage convention, one might look at combining the Valletta and Faro treaties – one calling for preservation, the other for communication and dissemination of heritage to increase quality of life.

References

Andersson, C., D. de Jager, E. Kars and V. Vandrup Martens. 2014. 'Preservation in situ or excavation?', *The European Archaeologist* 42: 39-40.

Aten, N.A., M.H. van den Dries, G.R.M. van den Eynde and D.H. de Jager. 2003. *Een goed begin …. Een verkennend onderzoek naar het gebruik van de Kwaliteitsnorm Nederlandse Archeologie als richtsnoer bij het opstellen van Programma's van Eisen*. RIA-rapport 1. Zoetermeer: Rijksinspectie voor de Archeologie.

Gemeente Almere. 2012. *Steentijd wildernis in Almere. Visie en toolbox voor inrichting, visualisatie en gebruik van de steentijdplaatsen*. Almere: Gemeente Almere.

Schute, I.A., M.E. Lobbes and M. Verbruggen. 2013. *Archeologie voor de toekomst. Kwantitatieve analyse van het behoud van archeologische waarden (2007-2011)*. RAAP-rapport 2618. Weesp: RAAP.

The invisible treasures of our past

Martijn Manders

Cultural Heritage Agency / Faculty of Archaeology,
Leiden University, The Netherlands

As an underwater archaeologist I often consider myself to be in one of the best professions in the world: it is adventurous and there is always new material to be discovered. Underwater archaeology involves picking up the pieces of a giant jigsaw puzzle, creating a picture of what might have happened in the past. The stories that unfold from these pictures can be shocking, moving and sometimes sad, but they can also be beautiful and joyous. I am also privileged to be working in the Netherlands, a maritime nation at heart, where water has shaped the country. We only have to think of all the land that would disappear if we got rid of the dikes: approximately half of the country would disappear! Cities have been built along important waterways, cultural and economic contacts were established over water, and the Netherlands had important colonies overseas. This rich maritime history has left an abundance of sites on the seabed, circa ten thousand well-preserved locations in Dutch waters alone. Scientifically I could not ask for more, but from an underwater cultural heritage management perspective, much remains to be done.

Drawing attention to underwater cultural heritage

The view of the importance of water within the Netherlands has changed over time. During the 19th and 20th centuries many maritime cities were opened towards the hinterland when roads were built and agriculture became more important. This latest view, that is, 'with our back to the sea', may have influenced cultural heritage management in the sense that it has been biased towards land monuments. Only relatively few underwater sites have been investigated, while this source of exclusive knowledge is ephemeral: erosion, biological deterioration, chemical and human deterioration all form serious threats. Underwater heritage has to be explored before it is lost forever. If we do nothing, then essential information to help us understand the past will be lost, at rapid speed. Is this negative? Well, some might say that 'if you cannot see it, you will not miss it', and others might say that 'the wreck did not belong in the sea anyway.' The discussion of whether 'mankind' should be allowed to leave his footprint on this earth will not be addressed here. What is important to mention though, is that shipwrecks are not just coincidental finds without any connection to their environment: they are always lying somewhere for a reason. The area, location or landscape says something about the wreck, and vice versa.

The value of shipwrecks

But does it all have any value, and if so, what kind of value? Can we establish value if we cannot see it? One particular type of value that is relevant for underwater archaeology is its economic value – however, I would like to stress that the selling of maritime artifacts is against my personal and professional ethics, as well as those of most other archaeologists. In my view, heritage is nobody's to sell – it belongs to all of us. Could tourism perhaps be an alternative way of making underwater cultural heritage economically attractive? Diving in the Netherlands does not make a great impact at the national level, but on a local scale it really can make a difference. This is because shipwrecks are a fantastic resource to draw upon as a source of enjoyment and learning. This is a perfect combination: value for knowledge, value for enjoyment, and on top of that, even economic value.

Heritage management, however, is built upon dealing primarily with the concept of cultural heritage value, as something we inherit from our ancestors and deem worthy to preserve. There are no universal criteria for this and no one has the exclusive right to determine what heritage is and what it is not. We can talk about 'our' heritage, but the 'we' is difficult to define – am I a European, a Dutchman maybe? Or do I – for example – belong to this professional group of 'archaeologists'? As part of the latter, I subscribe to a certain group of criteria to establish the value of cultural heritage as registered in the Dutch Quality Standards for Archaeology, but as an individual, this might be different. The phrase 'our heritage' in my opinion is rather impersonal, as one might question who this 'we' actually is. Instead, I want to determine my own personal identity: who I am, what I associate with, what makes me sad, and what makes me happy. I personally want to gain control over my environment, and feel and enjoy the spirit of the place I live in. For me, an investment in my environment is an investment in myself and my quality of life, and this may even become financially interesting. This is because a better living environment is more appreciated and thus house prices go up, in turn creating more willingness from others to invest in that same environment. In this sense, investing in my own environment is also investing in those of others -with cultural heritage as a binding factor.

Regional differences

Heritage management has been decentralized in the Netherlands, which means for instance that there is no additional financial compensation for it. As a result, people have become more involved themselves in processes of management and protection of what they value the most. But it is worth remembering that societies change and as a result, the ensuing valuing may become different. What is the value of an East Indiaman for the collective that calls itself Dutch? And how does this collective value the wrecks of British warships in the North Sea? Or the fishing ships connected with the closure of the Zuiderzee in 1932, turning it into the IJsselmeer? By contrast, how do the nearby villagers (including former fishermen) value those same ships? These are important examples of questions that draw attention to the diverse range of stakeholder values, but at the moment it is still normal procedure for archaeologists to exclusively determine the cultural heritage value. One might question whether archaeologists should have these exclusive rights, and who profits from exclusivity in the first place. If a large group of people declares something to be of high cultural historical value, who am I, as a professional archaeologist, to dispute this? In my view, being able to determine value together also means a joint responsibility.

The three English warships Hogue, Aboukir and Cressi are good examples. They sank 100 years ago and there was almost no professional or governmental attention given to them since, as World War I was not something high on the priority list in the Netherlands – even though it constituted a disaster unrivalled

> 'Safeguarding shipwrecks comes down to making well founded choices and taking different views and values into account.'

in Dutch waters. Interestingly, it has recently been due to a number of private individuals that came together under the umbrella of an initiative called *Duik de Noordzee Schoon* that this tragedy of 1914 is receiving so much attention. This bottom up initiative from civil society has made governments and politicians act, and the experience value has advanced. On the other hand, shipwrecks are also one of the very view hard substrates in the North Sea and therefore hotspots of biodiversity, as they are a nursing or hiding place for many fish. This in turn makes the experience of diving on such wrecks richer and thus has an economic value for more than just an individual. What this means is that different people and groups value the same object or place in different ways, but it also leads us to the question of how we can organise sound protection. This is because protecting the archaeological heritage for scientific reasons may be executed differently than for dive tourism. In the first scenario, the site may be covered up for *in situ* protection, whilst in the second, a site has to remain visible.

Participation and making choices

In the end it all comes down to making well founded choices and taking different views and values into account; a game of give and take by different stakeholders. With a new Dutch heritage law in the making for 2016 and hopefully also the ratification of the 2001 UNESCO Convention on the Protection of the Underwater Cultural Heritage, we will have better tools for law enforcement in the Netherlands. In addition, the referees – that is, law-enforcement agencies and the Ministry of Justice – are well informed and willing to cooperate.

Before this happens, however, we should all determine ourselves how much importance we are willing to attach to cultural heritage, and exactly what and how much we want to pass on to our children and grandchildren. Yes, we need to initiate a public debate, and support others that want to join, but ultimately this process starts with ourselves. Without heritage and no knowledge of the past, there is no understanding of who we are now and what tomorrow will bring. I would like to see everybody adding his or her own point of view and values to the playing field, be it cultural, economic or leisure-related. A government that guards the playing field, does not then really dictate anymore, but rather helps to explain and facilitate – and has archaeologists that are not determining, but guiding the narrative.

Fluctuating boundaries
Collecting policies in 19th century archaeological and ethnological museums

Ruurd B. Halbertsma

National Museum of Antiquities, The Netherlands

The ancient world with its rich cultures from Greece and Rome has been the focus of interest from the days of the Renaissance onwards. Splendid collections of Greek and Roman art were assembled, mostly by wealthy collectors, who used their antiquities to impress their fellow countrymen, to foster studies or to improve contemporary taste and art. When at the end of the 18th century the first National Museums came into being, which were open to the public and directed by professional scholars, the question of boundaries between museums began to emerge. A National Museum of Antiquities had to present the artefacts of ancient cultures, especially of the highly esteemed Greek and Roman world. But the scholarly debate started when the question was raised as to which other ancient cultures should be present in an archaeological museum, and which in an ethnological collection: where to place for instance ancient artefacts from India, Indonesia and America? According to the first director of the Leiden Museum of Antiquities, Caspar Reuvens (1793-1835), civilizations that had seen fundamental changes in religion and language could be regarded as 'extinct' and their artefacts therefore were suitable for a place in an archaeological museum (Halbertsma 2003: 34-38). Ethnologists strongly opposed these views. The debate continued throughout the 19th century and reflects contemporary views on the boundaries of the ancient world: the results of this difference in scholarly views are still visible in today's museums.

Indonesian artefacts: archaeology or ethnology?

In Reuvens' view, an archaeological museum should not focus on the classical world alone, but also on the cultures known by or influenced by the Greeks and Romans. For example, the influence of Greek and Roman art on the ancient Buddhist art of India and the later temple architecture and religious statuary of Indonesia, was for Reuvens a reason to include Indian and Indonesian antiquities in his collecting policy. Other archaeological material from *e.g.* the Americas was not included in this system. Reuvens wrote about American artefacts:

> *'I would not cut off the possibility of enlarging our Dutch museum collections with the so unknown objects from Mexico, but these objects should not be placed in a Museum of Antiquities, which should confine itself to classical antiquity and to those regions which were known by the Greeks and Romans and which were influenced by their civilization, e.g. India'* (Reuvens 17-2-1828, Museum Archive, 17.1.1/3, translation by the author).

In the Netherlands, Hindu and Buddhist art from the East Indies was dispersed among private collectors, the Royal Academy of Arts and Sciences in Amsterdam and the Ethnological Collection in The Hague. Reuvens published a monograph about the Amsterdam sculptures from Java in 1826 (Reuvens 1826). He was the first in the Netherlands to formulate a heritage policy with measures to safeguard the Indonesian monuments and antiquities *in loco* against vandalism, looting and neglect by his fellow countrymen: 'There seems to be a feeling on Java that those

> 'Extinct or living cultures? The debate continues in which museum archaeology should be shown.'

monuments are common property and that everyone, especially the higher civil servants, can take away what they like' (Reuvens 29-8-1832, Museum Archive, 17.1.1/4, translation by the author).

Reuvens formulated a strict policy to stop the destruction of these artefacts and to rescue this part of the heritage of Java by the creation of a 'Society for the Publication of Javanese Monuments'. Part of this policy was to combine all Indonesian antiquities in the museum in Leiden. Most of them were housed in the Ethnological Cabinet in the *Mauritshuis* in The Hague. When asked, the director of the cabinet refused to cede his Indonesian objects to Leiden, arguing that the statues were part of his cabinet because they *belonged to a still existing people*, and were therefore of ethnological value and not of archaeological interest. Reuvens replied that the ancient monuments from Indonesia were part of the extinct Hindu and Buddhist cultures, which were transformed in the course of the 15th and 16th century into an Islamic community. Civilizations that had seen such dramatic changes in religion could be regarded as 'extinct' and their artefacts therefore should be placed in an archaeological museum. Rèuvens wrote to the Ministry:

> *'It is important for scholarship that the Indian antiquities are not separated from the Egyptian and other artifacts. Otherwise, in the near future, there will be no longer a Museum of Antiquities, because Roman and Greek objects will also be placed in a Museum of Living People, the former labelled as Italian, and the latter among the objects from the Hellenic Commonwealth. The boundary, as I repeat, is this: the disappearance of a people, or its later civilization, by the complete transition to the Christian or the Muslim faith'* (Reuvens 25-11-1820, Museum Archive, 17.1.1/1, translation by the author).

American artefacts

As said above Reuvens' primary reason for placing the eastern artefacts in his museum was the cultural connection with the world of Greeks and Romans. After his untimely death in 1835 Reuvens was succeeded by Conrad Leemans, who developed new ideas about the collecting policy of the museum. Leemans decided to include the American continent in his collecting program in view of new theories about presumed connections between the earliest American cultures and European prehistory. Danish archaeologists had published influential articles about the similarities in form and function of for instance stone axes, arrowheads and other utensils (Randsborg 2001: 1-53). In his annual report of the year 1839 Leemans wrote about American archaeology as follows:

> 'During the last years the study of Nordic artefacts, initiated and fostered by the Royal Society in Copenhagen, has focused its attention to America and the old remains of that continent. It is impossible to deny the similarities between the old artefacts there and the ones that are found in our continent. [...] These and many other circumstances lead to the important decision that the civilization of the New World originated with the other civilizations from one point. This supposition finds new corroboration from old stories of the early Mexicans' (Leemans 1842, translation by the author).

For Leemans the boundaries were thus set: the archaeological museum of Leiden should collect objects from 'extinct' ancient cultures, including the Americas. During the whole 19th century this policy prevailed, which allowed the Buddhas a place next to Hercules and Apollo. In 1859 Leemans also became director of the Ethnographical Museum. On various occasions he argued that both the archaeological and ethnographical collections had to be combined in a new prestigious museum of ancient and modern ethnology. He regarded archaeology as the ethnology (or anthropology) of past civilizations.

Conflicts arose from within. In 1877 L. Serrurier became curator of the Japanese department of the Ethnographical Museum. His modern ideas and wishes to change the classification and presentation of the museum led to a conflict with Leemans, which resulted in Leemans' resignation as director of the ethnographical museum in 1880. He was succeeded by Serrurier, who continued to point his arrows at Leemans' collecting policy, which he described as 'unsystematic and haphazard'. He pleaded that the earliest artefacts of the cultures placed under his care had to be present in his museum, and not in the archaeological collection.

The question was raised again in 1903, when the Department of the Interior established a committee to decide the future of the Ethnographical Museum. Among other issues, the committee discussed the division of material between archaeology and ethnology and came to the following conclusion:

> 'Antiquities of the peoples of North-Africa, Western Asia and Europe, whose civilization can be considered the predecessor of our own, should find their place in the Museum of Antiquities. Everything else should go to the Museum of Ethnography. As far is known to the committee there are no objects in the latter which should move under that rule to the Museum of Antiquities. But the archaeological museum houses Indonesian, Indian and American antiquities, which belong without doubt in the Museum of Ethnography. The commission is of the opinion that as a rule the prehistoric artefacts of cultures, shown in an ethnological museum, should also be present in that museum.' (de Groot 1903: 8-9, translation by the author).

The question had been settled. In the years 1903 and 1904 the archaeological artefacts from India, Indonesia and the Americas left the National Museum of Antiquities, in total about 3600 objects. Protests from archaeological scholars were to no avail. The 'exotic' antiquities started a new future under the guidance of new curators. New boundaries had been set, which are still in full vigour today.

References

De Groot, J.J.M. 1903. *Rapport der Commissie van Advies betreffende 's Rijks Ethnographisch Museum (Leiden)*. Den Haag: Ministerie van Binnenlandse Zaken.

Halbertsma, R.B. 2003. *Scholars, Travellers and Trade – the Pioneer Years of the National Museum of Antiquities in Leiden*. London: Routledge.

Leemans, C. 1842. *Beredeneerde beschrijving der Asiatische en Amerikaansche monumenten van het Museum van Oudheden te Leiden*. Leiden.

Randsborg, K. 2001. 'Archaeological Globalization. The first Practitioners', *Acta Archaeologica* 72(2): 1-53.

Reuvens, C.J.C. 1826. *Verhandeling over drie groote steenen beelden, in den jare 1819 uit Java naar de Nederlanden overgezonden*. Amsterdam.

People rather than things, the *Haka* and the *Waka*

Steven Engelsman

Weltmuseum Wien, Austria

At the World Music Competition held in Kerkrade, the Netherlands in July 2013, the *Christelijke Muziekvereniging Kunst en Genoegen* (K&G) from Leiden came first in the 'world marching division'. In what was actually a derby with bands from neighbouring Sassenheim and Rijnsburg, the Leiden military marching band earned its decisive jury points with their spectacular *haka* (a traditional ancestral war dance from the Maori people). Yes, a real Maori *haka*, with all its shouting, abrupt and aggressive movements, clapping of hands on arms and legs, rolling of eyes and sticking out of tongues. Such a *haka* was the tipping point that earned the Leiden band first prize, which had gone to neighbouring Katwijk at the World Music Competition four years earlier. In this paper, I will summarize the string of events that lead to K&G adopting a Maori ritual in their artistic programme, and thus becoming World Champions of 2013. I will show that it resulted from an approach to cultural heritage that puts people before objects. And this – I believe – is exactly what Willem Willems was advocating during the last years of his active scholarly life, so I think it might be a proper subject in his memory.

Long-lasting partnerships

The story starts with Abel Tasman. On 13th December 1742 he was the first European to set sight on Aotearoa, which he then called New Zealand. At Golden Bay on the northern tip of South Island he sent a few crew ashore. However, local Maori were not amused, killed four of them, and Tasman left New Zealand as fast as he could. This meant he missed the Cook's Strait, which was just there for him to discover, and left New Zealand for the British to colonize nearly 200 years later. Hence, the Maori collection at the National Museum of Ethnology in Leiden is rather insignificant. All the good Maori *taonga* went to Britain and British collections.

In itself, there is nothing wrong with this; collections can be kept and safeguarded everywhere in the world, as long as they are well known and accessible. However, the lack of good Maori material was certainly a handicap at the National Museum of Ethnology in Leiden, when some 10 years ago the idea came up to stage a large exhibition about the Netherlands and New Zealand, with a special focus on Maori culture. There were a few good reasons to do this. Eventually, in the 1950s and 1960s – three centuries after Tasman – thousands of young Dutch men and women had emigrated to New Zealand in search of better opportunities. This in itself made New Zealand an interesting topic for exhibition in the Netherlands. One of those emigrants was Ans Westra from Leiden, who had become one of the top photographers of Maori social life. Another Dutch emigrant was museum curator Luit Bieringa, who had curated an exhibition of Ans Westra's photographic work, which he had already displayed in Leiden. And finally, in 2005, the National Museum of Ethnology had returned a *Toi Moko* – a mummified tattooed Maori head – to the New Zealand's national Te Papa Museum in Wellington, for eventual repatriation to its own *iwi*. So cultural ties between the Netherlands and New Zealand had already been strengthened, new partnerships had been forged. There was a need for more activities to be developed, such as a large exhibition.

But there was an issue over how to make an exhibition with little material to show. Loans from New Zealand's museums and official collections were not within budgetary reach. We decided to focus on story telling through filmed interviews

'The shift from tangible to intangible heritage made our exhibition much more engaging.'

rather than showing precious collections. The Leiden curator of audio-visual productions Herman de Boer spent months in New Zealand, interviewing a large range of very interesting people, both Maori and Pakeha. This shift from tangible heritage to intangible heritage was a very effective way out of the dilemma; even more, it made the exhibition much more engaging than a show of precious *taonga* would have been. There were many dynamics in the exhibition, many voices to be heard. However, the real big boost came through the *waka* project, which had been developed alongside the exhibition's preparation. After a visit to New Zealand's Minister of Culture in the summer of 2009, curator Luit Bieringa and I were pondering the issue that making and preparing an exhibition is great fun and takes years, whilst opening and showing the exhibition is rewarding but only lasts for a few months before the whole thing comes to an end and all fine partnerships become dormant again. How could we tackle this problem, in what way could we work around this dilemma and build something more long-lasting -that was what we were looking for.

And then, suddenly, Luit Bieringa had an idea; why not ask the Maori whether they would be willing to carve a real *waka*, a real traditional Maori canoe, for the Leiden museum? To be manned by a Maori trained Dutch crew, and to be used and operated on Dutch, or even European waters. We pitched the idea to Toi Maori Aotearoa, the organisation representing, dealing in and organizing Maori traditional craftsmanship and arts. They backed the idea, joined in the plan and pitched it among their elders (thanks to Garry Nicholas, Waana Davis and Robert Gable). Soon after, the Dutch Bankgiroloterij stepped in and boosted our plan with a donation of nearly half a million Euros; thus the dream came true.

From Maori waka to Dutch haka

Knocking the *waka* out of a Kauri tree was commissioned to master builder Hector Busby at Doubtless Bay. He liked the idea of making a *waka* in New Zealand that would sail back to Old Zealand, to the country were Abel Tasman had come from. The *waka* was ready by June 2010, baptised Te Hono Ki Aotearoa (the link with New Zealand). A Maori crew for the *waka* was trained and a special *haka* for Te Hono was composed. In October 2010, at a grand event at the canal in front of the Volkenkunde Museum in Leiden, the Maori crew handed over the *waka* to a crew recruited from the Royal Student Rowing Club Njord. They had been intensively trained by their Maori fellow crew in both sailing the *waka* and in all ceremonials that come with it, especially the *haka*.

Ever since, Te Hono Ki Aotearoa has been cruising through Leiden waters with its Njord crew under the leadership of Kaihautu Koos Wabeke performing their *haka*. This has attracted a lot of attention and generated enthusiasm and support in the small Leiden community, and so the *waka* and the *haka* have become a unique part of Leiden's cultural landscape.

This is how the agents of Leiden's marching band K&G came to know about the *haka* and how they presumably formed their plan to incorporate a *haka* into their show. They turned to Njord for help, and thus came about the grand innovation in their prizewinning show. Visual documentation of this training programme all the way through to the prizewinning performance of K&G at the World Music Competition in Kerkrade is available on YouTube (see for example www.youtube.com/watch?v=zXMyJ7qnEGo).

'Make it happen'
Presenting archaeology in a future-focused city

Dieke Wesselingh

City of Rotterdam Archaeological
Service (BOOR), the Netherlands

In December 2014 the City of Rotterdam presented its new slogan: 'Make it happen'. The second largest city in the Netherlands wants to emphasize its pioneering character: 'this is the place where ideas unfold, where things take off, where it happens.' Rotterdam is not frequented by large numbers of tourists. Most foreign visitors aim for Amsterdam and Delft, and Dutch holidaymakers might just go to Blijdorp Zoo or take a boat trip to the Port of Rotterdam. This has changed over the past two years. Modern architecture has always been a unique selling point for the city, which was rebuilt in a modern style after the German Luftwaffe bombed its historical centre in 1940. Several new icons, including the central railway station, the Koolhaas building 'De Rotterdam' and recently, a giant covered market (*Markthal*), have put Rotterdam high on people's 'must-see' lists. Because of the continuous (re)development activities, the city has employed archaeologists from as early as 1960 (Carmiggelt and Wesselingh 2010). Beneath the modern surface, where hardly any historical references are visible, archaeological vestiges are well-preserved, often covered by many layers of soil. Over the years numerous excavations have yielded detailed evidence about the medieval town dating from AD 1270, but also finds from the Roman and prehistoric periods. The question addressed in this essay is how to present such heritage in a city that prefers to look ahead rather than back.

Finds in a 'food-walhalla'

The *Markthal* was built just south of the spot where a dam in the river Rotte marked the beginning of the medieval town. Its four-level underground car park would destroy any archaeological remains, so extensive excavations were carried out. The research resulted in two comprehensive site reports and a small book in which the findings were presented to a broader public. Willem Willems visited the project as Dean of the Faculty of Archaeology, albeit just to have his photo taken when signing an agreement between Leiden University and the City of Rotterdam Archaeological Service (BOOR). He valued the work and role of municipal archaeologists and acknowledged the benefits gained by closer cooperation between the two organisations.

Apart from being an architectural icon, the *Markthal* is primarily a commercial enterprise. Besides apartments and parking spaces the building houses a large number of food stalls, food-related shops and restaurants. Although the archaeological interests were taken into account from the start, a visual reference to the history of the location was included at a fairly late stage. The idea of the *Tijdtrap* ('Time Stairs'), as the exhibition is called, was immediately embraced by all participants, including the City of Rotterdam, property developer Provast and a large number of financial contributors. Going down the escalators to the parking garage, visitors descend through the ages, as archaeological finds are displayed on each level, corresponding to the depth at which they were recovered. Touch screens provide extra information on the exhibits, while video images give an impression of the area in medieval times.

An archaeological exhibition in an extremely modern building, in the heart of a city where a single medieval church is the only reminder of the past – does it work? Is this what the public wants, could this 'add to the use of archaeological heritage as a source of collective memory', to quote the Valletta Convention? Although it is early days yet – *Markthal* and *Tijdtrap* opened in late 2014, while improvements and adjustments are under construction – and so far no evaluation or public survey has been carried out, some remarks can be made.

Visitors do not come to Rotterdam to admire heritage. Even its inhabitants generally have no idea of the medieval origins of the city, which were still clearly visible before World War II. People encountering the *Tijdtrap* probably do so because they have parked their car and / or want to visit the *Markthal*. Within the market hall, the *Tijdtrap* is somewhat hidden, it is easy to miss it altogether (there have been several accounts of this happening). It is a traditional exhibition, with objects in showcases. Apart from the touch screens it lacks any interactive element.

Layered city

Even though the *Tijdtrap* seems to be somewhat out of place as a conservative presentation in starkly modern surroundings, this is actually also a strong point. The fact that the objects were uncovered right there (illustrated by large photographs of smiling archaeologists showing the finds in their grubby hands) makes them a lot more interesting. The notion of a 'layered' city (archaeology deep down beneath the destroyed and rebuilt town) and the contrast between present-day Rotterdam and its medieval predecessor add to a sense of wonder. Although the *Tijdtrap* is freely accessible (it is open seven days a week and free of charge), Rotterdam archaeologists and architectural guides have given numerous tours these past months. Surprise at the depth of the finds is one of the most common reactions heard from visitors, especially from children. Archaeology may be a pleasant surprise, but it should not be hidden; therefore finding the location is an aspect of the *Tijdtrap* that is being improved as a matter of priority.

The district immediately surrounding the *Markthal* (Laurenskwartier) looks modern, but actually is the oldest part of town. Quite a lot of archaeological heritage is still preserved *in situ*, including the remnants of sluices that were part of the early river dam. Blaak railway station has displayed a large fragment of the medieval city wall since it was excavated in the 1990s, but it goes unnoticed by most travellers (Libert 2010). As the outdoor area is being redesigned in the next few years, there are plans to highlight these hidden treasures in different ways and to interconnect them by means of routes, apps and activities. Opening in January

2016, another architectural icon, the *Timmerhuis*, will house (historical) Museum Rotterdam as well as several exhibits of archaeological finds from the location.

In this way the *Tijdtrap* will become part of a larger story and of a broader repertoire of outreach activities and products, some of which already exist. These include ways of engaging the public that proved popular in a survey carried out in The Hague (Van den Dries and Van der Linde 2012: 13), such as local newspaper articles, radio and TV broadcasts and information panels. As for the conclusion

> 'Catering to the interests of different stakeholders means gaining support from parties outside the archaeologists' usual realm.'

from surveys that books might not always be what the public wants (idem: 13); in our case the reasonably priced popular book on archaeology is the best-selling product in the *Markthal* merchandise shop.

Future activities, such as workshops on medieval cuisine and preparing 3D prints of archaeological finds, will be organised in collaboration with local museums and the city archive, as well as with shopkeepers and restaurant owners based in the *Markthal*. Whether this mix of activities will enhance public engagement with Rotterdam's archaeological heritage will have to be evaluated in a few years' time.

Everybody happy

Besides public appreciation, there is another important success factor. The *Tijdtrap* is of interest to various stakeholders. The architect welcomed the addition to his creation and wanted the design of the *Tijdtrap* to match that of the building. The project developer uses it to promote the sale of apartments and to enhance the sustainability factor, one of the aspects that have won the building several international awards already. The investor asked us to show archaeological objects connected to food, drink and cooking, to emphasize the market function and to attract stallholders and customers. The city marketeers are happy with an extra attraction that fits with the image they chose for the Laurenskwartier.

Catering to different interests means gaining support from parties outside the archaeologists' usual realm of academic interest. Which in turn may help to enlarge public (and political) support, as the various stakeholders can act as ambassadors. Heritage will never be a primary tourist attraction in Rotterdam, but for a future-focused city, the *Tijdtrap* and related activities can add a surprising and worthwhile extra dimension and may well endorse the city's heritage policy.

In the meantime, plans are well under way for a National Archaeology Day in the Netherlands, an event that has rapidly found broad support among Dutch archaeologists. In Rotterdam activities will most probably concentrate around the *Tijdtrap*. Although Willem Willems highly appreciated local archaeology and public outreach, his focus was mostly on wider horizons and broader policy issues. But he would not have missed an event such as a National Archaeology Day, if his travel schedule allowed for it. I am sure we could have lured him to the *Markthal*, where archaeology, food and drink are proving a splendid combination.

References

Carmiggelt, A. and D. Wesselingh. 2010. 'Gemeentelijke archeologie in Rotterdam: het belang van kennis', *Vitruvius* 13: 22-27.

Libert, M. 2010. 'Public survey on archaeological public exhibits in the underground tunnels of Rotterdam and The Hague, Netherlands', in A. Degenhardt and S. Lampe (eds), *Out in the field – Internships Master students Archaeological Heritage Management 2009-2010.* Leiden: Sidestone Press (Graduate School of Archaeology Occasional Papers 5), 35-38.

Van den Dries, M.H. and S.J. van der Linde. 2012. 'Twenty years after Malta: archaeological heritage as a source of collective memory and scientific study anno 2012', in C.C. Bakels and H. Kamermans (eds), *Analecta Praehistorica Leidensia* 43/44, 9-19.

Crossing borders along the Dutch *limes*

How the famous Roman barges of Zwammerdam support people with multiple disabilities

Tom Hazenberg

1Arch / Hazenberg Archeologie, The Netherlands

Some readers may remember the picture of the Dutch queen Juliana visiting the excavation of Roman barge no.4 in Zwammerdam (South Holland) in 1974. In it the queen is listening attentively to the archaeologists' explanation of the oak planks of the shipwreck. The Zwammerdam 4 was part of the spectacular discovery of the limes fort *Nigrum Pullum* and six Roman shipwrecks: three barges and three canoes (De Weerd 1988). The ships were found on the estate Hooge Burch, now owned by Ipse de Bruggen, an institute for people with multiple disabilities. The site gave its name to this type of Gallo-Roman ship: the 'Zwammerdam type'. Since then, dozens of ships of this kind have been excavated in the Dutch *limes* area and throughout Europe. After forty years, the discovery of the Roman barges has led to the realisation of a first-class *limes* visitor centre, partly run by people with mental and physical disabilities. What has happened during these decades and how does the ship find of Zwammerdam support disabled people?

The discovery that makes it happen

The Zwammerdam fort is one of the sites along the Lower German *limes* on the south bank of the Rhine in the west of the Netherlands. It is known from the Tabula Peutingeriana as Nigrum Pullum. The *castellum* was founded in AD 47 and existed until the 70s of the third century. During its final stage, from AD 175 onwards, it was rebuilt in stone with a relatively large *principia*. Quite rare in the Dutch *limes* area is the discovery of foundations probably belonging to a bath-house. Outside the fort a *vicus* stretched out along some hundreds of metres of the *limes* road. The front of the fort lies just twenty metres from the bank of the Roman Rhine, which was transformed into a harbour here. In this area the shipwrecks were discovered. They were already wrecks at the time of deposition: they were sunk intentionally to strengthen the quay. Because of the high groundwater level in the area, the wood of the ships was in good condition at the time of excavation. For the first time, archaeologists were able to excavate, document and preserve some complete specimens of this type of Gallo-Roman barge. Especially the discovery of the barges (nos. 2, 4 and 6, measuring from c.20 to 34 m) drew wide attention. Ship no. 4 dates from AD 94. Ships nos. 2 and 6 date from AD 160-210 and were probably were probably used to transport building materials for the stone-built *castellum*.

Wider significance of the Zwammerdam ships

'Zwammerdam' was the starting point of a rich Dutch tradition of research on ship construction, inland navigation, transport and trade. In the following years comparable barges were excavated in Kapel-Avezaath, Druten (both in Gelderland) and nearby in Woerden (province of Utrecht). Four decades later, the *limes* area from Zwammerdam to Utrecht-Leidsche Rijn has yielded some twenty shipwrecks. This collection of ships, consisting of wood, nails, caulking remnants, small finds and their context, provides an outstanding set of data for research. Moreover, the ships represent the typical character of the Lower German *limes* as a river frontier, built in wetland, serving as a main transport route connecting the Germanic and Gallic hinterland with the North Sea basin. For this reason the ships play a principal role in the nomination of the Lower German *limes* as a UNESCO World Heritage Site (Willems *et al.* 2014: 15).

Public attention and tourism along the limes

The ship finds not only drew the attention of researchers from all over the world, but turned out to be real crowd-pullers as well. During the excavation the roads to Zwammerdam were too small for the crowd that followed in Queen Juliana's wake, whereas the more recent discoveries of the Roman shipwrecks De Meern 1 and Woerden 7, both in 2003, attracted 25,000 and 15,000 visitors respectively. There is sufficient evidence that the barges will play a prominent role in the tourist-oriented development of the Lower German *limes* connected to the UNESCO nomination programme.

The return of the Zwammerdam ships fits into the development of the old Roman border for the public. This development is quite a challenge, because the Roman remains are below ground and invisible. To expose the border, they are being rebuilt. From Katwijk to Nijmegen, small- and large-scale projects are under way. In Leiden, Utrecht-Leidsche Rijn, Bunnik-Vechten (Utrecht) and Arnhem-Meinerswijk (Gelderland) real-size forts are being reconstructed. In Woerden the public can sail on a Roman barge, while at Alphen aan den Rijn (South Holland) the archaeological park Archeon takes visitors back to Roman times. The final goal is the realisation of a 'string of pearls' along the *limes* that people can enjoy in their own region, but that also forms a line along which one can walk, cycle or sail.

Ipse de Bruggen's ambitions

Ipse de Bruggen, the organisation that owns the estate Hooge Burch, offers special care to the disabled. It supports clients in leading their own lives and participating in society. During the 1970s the estate was structured to guarantee the clients' peace and quiet. This resulted in an underground transport system to limit visible and audible traffic. Due to new medical insights and growing individualism, ideas have now changed regarding the relationship between clients and the rest of society. Cuts in health care also influence local changes and the treatments available. This development made Ipse de Bruggen decide to realise more interaction between clients and visitors on the Hooge Burch, while aiming at a more open connection to the village of Zwammerdam.

The organisation also wants to concentrate a large number of facilities that are currently scattered over the grounds in the estate's Community Centre, such as shops and canteens. The Community Centre already has many functions: daytime activities, recreation, open-air café, rehearsal space for the famous Josti Band, but also religious services and funerals.

The ambitions of both the *limes* network and Ipse de Bruggen resulted in a joint venture on the Hooge Burch, with the objective of establishing a first-class visitors' centre combining an exhibition with a Roman trail on the Roman part of the estate. In 2013 a feasibility study was carried out to bring the original ship finds

> 'The discovery of Roman barges has led to the realisation of a first-class visitors' centre that is partly run by people with mental and physical disabilities.'

back to the region of discovery, in which students in heritage management from the Faculty of Archaeology (Leiden University) also participated (Hazenberg *et al.* 2012; Boom and Nogarede 2013). In the summer of 2014 the Ipse de Bruggen board decided to reinforce the Community Centre's facilities and to strengthen the estate by investing in its Roman history. The Province of South Holland, which had already invested in the feasibility study, offered a grant for the realisation of the Roman ambitions on the estate, allowing Ipse de Bruggen to bring together a building team in which the Roman aspect is well represented.

Fleshing out the plans

On the estate visitors will see, hear and read that the world-famous Zwammerdam ships were discovered on this site and that research on Roman barges was born here. The discovery is presented in the context of the *castellum* and the other archaeological finds on the estate. This gives the site its own position on the Lower German *limes*: if you want to know about the Zwammerdam ships, the Hooge Burch is the place to go. The presentation also deals with other subjects, *e.g.* the military border system and life on the *limes*. Visitors who wish to learn more about these subjects are referred to other presentations along the former border, such as the above-mentioned Archeon or Park Matilo and the Dutch National Museum of Antiquities (RMO), both in Leiden. This anticipates the creation of the planned Interpretative Framework for the Lower German *limes* as it exists for Hadrian's Wall (Adkins and Mills 2011).

The means to tell the Roman story and entertain visitors have been concentrated in a Roman trail over the estate. Visitors following the trail will learn about the way the landscape was structured in Roman times: the course of the Rhine as it was then, the quay with the ships, the *castellum*, the baths and the neighbouring trade settlement. The information is provided not only on static panels, but also in an augmented-reality presentation for mobile devices. The current visualisation of the *principia* – one of the oldest in the Netherlands – will be upgraded on the site of discovery and extended with a visualisation of the gates and walls of the stone construction phase. In the Grand Café in the middle of the Roman trail, an extensive Roman exhibition tells the story of the fort and the ships on three levels: for clients of Ipse de Bruggen, for other users of the building and for *limes* tourists. The Zwammerdam 6 takes pride of place in the exhibition, with real-size images at the entrance and in the central space. The high-quality collection of archaeological finds from the estate is another mainstay of the exhibition. Spectacular objects include the bronze purses and bronze shield knob on which two successive owners, both serving in the Roman cavalry, wrote their names.

The arrival of *limes* tourists, recreational cyclists and groups of school children will guarantee a good turnover of the products (*limes*-related and otherwise) that clients of Ipse de Bruggen make during daytime activities. It will also mean more jobs for these clients and inhabitants: waiting on people at the Grand Café, assisting in the shop, maintaining the Roman trail, adapting the mobile parts of the exhibition to the planned activity, and providing support at larger events. Tourist-oriented development of the *limes* has also occasioned the development of a Roman teaching module specially for clients, a Roman theatre, extended opening hours for the Grand Café and a more attractive decoration of the Community Centre, making the estate more appealing. Above all, the integration of the estate Hooge Burch into the tourist highway of the Roman *limes* reinforces the open character of the health-care institute and stimulates interaction between its clients and inhabitants and the general public in a natural way, in a cultural and economic environment.

All interests united

Over forty years of trying to bring back the Zwammerdam ships to the place of discovery, many small steps have been taken and many disillusions experienced. The present cooperation however will finally achieve the greatest success possible. Different parties have succeeded in uniting their interests in a joint venture. On the Hooge Burch, Roman history now makes a positive contribution to the daily life of clients, inhabitants and employees. In this way, the famous Roman barges of Zwammerdam support people with multiple disabilities and their caregivers.

The Roman development of the Hooge Burch in Zwammerdam perfectly fits UNESCO's World Heritage 'values which seek to share heritage and experience of people around the world to foster understanding, respect, tolerance, co-operation and peace' (Adkins and Mills 2011: 2). A goal that was the motto of my professor (Leiden University), director (State Service for Cultural Heritage) and colleague Willem Willems for the major part of his career. An example that I am proud to follow.

References

Adkins, G. and N. Mills. 2011. *Frontiers of the Roman World Heritage Site – Hadrian's Wall Interpretive Framework – Overview and Summary*. Hexham: Hadrian's Wall Heritage Ltd.

Boom, K. and S. Nogarede. 2013. 'The return of the Zwammerdam ships', in K. Boom, C. Hageraats and C. Slappendel (eds), *Out in the field – Internships Master Students Archaeological Heritage Management 2012-2013*. Leiden: Sidestone Press (Graduate School of Archaeology Occasional Papers 13), 9-11.

Hazenberg, T., A.A. Zandbergen, S.-J. Nogarede and K. Boom. 2014. 'De terugkeer van de Zwammerdam-schepen. Een haalbaarheidsonderzoek', *Hazenberg AMZ-publicaties 2014-1*, Leiden.

Weerd, M.D. de. 1988. *Schepen voor Zwammerdam*. Amsterdam: University of Amsterdam (dissertation).

Willems, W.J.H., E. Graafstal and C. van Driel-Murray. 2014. *Draft Statement OUV & Comparative Analysis World Heritage Nomination Lower German Limes* (version July 15th 2014). Leiden: Leiden University (unpublished report).

Bibliography W.J.H. Willems

Edited volumes

2001-2015

2015 (with H.P.J. van Schaik)(eds) Water & Heritage. Material, conceptual and spiritual connections. Leiden.

2010 (with J. Bazelmans & C. Bakker) Conference Handbook 16th Annual Meeting of the EAA The Hague, Leiden/Den Haag.

2010 (with J. Bazelmans, C. Bakker & M. Verrijth) Conference Abstracts Book.16th EAA Annual Meeting of the EAA The Hague, Leiden/Den Haag.

2009 (with H. van Enckevort) Vlpia Noviomagvs – Roman Nijmegen. The Batavian capital at the imperial frontier, Portsmouth Rhode Island (Journal of Roman Archaeology Supplement 73).

2007 (with M.H. van den Dries)(eds) Quality Management in Archaeology, Oxford.

2005 (with M.H. van den Dries)(eds) Innovatie in de Nederlandse Archeologie, Gouda.

2005 (with H. Van Enckevort, J. Thijssen & J.K. Haalebos)(eds) Nijmegen. Geschiedenis van de oudste stad van Nederland. Prehistorie en Oudheid, Wormer.

2004 (with R.W. Brandt), Dutch Archaeology Quality Standard, Den Haag.

2000 Challenges for European Archaeology, Zoetermeer.

1990-2000

1999 The future of European Archaeology, Oxford (Archaeology in Britain Conference 1997), Oxbow Lecture 3.

1997 (with W. Groenman-van Waateringe, B.L. van Beek & S.L. Wynia)(eds) Roman Frontier Studies 1995. Proceedings of the XVIth International Congress of Roman Frontier Studies, Oxford.

1997 (with H. Kars & D.P. Hallewas)(eds) Archaeological Heritage Management in the Netherlands, Amersfoort/Assen.

1997 (with H. Koschik) Der Westwall. Vom Denkmalwert des Unerfreulichen, Köln/Bonn (Führer zu archäologischen Denkmälern des Rheinlandes, Bd 2).

1995 (with T. Bechert) Die römische Reichsgrenze zwischen Mosel und Nordseeküste, Stuttgart.

1995 (with T. Bechert) De Romeinse rijksgrens tussen Moezel en Noordzeekust, Utrecht.

1995 (with S.T. Mols, A.M. Gerhartl-Witteveen, H. Kars, A. Koster, W.J.Th. Peters) Acta of the 12th international congress on Roman bronzes, Nijmegen 1992, Amersfoort (Nederlandse Archeologische Rapporten 18).

1991 Oorzaak en gevolg van een opgraving, inaugurele rede, Leiden University.

1991 (with G. Bauchhenß & M. Otte)(eds) Spurensicherung. Archäologische Denkmalpflege in der Euregio Maas-Rhein, Mainz (Kunst und Altertum am Rhein 136).

1990 Romeins Nijmegen. Vier eeuwen stad en centrum aan de Waal, Utrecht.

1980-1989

1988 (with J.W. van Lieshout)(eds) 40 Jaar Tafelronde 8 Amersfoort, Amersfoort.

1986 Romans and Batavians. A Regional Study in the Dutch Eastern River Area, diss. Amsterdam.

1979-1970

1977 (with R.W. Brandt): Het project Wijster, Amsterdam (IPP Working Paper 3).

Articles and book chapters

2010-2015

2015 (with E. Graafstal and T. Leene) A pearl necklace: the Lower German Limes World Heritage nomination, Analecta Praehistorica Leidensia 45, 191-208.

2015 (with H.P.J. van Schaik and M. van der Valk) Water and Heritage: conventions and connections, in: W.J.H. Willems and H.P.J. van Schaik (eds), Water & Heritage. Material, conceptual and spiritual connections, Leiden, 19-35.

2014a Malta and its consequences: a mixed blessing, in: V.M. van der Haas & P.A.C. Schut (eds), The Valletta Convention: Twenty Years After. Benefits, Problems, Challenges (EAC Occasional Paper No. 9), Brussels, 151-156.

2014b 世界遺産とともに生きる― ヨーロッパの事例 (Living with a world heritage site – European examples), in: Report on the International Expert Meeting for the Promotion of Mozu-Furuichi Kofungun for World Cultural Heritage Inscription, Osaka, 28-37.

2014c Cleere, Henry, in: C. Smith (ed), Encyclopedia of Global Archaeology, 1502-1503.

2014d (with D.C. Comer) International Committee on Archaeological Heritage Management (ICAHM) (Conservation and Preservation), in: C. Smith (ed), Encyclopedia of Global Archaeology, 3942-3944.

2014e UNESCO (1972) and Malta (1992) Conventions, in: C. Smith (ed), Encyclopedia of Global Archaeology, 7433-7434.

2014f Heritage and social conflict: a symbiotic pair, in: Korea Cultural Properties Investigation and Research Institute Association, Archaeological heritage and the public. Public awareness and conflict management (Conference proceedings 2014), 39-58/59-77.

2014g The Future of World Heritage and the Emergence of Transnational Heritage Regimes. Heritage & Society, Vol. 7 No. 2, 105-120.

2014h (with R. Hodges, D. Miles and A. Olivier) Roşia Montană, România, A Review of the Archaeological Project.

2013a On the Organization of European Archaeology, in: S. Bergerbrant & Serena Sabatini (eds), Counterpoint: Essays in Archaeology and Heritage Studies in Honour of Professor Kristian Kristiansen, Oxford, 17-20 (BAR S2508), 17-20.

2013b Kategorizacija in vrednotenje arheoloških najdišč (Evaluation of archaeological sites and system(s) of protecting and managing archaeological heritage, in B. Djurić (ed), Vrednotenje arheoloških najdišč ter sistem(i) varovanja in upravljanja arheološke dediščine, (Acts of the conference Lubljana 2013), ARHEO 30-2, 2013, 7-12.

2012a (with D.C. Comer) Tourism and Archaeological Heritage. Driver to development or Destruction? In C. Gottfried & S. Hidalgo Sánchez (eds), Heritage, a driver of development. Proceedings of the 17th ICOMOS General Assembly Symposium. Paris, 499-511.

2012b 欧洲考古遗产管理的机制 (The Organization of Archaeological Heritage Management in Europe), Dual Celebrations for the inauguration of the Institute for Cultural Heritage and the 40th Anniversary of the Archaeology Department SDU, Jinan, 34-38.

2012c Problems with preservation in situ, Analecta Praehistorica Leidensia 43/44, 1-8.

2012d Foreword, in: S.J. van der Linde, M.H. van den Dries, N. Schlanger & C.G. Slappendel (eds), European Archaeology Abroad. Global Settings, Comparative Perspectives. Leiden.

2012e World Heritage and Global Heritage: the tip of the Iceberg, in: A. Castillo (ed), Proceedings of the First International Conference on Best Practices in World Heritage: Archaeology, Madrid, 36-50.

2011a (with M. Dolmans, P. Van der Heijden, F. Hermans and G. Jansen) Venlo Vennelo Sablones. Twintig eeuwen wonen aan de Maas, Venlo.

2011b (with B. Gunchinsuren, Ch. Amartuvshin, S. Chuluun, J. Gerelbadrakh, K. Tsogtbaatar, J. H. Altschul, J. A. Homburg, J. W. Olsen & G. Wait) The Oyu Tolgoi Cultural Heritage Program, Ulaanbaatar.

2011c (with D.C. Comer) Africa, Archaeology and World Heritage, Conservation and Management of Archaeological Sites 13.2-3, 160-173.

2011d Van de ivoren toren naar de markt: en toen?, Archeobrief 15.4, 28-33.

2010a Laws, Language, and Learning. Managing Archaeological Heritage Resources in Europe, in: P.M. Messenger & G.S. Smith (eds), Cultural Heritage Management. A Global Perspective, Gainesville Florida, 212-229.

2010b   Introduction to 'Protecting and Developing the Dutch Archaeological-Historical Landscape' (PDL/BBO), in: J.H.F. Bloemers, H. Kars, A van der Valk & M. Wijnen (eds), The Cultural Landscape & Heritage Paradox, Amsterdam, 19-10.

2010c   Archeologie en het heden, in: R. Hermans e.a. (eds), Neerlands hoop. Erfgoed en politiek, Amsterdam, 46-53.

2000-2009

2009a   Prólogo, in: V.I. Ruíz Ortíz & M.E.R.G.N. Jansen (eds), El Lienzo de Otla. Memoria de un Paisaje Sagrado, Oaxaca 2009, 7.

2009b   European and world archaeologies, World Archaeology 41.4, 649-658.

2009c   EAA 16th Annual Meeting, The Hague (the Netherlands), 1–5 September 2010, The European Archaeologist 32, 41-42.

2009d   Archaeological resource management and academic archaeology in Europe: some observations, in A.L. D'Agata & S. Alaura (eds), Quale futuro per l'archeologia?, Roma, 89-99.

2008a   Sur la genèse de la convention de Malte, Archéopages, hors série, février (Festschrift J.-P. Demoule), 135-139.

2008b   Language and Archaeology, Archaeologies 4.1, 179-181.

2008c   (with M.H. van den Dries) Uncovering quality gold, Quality World, June 2008, 40-43.

2008d   Archaeological resource management and preservation, in: H. Kars & R.M. van Heeringen (eds), Preserving archaeological remains in situ. Proceedings of the 3rd conference 7-9 December 2006, Amsterdam, Amsterdam 2008, 283-289 (Geoarchaeological and Bioarchaeological Studies, 10).

2007a   (with M.H. van den Dries) The origins and development of quality assurance in archaeology, in: W.J.H. Willems & M.H. van den Dries (eds), Quality Management in Archaeology, Oxford, 1-12.

2007b   (with M.H. van den Dries) Quality assurance in archaeology, the Dutch perspective, in: W.J.H. Willems & M.H. van den Dries (eds), Quality Management in Archaeology, Oxford, 50-65.

2007c   The times they are a-changin': observations on archaeology in a European context, in: G. Cooney (ed), Archaeology in Ireland: a vision for the future, Dublin, 5-23.

2007d   Met Malta meer mans? Een persoonlijke terugblik, in: R. Jansen & L.P. Louwe Kooijmans (eds), Van contract tot wetenschap. Tien jaar archeologisch onderzoek door Archol BV, 1997-2007, Leiden, 45-58.

2007e   A new study of the Batavians, Journal of Roman Studies 20, 554-556.

2007f   The work of making Malta: the Council of Europe's archaeology and planning committee 1988-1996, European Journal of Archaeology 10.1, 57-71.

2007g   Review of: M. Pomeroy-Kellinger and I. Scott (eds), Recent Developments in Research and Management at World Heritage Sites, European Journal of Archaeology 10.1, 106-107.

2006a   RPA abroad, SAA Archaeological Record 6 (3), 6-8.

2006b   (with J. Altschul) The Register of Professional Archaeologists' Standards Are Voluntary, Anthropology News 47 (5), 24-25.

2006c   文化遺産の世界 (The current situation of Archaeological Heritage Management in the Netherlands), The World of Cultural Heritage 22, 12-15.

2006d   Review of John Hunter and Ian Ralston (eds), Archaeological Resource management in the UK. An Introduction. Second edition, European Journal of Archaeology 9(2/3), 294-298.

2005a   (with H. Hassman) Workshop 4: "Kernaufgaben der Archäologischen Denkmalpflege in Deutschland – Wo liegen unsere Stärken?", Archäologisches Nachrichtenblatt 10 (2), 134-138.

2005b   Romeinen aan de wieg van Nijmegen, in: Romeinen terug in Nijmegen, bijlage bij De Gelderlander vrijdag 24 juni 2005, p. 4-5.

2005c   (with M.H. van den Dries) Innovatie: waar rook is, is Brandt, in: M.H. van den Dries & W.J.H. Willems (eds), Innovatie in de Nederlandse Archeologie, Gouda, 5-6.

2005d   Contract Archaeology and Quality Management in the Netherlands, in: M.H. van den Dries & W.J.H. Willems (eds), Innovatie in de Nederlandse Archeologie, Gouda, 153-161.

2004a   How the EAA came into my life, The European Archaeologist 10th Anniversary Conference Issue, 7-9.

2004b   Book marks guest editorial – Current issues in archaeological heritage management, European Journal of Archaeology 7(3), 315-318.

2003a   Archaeology in Europe: Alles wird besser, aber nichts wird gut, The European Archaeologist 19, 19-20.

2003b   Draft European Charter on General Principles for Protection of the Environment and Sustainable Development, The European Archaeologist 19, 12-13.

2003c   The European Association of Archaeologists, Naturopa 99 [English version], 26-27.

2003d   L'Association européenne des archéologues, Naturopa 99 [French version], 26-27.

2002a   RIA van start, Archeobrief 21, 19-20.

2002b   The role of archaeological societies in preserving cultural memorials, in: Encyclopedia of Life Support Systems, Oxford.

2002c   Het archeologisch bestel in kaart, Archeobrief 22, 10-16.

2002d   Archäologische Vereine in den Niederlanden, Archäologische Informationen 25, 61-67.

2001a   Some thoughts on public archaeology from a European perspective, in: J. Moore (ed), Institute of Field Archaeologists Yearbook and Directory of Members 2001, Reading, 19-20.

2001b   Archeologie en internationale samenwerking, Archeobrief 18, 3-5.

2001c Naaste buren en verre familie: de archeologische professie in Europa, in: B. Goudswaard e.a. (eds), Een beroepsregister in een open bestel, Amsterdam, 19-27.

2001d Het verleden zit in de grond: cultureel erfgoed en archeologie, in: I. Strouken & A. van der Zeijden (eds) Het verhaal achter het erfgoed, Utrecht, 37-44.

2001e Gestione dei beni archeologici in Europa: recenti sviluppi, Studi di Antichità 10, 339-348 (Università di Lecce, Dipartimento di beni culturali).

2001f Současný vývoj archeologické památkové péče v Nizozemí a v Evropě, Archeologické rozhledy 53, 564-575.

2001g In de liefhebberij liggen de wortels van de archeologie, Westerheem 50-6, 240-249.

2001h Archaeological heritage management and research, in: Z. Kobyliński (ed), Quo vadis archaeologiae. Whither European archaeology in the 21st century, Warsaw, 83-91.

2001i De archeoloog en het kwaliteitssysteem voor archeologische werkzaamheden, in: E. Jacobs (ed) Derde Nationale Congres Nederlandse Vereniging van Archeologen, Amsterdam 2001, 25-34.

2000a (with F. Lüth en A. Olivier) Europas Landesarchäologen rücken zusammen, Archäologie in Deutschland 2/00, 4-5.

2000b Sparta aan de Noordzee. Cultuurhistorisch erfgoed en ruimtelijke ordening, in: Y. Ezendam, Het verleden van de toekomst, Utrecht, 7-11.

2000d The Europae Archaeologiae Consilium, in: W.J.H. Willems (ed), Challenges for European Archaeology, Zoetermeer, 13-18.

2000e (with F. Lüth, A. Olivier & K. Wollák) A Strategic Plan for the EAC, in: W.J.H. Willems (ed), Challenges for European Archaeology, Zoetermeer, 19-26.

2000f Archaeology and Europe: 'reflexiveness' and action, Archaeological Dialogues 7.1, 37-40.

2000g The Management of the Archaeological Heritage in the Netherlands, in: Z. Kobyliński (ed), Archaeological heritage management, Warsaw, 153-168 Archaeologia Polona, 38).

2000h Le système de contrôle de qualité de l'archéologie aux Pays-Bas, Les Nouvelles de l'Archéologie 82, 35-41.

1990-1999

1999a (with J. Deeben, B.J. Groenewoudt & D.P. Hallewas) Proposals for a Practical System of Significance Evaluation in Archaeological Heritage Management, European Journal of Archaeology 2.2, 177-199.

1999b (with J.K. Haalebos) Recent research on the limes in the Netherlands, Journal of Roman Archaeology 12, 247-262.

1999c The EAA Long-Term Plan, in The European Archaeologist 11, 1-5.

1999d (ed) Nieuwe ontwikkelingen in de Archeologische Monumentenzorg (Nederlandse Archeologische Rapporten, 20), Amersfoort.

1999e De koers van de archeologische monumentenzorg: nieuwe ontwikkelingen in vogelvlucht, in: W.J.H. Willems, Nieuwe ontwikkelingen in de Archeologische Monumentenzorg, (Nederlandse Archeologische Rapporten, 20), Amersfoort, 9-17.

1999f (with J.K. Haalebos) Der Niedergermanische Limes in den Niederlanden, 1995-1997, in: N. Gudea (ed), Roman Frontier Studies. Proceedings of the 17th International Congress of Roman Frontier Studies, Zalau, 77-87.

1998a Europese ROB's werken samen, Archeologische Monumentenzorg 1, 1998, 9-11.

1998b EAA in Göteborg, Archäologie in Deutschland 2/98, 71.

1998c Ter inleiding, Jaarverslag van de Rijksdienst voor het Oudheidkundig Bodemonderzoek 1995-96, 5-6.

1998d Von Bodendenkmalpflege zum Management des archäologischen Erbes: Entwicklungen in Europa und in den Niederlanden, Archäologisches Nachrichtenblatt 3, 172-80.

1998e European Association of Archaeologists. New Venue for Collaboration and Exchange, SAA Bulletin 16.3, 9.

1998f Brennpunkt: Archäologie im vereinten Europa, Archäologie in Deutschland 3/98, 4-5.

1998g The European Association of Archaeologists, SHA Newsletter 31.2, 9.

1998h Archaeology and heritage management in Europe: trends and developments, European Journal of Archaeology 1.3, 293-311.

1998i The Secretary's Report, Göteborg 1998, The European Archaeologist 10, 8-10.

1998j Holandia: zarzdzanie dziedzictwem archeologicznym, in: Z. Kobylinski (ed), Ochrona dziedzictwa archeologicznego w Europie, Warszawa, 206-218.

1997a 50 jaar ROB, Archeologische Monumentenzorg 1, 10-11.

1997b Een bijzondere Romeinse grafsteen, De Aanzegger 7, 17-19.

1997c (with S.G. van Dockum) Laag voor laag; de kracht van complementair bestuur in de archeologische monumentenzorg, in: R.J. Beuse et al. (eds): Besturen in het midden (Festschrift jhr. P.A.C. Beelaerts van Blokland), 's-Gravenhage, 156-177.

1997d (with T. Bechert) De Romeinse rijksgrens tussen Moezel en Noordzeekust, Utrecht (2e druk).

1997e (with H. v.d. Linden) Archeologie is een collectieve zorg, NRC/Handelsblad 29 oktober.

1997f (with H. v.d. Linden) Preface, Berichten ROB 42, 1996-1997, 5.

1997g (with H. v.d. Linden) Introduction, in: W.J.H. Willems, H. Kars & D.P. Hallewas (eds), Archaeological Heritage Management in the Netherlands, Amersfoort/Assen, 1-2.

1997h   Archaeological Heritage Management in the Netherlands: past, present and future, in: W.J.H. Willems, H. Kars & D.P. Hallewas (eds), Archaeological Heritage Management in the Netherlands, Amersfoort/Assen, 3-34.

1997i   (with J. Deeben, J.-N. Andrikopoulou-Strack, R. Gerlach & J. Obladen- Kauder) Cross-border Cooperation on Archaeological Heritage Management and Research: the Niers-Kendel Project, in: W.J.H. Willems, H. Kars & D.P. Hallewas (eds), Archaeological Heritage Management in the Netherlands, Amersfoort/Assen, 282-295.

1997j   (with H. Koschik) Vorwort, in: W.J.H. Willems & H. Koschik, Der Westwall. Vom Denkmalwert des Unerfreulichen, Köln/Bonn, 7-8.

1997k   The Secretary's Report, The European Archaeologist 8, 4-6.

1996a   (with H.L.H. van Enckevort) Roman cavalry helmets in ritual hoards from the Kops Plateau at Nijmegen, the Netherlands, Journal of Roman Military Equipment Studies 5 [1994], 125-137.

1996b   Woord vooraf, in: P.G. Bahn (ed), Vondsten van eeuwen. De beroemdste archeologische ontdekkingen ter wereld, Utrecht/Antwerpen, 8-9.

1996c   De rol van de archeologische monumentenwacht in relatie tot consolidatie en beheer, in: R.R. Datema (ed), Archeologische Monumentenwacht Nederland 1990-1995 Lustrum, Amersfoort, 11-19.

1996d   In Memoriam Jules Bogaers, Scarabee 25, 48.

1996e   In Memoriam Jules Bogaers, Bulletin du Centre Interdisciplinaire de Récherches Aeriennes 19, 75.

1996f   Der Umgang mit archäologischen Naßholzfunden in den Niederlanden, in: Landschaftsverband Rheinland, Niederschrift über die Sitzung des Kulturausschusses: Hearing Gefährdung des Bodendenkmals "Römischer Hafen", Xanten, Anlage 8.

1996g   Heeft het verleden nog een toekomst?, Natuur en Techniek 64 (12), 87-93.

1996h   Ter inleiding, Jaarverslag van de Rijksdienst voor het Oudheidkundig Bodemonderzoek 1995/6, 5-6.

1995a   Ter inleiding, Jaarverslag van de Rijksdienst voor het Oudheidkundig Bodemonderzoek 1994, 5-7.

1995b   Die Villa Rustica von Voerendaal (NL) und die ländliche Besiedlung, in S.K. Palágyi (ed), Forschungen und Ergebnisse. Internationale Tagung über römische Villen (Balácai Közlemények, 3), Veszprém, 116-123.

1995c   Welkom en presentatie, in: R.R. Knoop & C.A.C. Jansen (eds), Verantwoord vergeten. Selectie in de archeologische monumentenzorg, Leiden, 5-7 (Archeologisch Informatie Cahier 8).

1995d   Een Romeins legerkamp op het Kops Plateau te Nijmegen / Ein römisches Militärlager auf dem Kops Plateau in Nijmegen, in: L.J.F. Swinkels (ed), Een leven te paard. Ruiters uit de Lage Landen in het Romeinse leger / Reiten für Rom. Berittene Truppen an de römischen Rheingrenze, Nijmegen-Köln 28-31.

1995e   (with S.T. Mols, A.M. Gerhartl-Witteveen, H.Kars, A. Koster, W.J.Th. Peters) Acta of the 12th international congress on Roman bronzes, Nijmegen 1992, Amersfoort (Nederlandse Archeologische Rapporten, 18).

1995f   (with T. Bechert) Der Niedergermanische Limes - Geschichte und Gestalt einer Grenze, in: T. Bechert & W.J.H. Willems (Hrsg), Die römische Reichsgrenze zwischen Mosel und Nordseeküste, Stuttgart, 9-28.

1995g   (with T. Bechert & H.L.H. van Enckevort) Von der Lippe zur Waal, in: T. Bechert & W.J.H. Willems (Hrsg), Die römische Reichsgrenze zwischen Mosel und Nordseeküste, Stuttgart, 63-76.

1995h   (with T. Bechert) De limes van Germania Inferior. Geschiedenis en vorm van een grens, in: T. Bechert & W.J.H. Willems (eds), De Romeinse rijksgrens tussen Moezel en Noordzeekust, Utrecht, 9-28.

1995i   (with T. Bechert & H.L.H. van Enckevort) Van de Lippe tot de Waal, in: T. Bechert & W.J.H. Willems (eds), De Romeinse rijksgrens tussen Moezel en Noordzeekust, Utrecht, 63-76.

1994a   Ter inleiding, Jaarverslag van de Rijksdienst voor het Oudheidkundig Bodemonderzoek 1993, 7-11.

1994b   Roman face masks from the Kops Plateau, Nijmegen, The Netherlands, Journal of Roman Military Equipment Studies 3 [1992], 57-66.

1994c   (with P.A.M. Beliën) Een bijzondere lamp uit Nijmegen, Westerheem 43, 11-15.

1994d   De toekomst van het verleden. Archeologische monumentenzorg in Nederland, Spiegel Historiael 29, 316-321.

1994e   Rijksarcheologie en gemeentelijke archeologie: complementair of supplementair?, in: R. Knoop & C.A.C. Jansen (eds), De plaats van de gemeentelijke archeologie binnen het archeologische vakgebied, Leiden, 11-16 (Archeologisch Informatie Cahier, 7).

1994f   Archaeological Heritage Management in the Netherlands: Perspectives and Problems, in: H. Koschik (ed), Aspekte europäischer Bodendenkmalpflege, Köln, 9-16.

1993a   Ter inleiding, Jaarverslag van de Rijksdienst voor het Oudheidkundig Bodemonderzoek 1992, 7-10.

1993b   Recentie van E.J. van Ginkel & J.A. Waasdorp, De archeologie van Den Haag. Deel 2: de Romeinse tijd, Den Haag 1992, Westerheem 42, 88-90.

1993c   Quo Vadis? Archeologische monumentenzorg op de drempel van de 21e eeuw, in: R. Knoop (ed), Archeologie, maatschappij en ethiek, Leiden, 54-59 (Archeologisch Informatie Cahier 5).

1993d   Archäologische Denkmalpflege und Forschung in den Niederlanden, in: S. Dušek (Hrsg), Archäologische Denkmalpflege und Forschung, Weimar, 22-27.

1993e   De Tabula Peutingeriana, in: A.A.J.J. van Pinxteren e.a., Pronkstukken. Venlo 650 jaar stad, Venlo, 39-41.

1993f   Preface, in: R.M. van Dierendonck, D.P. Hallewas & K.E. Waugh, The Valkenburg Excavations 1985-1988, Amersfoort, 7-9.

1992a   Ter inleiding, Jaarverslag van de Rijksdienst voor het Oudheidkundig Bodemonderzoek 1991, 5-15.

1992b   (with G. Bauchhenß & M. Otte)(eds) Spurensicherung. Archäologische Denkmalpflege in der Euregio Maas-Rhein, Mainz (Kunst und Altertum am Rhein 136).

1992c   Archäologie in den Niederlanden und der Rijksdienst voor het Oudheidkundig Bodemonderzoek (ROB) = L'archéologie aux Pays-Bas et le Rijksdienst voor het Oudheidkundig Bodemonderzoek (ROB) = De Nederlandse archeologie en de Rijksdienst voor het Oudheidkundig Bodemonderzoek (ROB), in: G. Bauchhenß, M. Otte, W.J.H. Willems (Hrsg), Spurensicherung. Archäologische Denkmalpflege in der Euregio Maas-Rhein, Mainz, 295-315.

1992d   Die kaiserzeitliche Villa von Voerendaal = La villa romaine à Voerendaal = De Romeinse villa van Voerendaal, in: G. Bauchhenß, M. Otte, W.J.H. Willems (Hrsg), Spurensicherung. Archäologische Denkmalpflege in der Euregio Maas-Rhein, Mainz, 526-534.

1992e   Preface, Berichten van de Rijksdienst voor het Oudheidkundig Bodemonderzoek 40, 7-8.

1991a   Preview of R.W. Brandt a.o. (eds), Assendelver Polder Papers I, Amsterdam 1987 (Cingula 10), American Journal of Archaeology 95, 562.

1991b   Review of R. Aßkamp (ed), 2000 Jahre Römer in Westfalen, Mainz 1989, American Journal of Archaeology 95, 362.

1991c   Early Roman Camps on the Kops Plateau at Nijmegen (NL), in: V.A. Maxfield & M.J. Dobson (eds), Roman Frontier Studies 1989. Proceedings of the XVth International Congress of Roman Frontier Studies, Exeter, 210-214.

1991d   Recentie van L.R.P. Ozinga e.a. (eds), Het Romeinse castellum te Utrecht, Utrecht 1989, Bulletin Antieke Beschaving 66, 199- 200.

1991e   Ter inleiding, Jaarverslag van de Rijksdienst voor het Oudheidkundig Bodemonderzoek 1990, 5-8.

1991f   Een Romeins viziermasker van het Kops Plateau te Nijmegen, Jaarboek Numaga 1991, 9-18.

1990a   Met de detector het bos in, Westerheem 39, 272-274.

1990b   Down to earth: a note on bolt-heads and rake-prongs, Arma. Newsletter of the Roman Military Equipment Conference 2, 22-23.

1990c   Ter inleiding, Jaarverslag van de Rijksdienst voor het Oudheidkundig Bodemonderzoek 1989, 5-9.

1980-1989

1989a   An officer or a gentleman? A Late-Roman weapon-grave from a villa at Voerendaal (NL), in: C. van Driel-Murray (ed), Roman military Equipment: the Sources of Evidence, Oxford (BAR S 476), 143-156.

1989b   Romeinse tijd, in: A. Gerhartl-Witteveen, A. Koster & L. Swinkels, Schatkamer van Gelderse Oudheden, Nijmegen, 24-25.

1989c   Rome and its Frontier in the North: the Role of the Periphery, in: K. Randsborg (ed), The Birth of Europe. Archaeology and Social Development in the First Millennium A.D., Roma (Analecta Romana Instituti Danici, Suppl. XVI), 33-45.

1989d   Das Rhein-Maas-Delta als Grenzgebiet vom 3. bis zum 8. Jahrhundert, Siedlungsforschung. Archäologie-Geschichte-Geographie 7, 31-49.

1989e   Ter inleiding, Jaarverslag van de Rijksdienst voor het Oudheidkundig Bodemonderzoek 1988, 5-7.

1988a   Review of S. Wolfram, Zur Theoriediskussion in der prähistorischen Archäologie Großbritanniens, Oxford 1986, American Journal of Archaeology 92, 123.

1988b   Rezension von P.T. Bidwell, The Roman Fort of Vindolanda at Chesterholm, Northumberland, London 1985, Germania 66, 235-237.

1988c   The Dutch river area. Imperial policy and rural developments in a Late Roman frontier zone, in: R.F.J. Jones, J.H. F. Bloemers, S.L. Dyson & M. Biddle (eds), First Millennium Papers. Western Europe in the First Millennium AD, Oxford (BAR S401), 241-256.

1988d   In: W.A. van Es e.a. (eds), Archeologie in Nederland, Amsterdam/Amersfoort: Midden-Romeinse tijd (50-270 n.C.) 88-91, De Archeologische Kaart van Nederland, 101-108, Meinerswijk en Rijswijk: forten aan de Romeinse grens, 148-151, Nijmegen: de stad der Bataven, 151-154, Voerendaal: een Romeinse villa, 154-156.

1988e   (with W. Groenman-van Waateringe) Een rijk graf uit de Vroege IJzertijd te Horst-Hegelsom, in: P.A.M. Geurts, T.J. van ensch, J.M.W.C. Schatorjé & G.F. Verheijen (eds), Horster Historiën 2, Horst, 13-29.

1988f   Het Romeinse fort in de Loowaard, Driepas 5, 15-19.

1988g   (with L.I. Kooistra) De Romeinse villa te Voerendaal. Opgraving 1987, Archeologie in Limburg 37, 137-147.

1988h   Die große Villa rustica von Voerendaal (Niederlande), in: H. Hiller (ed), Villa rvstica. Römische Gutshöfe im Rhein-Maas Gebiet, Freiburg, 8-13.

1988i   (with R.M. van Dierendonck & L.J.F. Swinkels) Reiche Gutsherren in Maasbracht, in: H. Hiller (ed), Villa rvstica. Römische Gutshöfe im Rhein-Maas Gebiet, Freiburg, 28-33.

1988j   Review of: Archäologische und naturwissenschaftliche Untersuchungen an ländlichen und frühstädtischen Siedlungen im deutschen Küstengebiet vom 5. Jahrhundert v. Chr. bis zum 11. Jahrhundert n. Chr., Weinheim 1984 (DFG), American Journal of Archaeology 92, 600-601.

1988k   Heerlen: Romeins grafveld bij Vrank, in: H. Stoepker, Archeologische kroniek van Limburg over 1987, PSHAL 124, 371-373.

1988l   Voerendaal. Romeinse villa, in: H. Stoepker, Archeologische kroniek van Limburg over 1987, PSHAL 124, 404-417.

1987a   (with L.I. Kooistra) De Romeinse villa te Voerendaal. Opgraving 1986, Archeologie in Limburg 32, 29-38.

1987b   Romeinse wegen in Limburg, Historisch-Geografisch Tijdschrift 1/2, 6-11.

1987c De grote villa van Voerendaal, in: P. Stuart & M.E.T. de Grooth (eds), Langs de weg, Heerlen/Maastricht, 46-50.

1987d (with R.M. van Dierendonck & L.J.F. Swinkels) Rijke hereboeren uit Maasbracht, in: P. Stuart & M.E.T. de Grooth (eds), Langs de weg, Heerlen/Maastricht, 62-67.

1987e Zusammenfassung: Romans and Franks in the Dutch River Area, Die Kunde 38, 246.

1987f Voerendaal. Romeinse villa, in: H. Stoepker, Archeologische kroniek van Limburg over 1986, PSHAL 123, 223-235.

1986b (with E. Milikowski) De Romeinse villa van Voerendaal. Instructieopgraving voor amateur archeologen, Vondsten uit het verleden. Archeologisch Jaarboek 1986, Maastricht/Brussel, 44-45.

1986c De Romeinse villa te Voerendaal. Opgraving 1985, Archeologie in Limburg 28, 143-150.

1986d (with J. Jamar) De Romeinse bewustwording, Limburgs Dagblad, Heerlen 22 maart 1986.

1986e Review of T.F.C. Blagg and A.C. King (eds), Military and Civilian in Roman Britain. Cultural Relationships in a Frontier Province, Oxford 1984, American Journal of Archaeology 90, 500-501.

1986f Archeologische kroniek van Limburg over 1985, PSHAL 122, 203-246.

1986g New Discoveries along the Limes in the Dutch Eastern River Area, in: C. Unz (Hrsg), Studien zu den Militärgrenzen Roms, III, Stuttgart (Forschungen und Berichte zur Vor- und Frühgeschichte in Baden-Württemberg 20), 291-299.

1986h De Bataven. Archeologisch onderzoek in het rivierengebied, Hermeneus 58, 281-289.

1985a Een Angelsaksisch zwaard, Bonnefans 1, 22-23.

1985b (with M.E.T. de Grooth & W. Dijkman) Fabricage van aardewerk in de IJzertijd, Maastricht (Informatieblad Bonnefantenmuseum zomer 1985).

1985c Archeologische kroniek van Limburg over 1984, PSHAL 121, 146-196.

1985d (with J. Ypey) Ein angelsächsisches Schwert aus der Maas bei Wessem, Provinz Limburg (Niederlande), Archäologisches Korrespondenzblatt 15, 103-113.

1984a Archeologische kroniek van Limburg over 1983, PSHAL 120, 354-393.

1984b Römer und Bataver. Regionale Entwicklungen an der Grenze des Reiches, in: L. Pauli (Hrsg), Archäologie und Kulturgeschichte 2, Saerbeck, 69-84.

1984c Recentie van G. Bauchhenß (Hrsg), Aqvae Granni. Beiträge zur Archäologie von Aachen, Köln 1982, Babesch 59, 218-219.

1984d Romans and Batavians. A Regional Study in the Dutch Eastern River Area, II, Berichten van de Rijksdienst voor het Oudeidkundig Bodemonderzoek 34, 39-331.

1983a (with A, van Doorselaer & W.J.H. Verwers) Kroniek District D 1978-1980, Helinium 23, 57-73.

1983b Jaarverslag van de provinciaal archeoloog van Limburg over 1982, Archeologie in Limburg 17, 12-16.

1983c Jaarverslag van de provinciaal archeoloog over 1982, deel II, Archeologie in Limburg 18, 2-5.

1983d Archeologische kroniek van Limburg over de jaren 1980-1982, PSHAL 119, 197-291.

1983e Romans and Batavians: Regional Developments at the Imperial Frontier, in: R.W. Brandt & J.Slofstra (eds), Roman and Native in the Low Countries. Spheres of Interaction, Oxford (BAR S 184), 105-128.

1982a Belfeld, Bulletin KNOB 81, 73-74.

1982b Romeinse ijzerindustrie in Lomm, in: A.J. Geurts, Verwoord Verleden. Opstellen over het Noordlimburgse Maasdal en aangrenzend Duits gebied, Lomm (Festschrift J.G.M. Stoel) 111-115.

1982c Archeologisch Congres Limburg 1982: Openingswoord, Archeologie in Limburg 15, 2-4.

1982d Belangrijke recente vondsten in Limburg, Archeologie in Limburg 15, 14-17.

1982e Romeinse ijzerindustrie in Lomm, Archeologie in Limburg 15, 20-21.

1981a Vondsten uit Noord Limburg, Archeologie in Limburg 10, 3-4.

1981b Het oostelijk rivierengebied tussen 250 v. Chr en 750 n. Chr., in: INQUA commissie Nederland, Symposium 'Het Rivierengebied', Ede, 18.

1981c Twee maalstenen uit Heijen, Archeologie in Limburg 11, 16-17.

1981d Bronzen bijl uit Schimmert, Archeologie in Limburg 11, 20.

1981e Over een fossa, een castra en een tabula, Westerheem 30, 168-171.

1981f Venlo, Bulletin KNOB 80, 167.

1981g De Koning van het Jammerdal, Maria Auxiliatrix Post 11(3), 8-9.

1981h (with J.H.F. Bloemers) Archeologische Kroniek van Limburg over de jaren 1977-1979, PSHAL 116-7, 7-94.

1981i Romans and Batavians. A Regional Study in the Dutch Eastern River Area, I, Berichten van de Rijksdienst voor het Oudheidkundig Bodemonderzoek 31, 7-217.

1981j (with J.H.F. Bloemers) Jaarverslag van de provinciaal archeoloog van Limburg over het jaar 1980, Archeologie in Limburg 12, 2-5.

1981k Ter aanvulling... Project Oostelijk Rivierengebied: Landesaufnahme AWN afd. Nijmegen en omgeving, in: R. Borman (ed), Archeologie in de gemeente Duiven, Duiven.

1981l Het werk van de provinciaal archeoloog, Jaarboek van de Heemkundevereniging Maas- en Swalmdal 1, 21-23.

1980a Meinerswijk (gem. Arnhem), Bulletin KNOB 79, 30-32.

1980b Arnhem-Meinerswijk: een nieuw castellum aan de Rijn, Westerheem 29, 334-348.

1980c Malburgen, gem. Arnhem, Bulletin KNOB 79, 128-129.

1980d Arcen (gem. Arcen en Velden), Bulletin KNOB 79, 129-130.

1980e Hegelsom (gem. Horst), Bulletin KNOB 79, 130-132.

1980f Nederweert, Bulletin KNOB 79, 132.

1980g Castra Herculis, een Romeins castellum bij Arnhem, Spiegel Historiael 15, 665-671.

1980h Castra Herculis, De Nieuwe Krant Arnhem, 4 oktober 1980.

1980i (with J.H.F. Bloemers & R.S. Hulst) A Short Introduction to the Eastern River Area Project, Berichten van de Rijksdienst voor het Oudheidkundig Bodemonderzoek 30, 277-280.

1970-1979

1978 Burial Analysis: A New Approach to an Old Problem, Berichten van de Rijksdienst voor het Oudheidkundig Bodemonderzoek 28, 81- 98.

1977a (with R.W.Brandt) Het project Wijster, Amsterdam (IPP Working Paper, 3).

1977b Ongoing Research Projects: The Netherlands, Old World Archaeology Newsletter 1.2, 8-10.

1977c National Research Organisation: Netherlands, Old World Archaeology Newsletter, 1.2, 16-18.

1977d A Roman Kiln at Halder, gemeente St. Michielsgestel N.B., in: B.L. van Beek & W. Groenman van Waateringe (eds), Ex Horreo, Amsterdam (Cingula, 4), 114-129.

Contributors

Jeffrey Altschul
Nexus Heritage
United Kingdom
Statistical Research, Inc.
United States of America
jhaltschul@sricrm.com

David Barreiro
Institute of Heritage Sciences (INCIPIT),
Spanish National Research Council (CSIC)
Spain
david.barreiro@incipit.csic.es

Tom Bloemers
University of Amsterdam (Emeritus professor)
The Netherlands
j.h.f.bloemers@kpnmail.nl

Alicia Castillo
Department of Prehistory, Universidad Complutense de Madrid
Spain
alicia.castillo@ghis.ucm.es

Henry Cleere
Council for British Archaeology (1974-1991) / ICOMOS (1992-2002)
United Kingdom
henry.cleere@btinternet.com

Douglas Comer
ICAHM / Cultural Site Research and Management
United States of America
d.c.comer@gmail.com

Felipe Criado-Boado
Institute of Heritage Sciences (INCIPIT),
Spanish National Research Council (CSIC)
Spain
felipe.criado-boado@incipit.csic.es

Timothy Darvill
Department of Archaeology, Anthropology & Forensic Science, Bournemouth University
United Kingdom
tdarvill@bournemouth.ac.uk

Mariana de Campos Françozo
Faculty of Archaeology, Leiden University / ERC-synergy project NEXUS1492
The Netherlands
m.de.campos.francozo@arch.leidenuniv.nl

Jos Deeben
Cultural Heritage Agency
The Netherlands
† November 2015

Dick de Jager
Department of Urban Development, Municipality of Almere
The Netherlands
dhdjager@almere.nl

Leonard de Wit
Cultural Heritage Agency
The Netherlands
L.de.Wit@cultureelerfgoed.nl

Cynthia Dunning
Archaeoconcept
Switzerland
cynthia.dunning@archaeoconcept.com

Steven Engelsman
Weltmuseum Wien
Austria
steven.engelsman@gmail.com

Margaret Gowen
Ireland
mmgowen@live.com

Ruurd Halbertsma
National Museum of Antiquities / Faculty of Archaeology, Leiden University
The Netherlands
R.Halbertsma@RMO.NL

Jay Haviser
Sint Maarten Archaeological Center
Sint Maarten
jhaviser@hotmail.com

Tom Hazenberg
1Arch / Hazenberg Archeologie
The Netherlands
tom@hazenbergarcheologie.nl

Corinne Hofman
Faculty of Archaeology, Leiden University / ERC-synergy project NEXUS1492
The Netherlands
C.L.Hofman@arch.leidenuniv.nl

Monique Krauwer
Department of Arts and Heritage, Ministry of Education, Culture and Science
The Netherlands
m.krauwer@minocw.nl

Kristian Kristiansen
University of Gothenburg
Sweden
kristian.kristiansen@archaeology.gu.se

Ian Lilley
University of Queensland
Australia
i.lilley@uq.edu.au

Martijn Manders
Cultural Heritage Agency / Faculty of Archaeology, Leiden University
The Netherlands
M.Manders@cultureelerfgoed.nl

Arkadiusz Marciniak
Adam Mickiewicz University, Poznań,
Poland
arekmar@amu.edu.pl

Adrian Olivier
Institute of Archaeology, University College London
United Kingdom
adrian.olivier@btinternet.com

Nelly Robles
Instituto Nacional de Antropología e Historia
Mexico
nellym_robles@yahoo.com.mx

Nathan Schlanger
Ecole nationale des chartes / UMR Trajectoires
France
RARI, University of the Witwatersrand
South Africa
schlanger1@gmail.com

Chen Shen
Royal Ontario Museum
Canada
chens@rom.on.ca

Björn Smit
Cultural Heritage Agency
The Netherlands
B.Smit@cultureelerfgoed.nl

George Smith
Florida State University
United States of America
gsmith4790@comcast.net

Amy Strecker
Faculty of Archaeology, Leiden University / ERC-synergy project NEXUS1492
The Netherlands
a.strecker@arch.leidenuniv.nl

Pieter ter Keurs
National Museum of Antiquities / Institute of Cultural Anthropology, Leiden University
The Netherlands
P.terKeurs@RMO.NL

Monique van den Dries
Faculty of Archaeology, Leiden University
The Netherlands
m.h.van.den.dries@arch.leidenuniv.nl

Sander van der Leeuw
ASU-SFI Center for Biosocial Complex Systems, Arizona State University
United States of America
vanderle@asu.edu

Sjoerd van der Linde
CommonSites
The Netherlands
sjoerd@commonsites.net

Rocío Varela-Pousa
Institute of Heritage Sciences (INCIPIT), Spanish National Research Council (CSIC)
Spain
rocio.varela-pousa@incipit.csic.es

Gerry Wait
Nexus Heritage
United Kingdom
gerry.wait@nexus-heritage.com

Dieke Wesselingh
City of Rotterdam Archaeological Service (BOOR)
The Netherlands
da.wesselingh@Rotterdam.nl

Annemarie Willems
Archaeoconcept
Switzerland
amvwillems23@gmail.com

Tim Williams
Institute of Archaeology, University College London
United Kingdom
tim.d.williams@ucl.ac.uk

Pei-Lin Yu
Boise State University
United States of America
pei-linyu@boisestate.edu